Global Revival of Left and Socialism Versus Globalization and China's Share

Pu Guoliang, Xiong Guangqing

Translated by Guo Hui

CANut

Originally published as The Relationship Between Socialism and Capitalism in the Process of Globalization in 2006 by China Renmin University Press.

Original Chinese Edition Copyright © 2006 by Pu Guoliang and Xiong Guangqing
ISBN: 978-7-300-07314-9

Global Revival of Left and Socialism Versus Globalization and China's Share
ISBN: 978-3-942575-00-3

Published by
Canut International Publishers
Yorck Street. 66
10965 Kreuzberg
Berlin-Germany

Canut International Publishers
12a Guernsey Road E11
Lodon 4BJ-England-U.K.

URL: http//www.canut.us
E-Mail: canut@aol.com

Acknowledgements

This book is the result of a research sub-topic, titled as "The Relations of the Two Systems and China's Foreign Strategies in the Process of Globalization in the Post-Cold War Era". The main research project topic was "International Political Economy and China's Diplomatic Strategies in the Era of Globalization" (Project 211) undertaken by Renmin University of China. This Research had started in 2003 with group members from World Socialism Research Institute, School of International Studies under Renmin University of China. Initial group members were Pu Guoliang, Zhang Weiying, Feng Qingshu, Xiang Wenhua, Wang Tingyou, and Guo Chunsheng. Later on, each member of the group had also published papers and works on related issues, as periodical achievements of this research. Finally Pu Guoliang and Xiong Guangqing completed this book on behalf of the group. Pu Guoling set forth the outline for writing this book, finished the Introduction, Chapters 2 and 5; Xiong Guangqing finished Chapters 1, 3 and 6. Pu Guoliang polished the full text.

Due to our level of understanding and the limited materials we have access to, we believe there is still some room to make improvements in this book. We will be grateful for any suggestions.

Pu Guoliang
March 6, 2006

Foreword

The last two decades of the 20th century recorded dramatic and radical changes in capitalism, the world political configuration and especially the world socialist and left movement.

As the main part of the world socialist movement, the countries struggling for the cause of a socialist and communist future fell into grave setbacks and diverse forms of crises and many of them could not cure the deeply rooted problems posed in their development and construction efforts. One major root of the problem had been the relationship of socialist construction to existing capitalism and its realistic capabilities. Some countries through trial, error and tortuous efforts opened a brand new mode of socialist construction and a new type of engagement with external capitalism contrasting the previous mode of socialist construction. This transformation—with variations in time, pace and other characteristics—was generally carried out gradually and cautiously. This was called reform and opening up in China, Vietnam and Cuba. As compared to the previous mode—under their sovereignty—they have been allowing a certain degree of external capitalism in their territories and have adjusted the ideological and political superstructure to the whole new mode of socialist construction and reform.

The socialist and left movement in the rest of the world had greatly reflected developments in the socialist countries since the establishment of the first socialist power in 1917. And since diverse modes of socialist movements have continued to co-exist in the world socialist movement—most of the time—unable to bridge the differences and severe conflicts. Even socialist countries have had severe ideological, national and international disputes.

After the collapse of Soviet Union and many other socialist countries in

urope, nearly all schools of world socialist movements and thoughts
ᵾ an unprecedented setback or difficulties and have paid with high losses.

Many socialist parties and left movements were dissolved and some were
unable to resist capitalist arrogance arising after the "victory" of capitalism
won without battle. The shiny aspect of capitalist development had seemed
unmatchable and ideas about its demise had lost its relevance.

Thanks to intrinsic development of motive forces inherent in socialist
reality and its subjects, things have started to change and signs of recovery,
rectification, re-exploration, reform and revival have soon started to emerge
and even recorded some important achievements in many parts of the world.
Many important schools including (social) democratic socialism, autonomous
socialism-Trotskyism, new-left, green-left, post–Marxist left, Western and
Eastern communism and critical-Western Marxist thought have scored certain
remarkable achievements.

Globalism is a new objective trend motivated by capitalism and poses
important and new challenges to both capitalism and socialism since its vigorous
development in 1990s. Its content, modes, prospects and relation to capitalism
and socialism has been a major pressing and controversial issue debated between
and among socialist movements. It demands a creative renewal of ideas and
the socialist mode of development and also prepares new conditions in which
socialism can flourish.

Many Chinese scholars studying the world socialist movement and
international developments have adhered to Marxism and achieved original
findings in their researches. Prof. Pu Guoliang and Prof. Xiong Guangqing,
distinguished scholars in Renmin University of China, authors of this book, by
their analytical rigour, have indeed produced an innovative study of recent world
socialist movements faced by capitalism and globalism. The book offers many
facts, and numbers which comply with and support the analytical discourse. We
have also noted the scholars' sincere and keen pursuit of a fruitful dialog and
empathy with the many schools of socialist thought.

The book also offers a comprehensive analysis and in-depth information
about the Chinese case: how the communists in this country have developed

socialism and ideas about its construction in a country where capitalism and capitalist civilisation were so weak and shadow of its long pre-capitalist history was so obvious. Anyone interested in the fate of current capitalism, globalism and socialism in the new century will find ample stimulating material in this book.

Finally I would like to thank China Renmin University Press, and their encouragement to our publishing house for the realisation of this book.

Cem Kizilcec

Berlin, September 2010

Contents

Introduction ·· 1

**Chapter 1 Globalization and International Politics in the
Post-Cold War Era**··· **5**
1.1 The Rapid Progress of Globalization ·································· 6
1.2 The Basic Features of Globalization ······························· 19
1.3 The Impact of Globalization on Politics in the Contemporary
World ·· 34

**Chapter 2 Globalization and Capitalism in the Post-Cold
War Era** ·· **49**
2.1 The Role of Contemporary Capitalism in Globalization ·········· 49
2.2 Impact of Globalization on the Evolution of Contemporary
Capitalism ·· 60
2.3 The Overall Situation of the Evolution of Capitalism
in the Post-Cold War Era·· 70

**Chapter 3 Globalization and Socialism in the Post-Cold
War Era** ·· **85**
3.1 Opportunities for the Development of Socialism in the Process
of Globalization ··· 86
3.2 Globalization Brings Serious Challenges to Socialism············· 93
3.3 The Overall Situation of the Evolution of Socialism in the
World in the Post-Cold War Era ·· 106

**Chapter 4 A Review of Socialist Movements and Thoughts in
the Age of Globalization**··································· **139**
4.1 The New Changes of Capitalism Create Conditions for the

Realization of Socialism ·· 140

4.2 Socialist Movement Is an Immense Driving Force for the
Changes of Capitalism ·· 162

4.3 The Confrontation and Cooperation Between Socialism and
Capitalism in the Age of Globalization ································ 179

**Chapter 5 The Re-Positioning of the Contemporary
Socialism in China** ··**188**

5.1 The Complications and Relapses of Identifying Socialism with
Chinese Characteristics ·· 189

5.2 The Historical Re-Positioning of Socialism with Chinese
Characteristics ·· 206

5.3 The Relation Between Socialist China and the Contemporary
Capitalism ·· 218

**Chapter 6 China's Foreign Strategy and Prospects on
the Relations of Two Systems in the Age of
Globalization** ··**230**

6.1 Opportunities Brought to the Development of China by
Globalization ·· 231

6.2 Challenges Posed to the Development ································ 241

6.3 China's Strategic Choice in the Context of Two Systems ······· 260

Bibliography·· 281

Introduction

In the context of globalization, socialist countries with their special national attributes and identity are facing, more often than not, a dilemma in choosing appropriate foreign strategies. Globalization has become one of the important features and tendencies of the modern world, and socialist countries should opt for the strategy of merging into globalization in order to keep up with the historical tide and grasp the opportunity of development; but globalization is dominated by the developed countries, and the progress of globalization to a large extent is the expansion of capitalist values and institutional patterns. In the context of globalization, socialist countries need to absorb and refer to the outstanding achievements of developed countries in the West, at the same time adhere to the direction and principles of socialism and prevent any change of the nature of their socialist system. In exchanges with other countries, socialist countries need to transcend ideological limitations and make more friends. However, ideological factor can not be circumvented; clear-cut stance and attitude are always needed. In the process of globalization, it is essential and not ignorable for any socialist country to handle in an appropriate way the relationship between socialism and capitalism.

In view of Chinese reality and the world situation, this book studies the new changes of international politics against the backdrop of globalization, the development of capitalism, the interactive relationship between socialism and capitalism, the re-positioning of socialism in China in the process of globalization, as well as opportunities and challenges posed by globalization. The relationship between capitalism and socialism in the process of globalization is analyzed, and appropriate strategic choices China should make in the process of globalization are proposed from the perspective of the relationship of the two different systems.

Since the 1990s, globalization has accelerated and expanded into new territories and scope, and an integrated world economic system has taken shape once again. Political, cultural, technological and educational exchanges between nations, regions and different races are getting increasingly closer, and in turn they become more interdependent. Meanwhile, the process of globalization shows some basic features, such as uneven development, uneven distribution of benefits and causes diverse type of uncertainties. On the other side, globalization has different impacts on each particular country. This consequently influences different countries to adopt different measures and strategies. As globalization proceeds, the interests of different countries have intertwined and countries have become more interdependent, and this greatly influences international politics. Thus the relations between countries with socialist or capitalist systems have changed dramatically.

Globalization is closely linked to capitalism. First, contemporary capitalism plays a very important role in the process of globalization. Globalization is the result of capitalist development over a long time. Developed capitalist countries are the dominant force for the process of globalization, and many drawbacks arising in the process of globalization have their roots in capitalism. Secondly, globalization exerts major impacts on the development of modern capitalism. On the whole, globalization promotes and motivates global expansion of capitalism. The impact of globalization on developed and developing countries is not the same and varies remarkably. On the other side, globalization poses new challenges to capitalism. Thirdly, in the context of globalization, capitalism still displays strong vitality. Capitalism "winning" over the Soviet Union and Eastern Europe in the long-standing confrontation has expanded its space and influence. Throughout its history, capitalism has experienced quite many self-adjustment and renewal practices and has enhanced its risk-bearing capacity. Thus in some aspects, capitalism still holds a stronger position than socialism.

With respect to socialism, globalization is both an opportunity and a challenge. Globalization provides opportunities offering advantage of external investment, advanced technology and managerial expertise and thus accelerates socialist development, and promotes industrial restructuring and modernization. Globalism—to a certain extent—pushes political civilization process in socialist countries, while on the other hand may pose severe challenges for economic, political and cultural security of socialist countries. From the perspective of the situation of socialist development in the world, in general socialist movement is still at a low tide, while new waves of socialist development surge. In the long run, socialism certainly has a bright future and broad space for development.

Despite globalization, the historical trend of capitalist and socialist development remains unchanged, but the relationship between these two systems has undergone certain changes. And new changes brought by capitalism still creates and prepares conditions for the realization of socialism, and socialist movement still plays an important driving force for the renewal and evolution of capitalism. The two systems will follow a pattern of co-existence including both confrontation and cooperation in the same process. In the process of globalization, conflicts between them still remain, but the nature of conflicts and the means of solving these conflicts have altered. The irreconcilable confrontation turns into more cooperation, and the cooperation spheres may expand in the long run.

As far as China is concerned, a clear positioning of socialism is fundamental to establishing the development strategies and foreign strategies for this country. The Communist Party of China has been exploring for a long period the issue of how to position China's socialism applying a historical and global perspective. The re-positioning of socialism with Chinese characteristics designed by Deng Xiaoping has become the foothold of modernizing socialist China. After the reform and opening strategy was set, all policies and regulations stipulated have taken account of this position. In the current age of globalization, the relationship between socialist China and contemporary capitalism is quite sophisticated. China criticizes, competes and at the same time learns selectively from capitalism. To a large extent, China seeks to adopt favorable things and oppose to unfavorable in that of capitalism.

As an objective reality and a trend of development, globalization exerts great influence on the progress of world history, and undoubtedly on the development of China. Globalization in the 21st century will progress in both scope and depth at a fast speed. In the context of globalization identifying opportunities and challenges properly is a prerequisite for differentiating advantages and disadvantages and establishing a correct national strategy. China needs to take a global perspective and actively participate in and respond to globalization. A new concept of security needs to be worked out for China to enable her take part in solving global security issues and handle social risks and security issues she faces. The ideological element in international relations should be fully understood and properly handled, and this also applies to relations between socialism and capitalism. Socialism should inherit, refer and absorb all outstanding achievements of human civilization. This book partly focuses on suggestions how China should maintain self initiative in her development road and socialist cause.

Globalization and International Politics in the Post-Cold War Era

As one of the major trends of the world history, globalization has accelerated since the 1990s. In this context, production factors, such as capital, technology and labor force, have flowed and been allocated globally. Almost every economy has been integrated into the world economic system. With the trend of globalization, political and cultural exchanges between nations get closer, and interdependence of nations deepens. Currently some basic features of globalization have been revealed, such as uneven development, uneven distribution of benefits and the uncertainty of the impact of globalization, which in turn results in remarkable differences of the impact of globalization on countries with different systems. Consequently, countries with different systems take different measures and strategies. Globalization is having a huge impact on the way of living of human society and on international relations. Under this impact, relations between countries adopting the principles of socialism or capitalism will changes remarkably.

1.1 The Rapid Progress of Globalization

Globalization has become one of the most important characters of the contemporary era. Though there is a lack of a clear and universally-accepted definition of "globalization"[1], the presence of globalization is felt everywhere.

1.1.1 Driving factors in the rapid expansion of globalization

The term "globalization" came into being as early as in the 1940s.[2] Due to turbulences, polarization and restructuring of forces in the world in the 1960s, and in particular the impact of oil crisis in the 1970s, global factors began to become the focus in the world economy, politics and culture and drew general attention. Some terms referring to globalization were firstly recognized and used generally in different domains, for instances, "integration" and "economic integration"[3] in international political economics, "integration," "political integration" and "interdependence"[4] in international politics, and "world culture", "global culture" and "global village"[5] in international culturology. Correspondingly, "globalization," a relatively normative definition in social sciences, has been fixed. In the mid-

---

[1] In terms of the definition and understanding of globalization, scholars put forth varying views. Wang Yizhou, *Analysis on Modern International Politics*, pp 9-16, Shanghai: Shanghai People's Press, 1995; Hu Yuanzi and Xue Xiaoyuan as chief compilers, *Globalization and China*, pp 2-3, Beijing: Central Compilation and Translation Press; Wu Jiang, "World Polarization and Economic Globalization", in *The Paradox of Globalization* with Yu Keping and Huang Weiping as chief compilers, Beijing: Central Compilation and Translation Press, 1998; Li Cong as chief compiler, *A New Anthology of World Economics*, p 510, Beijing: Economic Science Press, 2000.

[2] *Webster's Ninth Collegiate Dictionary*, Webster Co Ltd., Massachusetts, 1991, p 521; Gao Fang, "The Origin of the Term 'Globalization'", *Study Times*, 2001.

[3] Li Cong, "On Economic Integration", *Journal of China Social Sciences*, 1993 (1).

[4] Johan K. De Vree, *Political Integration: The Formation of Theory and Its Problems*, the Hague-Paris, Mouton, 1972, p 45; Ernst B. Haas, *Beyond the Nation State*, Stanford: Stanford University Press, 1964, p 29; Karl W. Deutsch, *The Analysis of International Relations*, 2nd ed., Englewood Cliffs, New Jersey: Prentice Hall Inc. 1988, p 198; R. Keohane and J. Nye, eds. *Power and Interdependence: Transnational Relations and World Politics*, Cambridge, Massachusetts: Harvard University Press, 1977, p 3.

[5] Wang Yizhou, *Analysis on Modern International Politics*, pp 31-32.

1980s, "globalization" became a basic concept defining the future trend and features of the human society.[1] In the 1990s, systematic research on globalization peaked in academia. At present, "globalization" turns to be one of the most popular and trendy words across the world. Various viewpoints have come into being, largely out of systematic researches on the concept, attributes, contents, manifestations, consequences as well as measures from various perspectives, forming different theories of globalization. Gradually, from a mere term in vogue, "globalization" has turned into a famous school of study with much influence.

When was globalization originated? It remains one of the controversial issues in the international academia.[2] However, what is basically indisputable is that globalization has gained unprecedented progress since the 1980s. What kinds of forces, then, are pushing forward this progress at an all-time speed?

First, the unremitting development and application of new technologies has laid a solid material and technological foundation for globalization. In the second half of the 20th century, an unparalleled breakthrough in technology was achieved and the speed of technical updating became ever faster. Technological progress has shortened continuously the distances between nations, races, and turned our planet into a small village.[3] The information revolution, including extensive application of computers, large scale improvement of communication capacity and sharp decrease of communication expenses, is essential factor turning globalization increasingly into a reality in the 1990s. The revolution has completely changed people's way of production, living as well as thinking. People

---

[1] *Oxford Dictionary of New Words*, p133, London: Oxford University Press, 1991.

[2] Li Shenzhi, "Globalization and Chinese Culture", *Journal of Pacific Studies*, 1994 (2); Li Cong, *The New Evolution of Modern Capitalism*, pp 235-236, Beijing: Economic Science Press, 1998; Gang Fang, *Probe into the World Affairs*, pp 259-260, Beijing: China Books Press, 2002.

[3] "Global village" first appeared in the 1960s in *Exploration in Communication* written by Marshall McLuhan, and soon gained popularity throughout the world. The fact of the spread of this term shows that the world has indeed become smaller. Li Huaju as chief compiler, *21st Century English Chinese Dictionary*, p 990, Beijing: China Renmin University Press, 2003.

could obtain and control information from all over the world at an extremely cheap cost anytime and anywhere. Since the mid-1980s, the popularization of computer and other information technologies, and the swift expansion of the use of the Internet have linked economic activities globally. Today, information industry has grown as a new giant, and the economy of many nations and of the world has applied information technology. Since the mid-1990s, developed countries in the West have brought forward the idea of transforming the traditional economy into knowledge economy, an economy based on the production, dissemination, management and application of knowledge. Sectors of knowledge economy, such as high-tech manufacturing, agriculture and high value-added service industry, are depending on the extensive application of information technology. Information revolution also offers more opportunities to more people to take part in global affairs. Global business operations of transnational corporations, cooperation and exchanges between countries and governments, and non-governmental organizations all witness rapid growth. For instance, there were about 6,000 non-governmental organizations internationally in 1990, and within 10 years time the number increased to 26,000. Reduced cost of Internet communication enables small organizations with even only one computer and one modem to deliver messages to all continents, within a few seconds at very low cost, helping them assume growing roles in world politics. In short, new technological revolution brings material possibilities for the wave of globalization.

Secondly, in economic sectors, depth and breadth of the flow of trade, investment and finance has been developing internationally at an unprecedented speed, which remarkably deepens the interdependence among countries and regions. International trade, as an important medium connecting different economies, has achieved rapid progress in the 20th century. Meanwhile, forces hindering international economic exchanges have weakened increasingly. So far, the average custom tariffs in the world has decreased to one tenth of that in 1948 when the General Agreement on Tariffs and Trade (GATT) was established. Tariffs on imported finished goods in developed countries were reduced to below 4%, and to about 10%

in developing countries which were on average 34% in the early 1980s. The growth of international trade volume has reached to three times of the growth of world production. Free flow of international capital is also one of the driving factors for economic globalization. At present, the average annual growth rate of international capital flow has reached 20%. Continuous growth of international direct investment connects different economies in terms of production, pushing forward economic globalization and spurring a full-scale growth of world economy. Transnational corporations have become the main carrier of international investment. The output value of nearly 60,000 transnational corporations accounts for 30% of total output value in the world. Their trade volume accounts for 60% and direct investment accounts for 90% of the world total. The rapid growth of international direct investment changes the economic structure, featuring international division of labor between departments and units, creating and distributing production and wealth worldwide. At the same time, international financial market booms at an unprecedented speed. According to statistics, over 20 years from 1972 to 1995, international financial market transaction volume swelled over 40 times, while the world production only increased by seven times and world export volume by 12 times in the same period. The rapid expansion of international financial market stimulates investment, fund raising and financing among enterprises and countries. Conventional geographical territory of international capital is being replaced by a new and global "flowing space". Continuous improvement of various financial derivatives and the means of trading, especially wide use of remote terminals of computers and international information network technologies, facilitates swifter capital flow in the world on the one hand, and intensifies the intangibility of the world economy on the other. The rapid growth of international trade, investment and finance enables the factors of economic activities, including capital flow, labor force market, information transmission and raw material supply, as well as management and organization, breaking through the boundaries of countries and becoming internationalized. The global nature of economic activities becomes prominent.

Thirdly, the innumerable economic contacts and the expansion of political and cultural exchanges between countries make internal affairs that were traditionally domestic turn internationalized, either intentionally or unintentionally. For instance, economic globalization leads to the transfer of sovereignty, internationalization of human rights issues and other issues such as peace, environment and human development, which have exceeded the domain of a single country's sovereignty and become global affairs. It is not right for some countries to intervene or involve in other countries' internal affairs taking these issues as an excuse. Anyhow an increasing number of affairs and issues, political, military, cultural or social, requests to ignore national boundaries and turn international and global, along with the ever growing and deepening contacts, exchanges and cooperation between countries.[1]

Finally, international organizations and coordinating mechanisms and their activities push forward the process of globalization. International economic organizations and coordinating mechanisms play significant roles in economic globalization through chiefly two channels, either implementing organizational management or stipulating rules and regulations. International economic organizations have contributed greatly in implementing organizational management. The outstanding example is the GATT, the predecessor of World Trade Organization (WTO), which has implemented concrete management on international trade through rounds of multilateral negotiations and through the results of these negotiations over the past half century. The Uruguay Round, the 8th multilateral trade negotiations, reached an agreement at the end of 1993 and World Trade Organization was founded on January 1, 1995. International economic organizations have made great efforts in establishing rules in the world's economic activities, and a series of rules have been set forth. Though displaying a notable mark of developed countries, especially the United States, the influences of these

---

[1] Adam Roberts, "Humanitarian War: Military Intervention and Human Rights", *International Affairs*, Volume 69, No. 3, July 1993; Michael Glennon, "The New Interventionism", *Foreign Affairs*, May/June 1999.

rules on international economic activities and the merits of these rules can not be ignored. At regional levels, international economic coordination and cooperation has been remarkably enhanced, and numerous regional organizations have emerged, such as North American Free Trade Area (NAFTA), European Union (EU), South Common Market, Organization of African Unity (OAU), Association of Southeast Asian Nations (ASEAN), Asia-Pacific Economic Cooperation (APEC), etc. Politically and culturally, all kinds of international organizations and coordination mechanisms at all levels are also emerging and playing ever greater roles. The United Nation, for example, is the most influential.

1.1.2 The expanding scope of globalization

When we are discussing globalization or issues related to globalization from different perspectives or at different levels, we are referring not only to the facts, but also to the processes and trends. As a reality, the typical form of globalization is economic globalization. As a process and a trend in progress, economic globalization, as well as the expansion and spreading of globalization in other spheres of the society, needs to be followed with interest.

1.1.2.1 The most typical and basic form of globalization is economic globalization.

Economic globalization is the result of the development of world economy, technology, the international division of labor, and an unstoppable historical trend. Most countries in the world are involved in the process of economic globalization. Economic globalization is a process and status in which the market of a country merges with the world market and eventually transcend national boundaries, promoted by the flow of production factors with unprecedented scale and speed, and by the constant rise of variables in international economic relationships. In this process, capital flow, labor market, information transmission, raw material supply, management and organization have all become internationalized. The development of economic globalization is amazingly developing one wave after another, initially in the trade sector, then in the financial sphere, followed by information and knowledge economy sectors. The flow of products, services, capital as well as information transcend national boundaries, and most countries are engaged to global markets. Thus, the comparative advantages of each country can play their role, and resources can be allocated to regions and areas where they can be utilized optimally. It implies increased trade opportunities, and broader channels for acquiring international capital, technology and knowledge. It also means that opportunities are not evenly distributed among different regions and countries which are at different levels of development and possess or have different resources. The issue of inequalities stands out remarkably. Anyhow, as economic globalization has become a reality and a trend, no country can stay aloof. Attempting to avoid or refusing to ignore will only make a country move backward. There are opportunities for each country, and the key is to form comparative advantages, build up capacity and improve adaptation to the process.

1.1.2.2 Science and the advance of technology is the fundamental and sustained driving force of globalization.

Globalization of science and technology means allocation of technological resources, appraisal and application of those technological results, as well as the development and research of science and technology are conducted or exchanged globally, and technological collaboration and exchanges are realized in a frequent and globalized manner. The global allocations of technological resources are represented by the following facts: the number of researchers, scholars and technological staff exchanged increases remarkably; governmental collaboration, direct investment of transnational or foreign companies, international capital input into academic collaboration or research programs of research institutions or private organizations also grow at a large margin; technological equipment, large-scale laboratory installments in particular, are jointly established or shared; and scientific or technological information and resources from one country are obtained by scientists of other countries. The appraisal and application of technological results conducted globally are embodied through the following phenomena: research papers from different countries are published in world-renowned journals and cited extensively by scientists from other countries, the movements of patents, exclusively owned technologies and products are speeded up and grow in number, and the appraisal systems for technological results are standardized internationally. Economic globalization pushes enterprises to apply the latest technology worldwide, and ensure that new technologies enter and penetrate the international market more rapidly. As a result, it has become a most remarkable tendency of technological globalization that transnational corporations establish research and development centers outside the native country. The purpose of such a practice is to take advantage of cheap and qualified technological human resources in host country, and to guarantee largest market share therein. As the majority of researchers are from the host countries, the transfer and dissemination of knowledge and technology can be speeded up in the host countries. Technological exchange and collaboration between countries consists of two parts, namely, those between peoples and those between governments. The basic driving force comes from various interests, direct or indirect, such as improving technology through obtaining overall knowledge, experience and expertise, directly using scientific and technological resources of other nations, sharing the costs and risks of research and development, as well as enhancing the reform in technological system of a nation. In addition, there are many acute scientific challenges and technological puzzles that call for global collaboration. While bringing about economic benefit for mankind, technological development produces some negative effects which impact lives of many people in different countries and become common problems to be faced by the human society.

1.1.2.3 Globalization covers other domains apart from economy and technology.

In the political domain, though sovereign nations remain to be main actors in the international political arena in the foreseeable future, the emerging global issues transcending state sovereignty and boundary poses increasingly serious challenges to the traditional idea of state sovereignty.

To solve some global economic or social issues, political domain will have to be touched upon. Political issues are more prone to go beyond domestic or bilateral territories and turn regional or global. It may seem too early to discuss political globalization, and yet many people don't even accept or refuse to accept the phenomenon of political globalization. But it is obviously inappropriate to neglect this tendency in the study of issues of globalization. In the military domain, with the appearance and proliferation of mass destructive nuclear weapons, the appearance of long distance military attack and threats, and hence the formation of an interdependent military network, military and security issues have transcended not only the conventional national boundaries, but also the conventional restraints of military alliances and regional security. Military and security issues have become globalized. Such a feature was initially shown in the "balance of terror" between the United States and the Soviet Union during the Cold War period.[1] But global armament controls, disarmament, nuclear non-proliferation efforts transmit a clear and common message, that is, in today's world, similar to economic issues, military and security issues are also becoming increasingly globalized. This was clearly seen when the strong reaction arouse from all over the world after President Bush put NMD (preemptive defense) on his agenda. Terrorist attack of 9.11 indicates even more clearly that the world security is totally interconnected and no country could stay aloof. In terms of social life, many social issues on a global basis surge, such as environmental pollution, greenhouse effect, Aids epidemic, mouth and feet disease, mad cow disease, SARS, bird flu, which in turn result in the globalization of issues including environmental protection. In the cultural sector, globalization is represented in the global mobility of ideas, information, images as well as people with their own ideas and information, such as the dissemination of religion, scientific knowledge, and even recreation, fashion and languages. The most interesting phenomenon is the globalization of the concept of "globalization".

---

[1] William W. Kaufmann, "The Requirements of Deterrence", in W.W. Kaufmann, ed. *Military Policy and National Security*, Princeton: Princeton University Press, 1956; Albert Wohsstetter, "The Delicate Balance of Terror", *Foreign Affairs*, XXXVIII (January 1959).

1.1.3 Response to globalization: integration, anti-globalization, regionalization and localization

Globalization has become one of the major trends of the world development, and the rapid progress of globalization has posed a new challenge for the human society. Facing this unavoidable challenge, governments, political, economic and social organizations will have to respond and make their choices.

To actively promote globalization is the response of neo-liberalism to the process of globalization. Generally, globalization is a self-organizational behavior of social development, while global integration is a choice of the main body of the society of its own accord. First and foremost, globalization is an economic and social process driven by market forces, instead of a public (governmental) policy. Not being a governmental policy does not mean that the government has no policies promoting globalization. Take the economic sector as an example: Economic globalization refers to the continuous expansion of the market, and the transnational expansion of the operational mechanism of market economy, so that a world market is formed and resources are allocated in a rational way globally. But economic integration has a color of governmental intervention and is the result of governmental decision-making. The transnational expansion of the market requests objectively that market rules and the means of adjustment correcting the drawbacks of the market can expand across boundaries. This is what is generally meant by economic integration. If the process of economic integration seriously lags behind the process of economic globalization, it will become the shackles of global development. Theoretically, economic globalization brings participants more effective allocation of resources and greater economic efficiency. But the interest of developing nations taking part in economic globalization is usually affected by lagging economic integration. As many scholars do not differentiate strictly between economic globalization and integration, they tend to draw different conclusions at different time while analyzing the impact of economic globalization on developing nations. For example, when some developing nations obtain economic growth benefiting from globalization by adopting policies of economic opening up, some scholars regard economic globalization as "paradise" for developing nations. But when there are problems, these scholars regard globalization as a "pitfall". The completely different evaluations of economic roads taken by some emerging economies in Asia in and around 1997 indicate confused understanding of the process of globalization. The extent of globalization in other sectors is far less great than in the economic sector, but similar problems exist. In globalization dominated by the West, neo-liberalists try their best in advocating global integration. They believe that any government in pursuit of anti-market policies is against democracy, and production, distribution, exchange and social organizations all should follow market force. They also believe that people are living in a globally "competitive order", and the power of one country can not hinder the power of globalization; the market is no longer national, but global; moreover, with the process of economic globalization, politics, culture, law, as well as values should become globalized. Accordingly, various regulations and rules of the society should be integrated globally.

What opposes the call for global integration of neo-liberalism is the wave of anti-globalization which has appeared in the late 1990s worldwide. Like the fuzzy definitions of globalization, the agenda of anti-globalization movement is also very broad and quite vague. It can refer to the negation of globalization, or criticize the one-sidedness of globalization, or express concern for extreme globalization, to form a counter rebel to "global capitalism", the new-stage of capitalism represented by globalization, or express dissatisfaction for the increasing gap between rich and poor, social disintegration as well as environmental disasters, etc. The radical extremists see globalization as a catastrophe, rather than a blessing. According to them, globalization is not an inevitable trend of the development of human society, but a well-plotted conspiracy by developed nations and transnational corporations. At the end of 1999, when the WTO conference was held in Seattle, tens of thousands of people from other parts of the world protested and messed up the city. Since then, almost every international conference of

IMF, World Bank or WTO is confronted with large-scale radical protests and campaigns. The themes of those protests are no more than that globalization accelerates ecological damages and polarization of the rich and the poor, or express that there is only so little democratic participation from developing nations in globalization process and that they are discriminated, etc. The protestors are against the idea of regarding the world as a single commodity market, and they oppose freeing market to decide everything. Apart from large-scale protests, online Internet anti-globalization campaigns are very active. Anti-globalization activists study and discuss issues of globalization on the Internet, express their concerns over social justice and environmental issues extensively, and coordinate their anti-globalization actions worldwide. They've established several well-known websites, including "Destroy IMF", "Multinational Monitor", "Peoples' Global Action against Free Trade and the WTO", "Socialist Option", all of which are very influential. The anti-globalization activists are mixed, including all kinds of associations, trade unions, ecological and environmental organizations and non-governmental organizations, as well as individuals such as socialists, feminists, and anarchists. They join their efforts for the same goal of anti-globalization. Anti-globalization campaign is a result of and a response to globalization. It reflects a confrontation—though fairly weak—of those in the lower classes or stratum or victims and losers of globalization and poses a challenge to the inevitability of globalization. Anti-globalization campaign has raised or revealed various impeding and serious issues facing the whole world, and it will undoubtedly encourage profound retrospection or renewed understanding on globalization.

At the time when globalization is deepening, the trend of regionalization is also strengthening, which is most typically shown in the economic sphere. Over the recent years, like the accelerating economic globalization and global economic integration, regional economic integration is also growing quickly, and nations participating in the regional economic integration continue to increase. Currently, economic integration shows a pattern of coexistence of regional economic integration and global economic integration, the fundamental reason of which is the uneven growth of world economy. For Western countries, regionalization in North American or in West Europe is to protect the interests of countries in these regions, and serve as bargaining counters to contend for more interests. For developing countries, regionalization can not only protect their interests, but also serve as a ladder leading to globalization. From this angle, regionalization not necessarily serves as a reliable ladder to globalization, it may well become a new source of international conflict. But from a different angle, the driving force for both regional and global economic integration is that economic entities pursue the maximum interests driven by market force. Regional economic integration aims to achieve the maximum interests in specific regions, while global economic integration pursues the maximum interests globally. For both kinds of integration, the basic requirement for achieving the goal is to remove trade and investment barriers among economic entities. In this sense, both regional and global integrations are going toward the same "integration". Regional economic integration will be the important driving force for the continuous and accelerating growth of global economic integration, and the future direction of regional integration draws close toward global economic integration and thus facilitates the growth of global economic integration. If the coordination and collaboration between regional economic organizations is to be constantly strengthened, economic rules and operational models accepted by a wider scope of countries will become the embryonic form of the internal mechanism of global economic integration. The coexistence of globalization and regionalization shows that the process of globalization is packed with conflicts and clashes.

What is contrary to the process of globalization is localization. Globalization involves almost every nation on earth and most of them are responding positively in the face of this great historical wave. It has become a common understanding for these countries to "get connected with the international community". But during the process of connection, there are inevitably conflicts between what is local and what is external, either in terms of systems and policies, or mindsets. Globalization weakens one nation or one country to a certain extent, but in the foreseeable future, neither a nation nor a sovereign state will retreat from the world historical arena. As long as a nation or a country exists, as long as different levels of cultural and social development exist, any nation or state will witness conflicts between what is local and what is external in the process of embracing the world, no matter how wide it opens up. During the process, each nation and country needs to combine international practices with its own reality and localize international practices in line with its own historical and current situation. If this issue is well handled, the sufferings during the globalization process will be eased, and if not, the pain will be sharpened. For any nation and country, globalization is not limited to mutual exchanges, but a mingling and merging process. What mankind needs is a win-win pattern globalization, an equal footing globalization and a coexisting globalization.

1.2 The Basic Features of Globalization

Globalization transforms economic, political and cultural life of people, as well as the traditional lifestyles, values and moral concepts of people. It is also remoulding the old world and the established orders or norms, and changing the direction of the development of human history. At present, some basic features of globalization are exposed, such as uneven development, uneven distribution of benefits and uncertainties brought by globalization.

1.2.1 The uneven development

In the context of globalization, almost all countries and regions are included in a universal world system, and interdependence among nations is ever deepening. However, the progress of globalization in different regions is not at the same level; extent of involvement of each country varies; and the development is markedly uneven.

Though globalization witnesses a quite strong development, the process

is not yet completed. We still live in a partially globalized world.[1] Kearney/
Foreign Policy Globalization Index is the first comprehensive empirical
index measuring the degree of globalization and its impacts. It examines the
integration of economy, personnel, technology and politics of 62 countries
and regions, which account for 96% of the world GDP and 85% of the world
population. In the fifth release of Kearney/Foreign Policy Globalization Index
in 2005, 10 countries ranking top were: Singapore, Ireland, Switzerland, the
United States, Holland, Canada, Denmark, Sweden, Austria, and Finland.
It was the first time that the United States had been ranked in the top 5,
ascending from the previous 7 up to 4. Connections between the United
States and other countries in political and economic sectors had weakened,
but technological advantage had helped the United States improve its
ranking. The United States ranked No. 1 in the world in terms of the number
of Internet users and safe Internet servers. Singapore ranked top in the index
because of its intensified political contacts and international trade links,
replacing Ireland who had been the top of the index for three consecutive
years. Russia experienced the sharpest decline by eight ladders places
and ranked 52 among the 62 countries and regions covered by the index.
Mainland China ranked 54, climbed up three ladders places. The percentage
of export commodities of mainland China increased from 1.9% in 1990 to
6% in 2003. Though China has gained major economic growth, it should be
yet to make more efforts in improving its ranking in the globalization index.
Because many indexes are measured by per capita average figures, in reality
the benefits of globalization will be slowly passed on to the majority general
public of each country.

   The feature of imbalanced development of globalization is best shown
by the status of economic globalization. Economic globalization is an organic
whole, driven by the evolving scientific revolution and internationalization of
production, in which the interdependence and mutual interaction of different

---

[1] Robert Keohane, Men Honghua as compilers, *Liberalism, Power and Governance in a Partially
     Globalized World*, p 280, Beijing: Peking University Press, 2004.

economies are increasingly deepening, and that any change in any part affects the whole situation. Almost all the economic departments and links of every country, region and national group have become integral parts of a whole.[1] The economic globalization is mainly represented in the following aspects: firstly, the scope of trade liberalization is rapidly expanding, and the interdependence and interaction of each economy is deepening. Secondly, the process of financial internationalization is remarkably accelerating, and financial policies of different nations tend to become integrated. Thirdly, globalization of investments proceed remarkably, and foreign direct investment grows rapidly. Fourthly, the network of production cooperation is established and level of international division of labor is further improved. Fifthly, the trend of internationalization of operating entities can not be stopped and the functions of multinational corporations are further enhanced. According to information released by the UN Trade and Development Conference, by the end of the 1980s, there were 385 bilateral investment agreements that had taken effect, which later increased to 1,857, involving 173 countries, by the end of the 1990s. There were about 140 countries that had abolished foreign exchange controls. In 1993, the net volume of foreign direct investment in the world amounted to 193.4 billion US dollars, which increased to 865 billion US dollars in 2000. In 1993, the total volume of commodities and service exports in the world accounted for 19.2% of the world GDP, which increased to 23.3% in 2000. Both developed and developing nations, and transforming economies are increasingly becoming dependent on the world economy.[2]

Chinese scholars Liu Yumei and Zhang Peng have conducted quantitative research on the extent of some countries participation in economic globalization. Their research shows that different countries have

---

[1] Li Jingzhi, Lin Su, *Economy and Politics in Contemporary World*, p22, Beijing: China Renmin University Press, 2003.

[2] Su Jingxiang, "Asian Consciousness and East Asian Economic Cooperation", from http://www. blogchina.com/new/display/29615.html, 2004-04-24.

different degree of participation in economic globalization. Data of 16 representative countries have been chosen and analyzed.[1] The overall scores of the degree of participation in economic globalization of these countries are shown in Table 1-1.

Table 1-1   The Overall Scores of the Degree of Participation in Economic Globalization of Some Countries

Ranking	1	2	3	4	5	6	7	8
Country	the United States	the United Kingdom	Germany	Japan	France	China	Singapore	Italy
Score	1.57	0.90	0.41	0.28	0.21	-0.02	-0.12	-0.16
Ranking	9	10	11	12	13	14	15	16
Country	Canada	Brazil	Australia	Mexico	Korea	New Zealand	Russia	India
Score	-0.17	-0.34	-0.38	-0.40	-0.41	-0.41	-0.46	-0.49

Note: The negative scores of some countries do not indicate that these countries have not participated in the process of economic globalization. For the sake of standardizing the data in analysis, the average level of world economic globalization is treated as zero. The positive or negative relations are indicating the degree of participation in economic globalization and the comparison of the average levels of world economic globalization.

Source: Liu Yumei, Zhang Peng, "Quantitative Research of the Degree of Economic Globalization", published in *Statistics Research*, 2003 (12).

These countries can be categorized into four types according to their scores (See Table 1-2). Type 1 and Type 2 include five developed countries. Type 3 includes two developed countries and two developing countries with contrasting situations. The overall level of participation of Italy and Canada is high, and their dependency on the globalization of production and trade and the dependency on investment globalization are both low, which is a common feature of big economic powers. The high degree of participation of Singapore is due to its highly developed foreign trade. The dependency on

---

[1] For the contents of quantitative research on economic globalization, see Liu Yumei and Zhang Peng, "Quantitative Research of the Degree of Economic Globalization", *Statistics Research*, 2003 (12). See this research paper for the method employed and their detailed conclusions.

the globalization of production and trade and the dependency on investment globalization of China is fairly high; meanwhile China had absorbed a large amount of foreign investment. As a result, China ranks high in terms of the level of economic globalization. The level of participation in economic globalization of China is less than that of developed nations, but China is leading developing country and ranks in the middle on the global level. Type 4 mainly includes developing nations, with lower degree of participation in economic globalization and smaller economic scales, which have great potential of development.

Table 1-2   Categorization of Some Countries in Terms of the Degree of Participating Economic Globalization

Type	Country
1	the United States
2	the United Kingdom, Germany, Japan, France
3	China, Singapore, Italy, Canada
4	Korea, Mexico, New Zealand, Australia, India, Russia, Brazil

The conclusion of researches may vary because of different perspectives, methods applied or data collected. But there is one thing for certain, that is, the degree of participation in economic globalization of different countries are different. Ranking from high to low degree of participation in economic globalization of countries is: developed countries—developing countries (newly industrialized countries—other developing countries). Shi Yinhong, a Chinese scholar, believes that the interdependence resulted from globalization is not evenly distributed, and the imbalance forms an intrinsic structure and an internal operational pattern. Globalization at current stage has resulted in three basic situations: extensive and genuine interdependence seen inside the developed world, the dependency of less developed countries on the developed world, and fragmentation and divisions seen inside the underdeveloped world.[1] In summary, the promotion and development of

---

[1] Shi Yinhong, "On the Limitation of Interdependence and the Restraint of National Policies on the Impact of Globalization", *Research of International Issues*, 2002 (2).

globalization does not touch every corner of the world at the same pace, and the progress of globalization is markedly uneven.

1.2.2 The differential distribution of benefit

It seems that globalization can result in the aggregation of wealth in the world and improve welfare of the citizens. But to a large extent, globalization is global expansion of market economy, and globalization at current stage is dominated by developed countries, which are positioned quite advantageously. Thus in the process of globalization, wealth is increasingly accumulated in a small number of developed countries, which are the main beneficiaries of economic globalization. As a scholar pointed out, "Despite the utopian promises of globalization and advantages of an information society, benefits have not been universal and inequality in the world has grown wider. To some extent, globalization may have exacerbated the discrepancy between the rich and the poor (at the international, national and individual levels) through its relentless progress.[1] To put it simply, the distribution of benefit is markedly uneven in the process of globalization.

The United States is the major promoter and the largest beneficiary of the current economic globalization. After the Cold War, the American government has adopted a series of measures to strengthen its efforts in promoting economic globalization. These efforts include: promoting the liberalization of trade and investment, maintaining the stability and authority of multilateral trade system, actively taking part in creating WTO, facilitating the implementation of the results of Uruguay Round talks, exercising international economic diplomacy, and promoting bilateral and regional economic, trade and technological cooperation. What is then the fundamental reason for U.S. to promote economic globalization? According to Robert

---

[1] Ryokichi Hirono, "Globalization in the 21st Century: Blessing or Threat to Developing Countries". *Asia Pacific Review*, Nov. 2001, Vol. 8, Issue 2.

Gilpin, "Most countries certainly benefit from the operations of world market economy, but economies with higher efficiency and more advanced technology have greater benefits. They enjoy higher profit rate and more favorable trade terms. As a result, market economy and wealth is accumulated by more advanced economies."[1] It is of important strategic significance for the United States to dominate the international economic order with American style systems, and to promote economic globalization. The purpose of this strategy is to reduce the cost of deals in the international market, to promote cross-border flow of capital, goods and services by taking technological and capital advantages, and to advance the restructuring of global resources. As clearly seen from the relationship between American economic prosperity and development and economic globalization since the 1990s, economic globalization has brought about enormous economic benefit for the United States, and to a large extent promoted the model of "new economy" in that period. First of all, globalization of production has provided opportunity for upgrading industrial structure of the United States, in particular, for the development of information industry; secondly, the expanding international trade has offered broad space for the economic growth in the United States; thirdly, the huge amount of capital out and inflow has injected great vitality for the American economy.[2] American economy regained its new energy in March 1991, and maintained a fast and steady growth until March 2001 when a new recession set in. That decade witnessed the longest economic expansion; after since data records for economic cycles were being gathered. That round of economic growth has distinctive features of two highs and two lows formula, as compared with traditional economy: high economic growth rate, and high growth rate of labor productivity, low unemployment rate, and low inflation rate. The fundamental purpose for the United States to spare

[1] Robert Gilpin, *War and Change in World Politics*, p 139, Beijing: China Renmin University Press, 1994.
[2] Xiong Guangqing, "Economic Globalization: Major Driving Force of America's New Economy", *Chongqing Business School Journal*, 2002 (4).

no effort in promoting economic globalization is that it brings about huge economic interest for the country.

In the process of globalization, benefit received by different types of countries is unevenly distributed, which will further result in or deepen the imbalanced development of different countries and regions in the world. The imbalance is shown in two aspects. One is that the wealth gap between developed and developing nations continues to grow. The other is the polarization of the rich and the poor in developing nations, in particular, developing countries located in forgotten corners of the world are getting poorer and more backward. Theoretically, as a member of the international community, any developing country is entitled to share world wealth and economic growth. However, "as a matter of fact, financial system and its liberalization have benefited countries enjoying privileges and made them dominate the world economy. But the cost is borne by developing countries, in particular, the poorest countries."[1] This is cruel reality of economic globalization. At present, there are 48 least underdeveloped countries in the world, most of them are far away from world or regional economic centers. The extent of their taking part in economic globalization is far less than that of other developing countries with relatively more advanced economy. Most of the least underdeveloped countries either have not benefited at all from economic globalization, or benefited little.[2]

In the process of economic globalization, one of the important outcomes of the concentration of world income in a small number of countries is that GDP is not evenly distributed. The well-known chart of Robert Hunter Wade, resembling a champagne drinking glass, shows the distribution of world income by population quintiles (See Chart 1-1).

---

[1] Gerald Boxberger and Harald Klimenta, *Die 10 Globalisierungslügen*, p 143, Beijing: Xinhua Press, 2000.

[2] Guo Liancheng, "Positive and Negative Effects of Economic Globalization", *World Economy and Politics*, 2000 (8) .

Chart 1-1 World Population Quintiles and Income Distribution

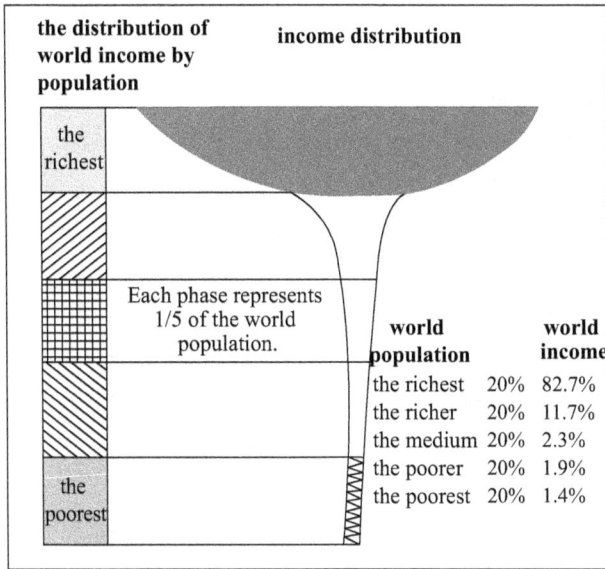

the distribution of world income by population	income distribution		
the richest			
	Each phase represents 1/5 of the world population.	world population	world income
		the richest 20%	82.7%
		the richer 20%	11.7%
		the medium 20%	2.3%
		the poorer 20%	1.9%
the poorest		the poorest 20%	1.4%

Source: Robert Hunter Wade, *Inequality of World Incomes: What Should Be Done?*, http://www.opendemocracy.net/globalization/article257.jsp.

Statistics on the World Bank website show that, in 2002, world GDP was 32,252.480 billion US dollars; countries with low income accounted for 40.6% of world population, and GDP of these countries only accounted for 3.51% of the world total; countries with high income accounted for only 14.9% of world population, and GDP of these countries accounted for 80.59% of world GDP.[1] If the uneven GDP distribution in the world can not fully reflect the gap between the rich and the poor, a comparison with purchase power parity can show that more clearly. In 2002, the purchase power of countries with low income is only 7.4% of those countries with high income. According to the classification of World Bank which generally regards countries with low and medium income as developing countries, the purchase power of developing countries (3,910 US dollars) is just

---

[1] Xie Hao, "Uneven Distribution of Benefit in Economic Globalization and the Theoretical Origin", *Economic Issue Studies*, 2004 (7).

over a half of the world average (7,570 US dollars), and only 14% of that of developed countries (27,590 US dollars). On top of the list in terms of purchase power is Luxemburg (51,060 US dollars) and Sierra Leone ranks 208th (490 US dollars), and the purchase power of the former is 104 times of that of the latter.[1] What's worth noting is that as globalization proceeds, the income gap between developing and developed nations is not narrowed but enlarged. The income of countries in Latin America, Middle East and Africa as compared with developed nations decreased from 14% in 1965 to 7% in 1995. In particular, the majority of African countries are further pushed to edges in the world economy, and their economy either grows very slowly or stops to grow. Trade terms of primary product exports from these countries are instable and tend to be worsened; the proportion of export in GDP is not markedly increased; capital outflow far exceeds inflow; over the past 20 years the actual income per capita has not increased but decreased. It is generally believed that the major mistake of these countries is that they have not taken effective measures to develop labor-intensive processing sector oriented for export. When other developing nations are encouraging free trade policies, trade barriers in African countries are still high; when other developing nations are diversifying their export commodities and lowering the proportion of primary products in their exports, the proportion of primary products in the export of African countries are remarkably increasing.

World income gap is also rapidly widening, both in relative and absolute terms. Take the situation of 1980 for example. The average income per capita in countries in the top quintile was 16 times on average of that in countries in the lowest quintile, with a gap of 19,000 US dollars in terms of absolute income (as calculated according to the price in 2002 and adjusted with purchase power parity). The gap was 22.5 times and the absolute income difference was 26,500 US dollars. If we focus on the average income of individuals instead of that of nations as a whole, to certain extent it looks more encouraging. It is obvious that the income of 70% of the population

---

[1] Xie Hao, "Uneven Distribution of Benefit in Economic Globalization and the Theoretical Origin", *Economic Issue Studies*, 2004 (7).

with the lowest income has increased. However, despite progress made in this regard, there is still great inequality of income in the world. As calculated by weighted population, 40% of the poorest nations account for just over 10% of the total national income in the world, while 20% of the richest nations account for over 60% of the total national income in the world. The ratio of average income per capita between the top 5% nations and the lowest 5% nations is 32:1.[1]

Since the 1990s, with the growth of new information and communication technology represented by the explosive growth of the Internet, new gap between the rich and the poor has appeared, that is, the increasingly expanding "digital gap". The digital gap between countries with high and low income largely results from economic gap between developed countries and developing countries. Shortage of computers, poor electricity infrastructure, lack of telephones and the low capacity of telephone lines all increase the difficulties of starting digital economy in developing countries; the fees charged for new software and the Internet service are hindering the development of digital economy. To a large extent, the users of new information technology are rich countries, and most countries with underdeveloped economy are digitally poor countries in the new digital revolution, or utterly poor.[2] With growing importance of the Internet, crises resulted from digital gap are getting serious. The survey conducted by the Conference on Trade and Development of the UN showed the importance of online transactions, and e-commerce has become an essential component of international trade. The volume of B2B trade online exceeded 5,000 billion US dollars. But the low participation rate of developing nations in digital economy has prevented them from profiting in the growing digital "cake", and as a result, the economic gap between different countries is further

---

[1] James Wolfensen, Francois, "Development and Poverty Alleviation: Review and Outlook—Before the Annual Meeting of the World Bank and IMF, 2004", Oct. 2004, http://www.worldbank.org.cn/Chinese/content/lblacn.pdf, 2005.02.03.

[2] Hu An'gang, Zhou Shaojie, "New Gap Between the Rich and the Poor in the World: Increasingly Expanding 'Digital Gap'", *China Social Sciences*, 2002 (3).

expanded.[1]

Economic globalization is a process of the integration of markets and the liberalization of international trade and investment. World economy being taken as a whole, the improvement of the levels of market exercises influences on the actual income of the poor through three channels. Firstly, general world productivity is to be improved through more efficient allocation of resources in the global scope in order to promote economic growth and improve average income. Secondly, through positive down-trickling effect and diffusion effect as well as negative Matthew effect, income distribution and the income of the poor will be alleviated. Thirdly, with the adjustment of market structure and information transfer, thus risks faced by the poor will be diminished. Yet it is still far from the expected ideal global market integration, and the role of economic globalization in economic growth is uncertain. In terms of income distribution, down-trickling effect and diffusion effect are not obvious since they are interrupted by national borders, but Matthew effect can play a greater role. Due to increased debts and financial risks of developing countries resulting from economic globalization, the risks for the poor are growing.[2] Robert Hunter Wade believes that there are two main causes for the rise in world income inequality. One is the differential population growth between poorer and richer countries, and another is technological change. Technological change in the past two decades tends to reinforce a tendency for high-value-added activities to cluster in the higher-cost Western economies rather than disperse to lower-cost developing countries.[3] In summary, it is true that wealth and income are growing when globalization proceeds, but income distribution inequality is rising too, thus benefits of economic globalization for different nations are uneven.

---

[1] Yang Mengying, Chen Demian, "Digital Gap Between Developing Countries and Developed Countries", *Modern Scientific Management*, 2003 (11).

[2] Qi Liangshu, "The Sustainable Growth of Developing Countries in the Trend of Economic Globalization", http://cedr.whu.edu.cn/cedrpaper/200429214116.pdf.

[3] Robert Hunter Wade, "The Rising Inequality of World Income Distribution", *Finance and Development*, December 2001, Vol. 38, Issue 4.

1.2.3 The uncertainty effect of globalization

For developing countries, the influence of the process of globalization has a very strong feature of uncertainty. While merging into globalization, developing countries will benefit from economic globalization if they choose appropriate policies and have favorable opportunities and better domestic conditions. They will suffer losses in economic globalization if they choose inappropriate policies and have unfavorable opportunities or weak domestic conditions.

1.2.3.1 Globalization has a double effect.

Globalization is an objective and historical process, and it is also the requirement and outcome of the progress of social productivity and technology. For developing countries, globalization is a sword with a double edge, with both positive and negative effect. Facing opportunities and challenges brought about by globalization, developing countries may take measures to improve their advantages and avoid the disadvantages and gain rapid growth in the context of globalization.

Take economic globalization as an example. Its positive effect includes the following: firstly, economic globalization provides conditions for the rational allocation of resources in the world. As economic globalization proceeds, international market is growing into an integrated one, obstacles and barriers for economic exchanges between countries are disappearing, and the possibility of engagement with each other's advantages are increasing. Secondly, economic globalization has made the competition in the world market ever keener. Fierce competition in the world market urges enterprises to keep improving their production and operational activities, to increase investment in research and development, and to promote technological progress. Thirdly, economic globalization has speeded up industrial restructuring in the world. In this process, developing countries can attract capital and advanced technologies from developed countries, draw on management expertise of developed countries, and speed up domestic industrial restructuring and upgrading, as well as industrialization and modernization. It is obvious that economic globalization has provided developing countries important opportunities for rapid economic growth.

But the negative effect of economic globalization should not be ignored, either. Firstly, economic globalization may intensify the imbalance of world economic development. Developed countries have great economic and technological strength and advantages in the world political and economic system, so it is highly possible that they may gain far greater benefits from the process of economic globalization than developing countries. As a result, the South-North gap tends to be expanded. Secondly, economic globalization has promoted the merger and acquisition operations of international enterprises, possibly resulting in a new international monopoly. Some large corporations in developed capitalist countries expand their advantage of scale through merger and acquisitions to increase competitiveness in international market, and thus occur waves of merger and acquisitions all throughout the world. Some countries even ignore anti-trust laws they had promulgated and this time support merger and acquisitions. In recent years, big corporation alliances have appeared, thus bringing about new international monopoly and increasing international competition. Thirdly, the progress of globalization also results in many global issues. When economic globalization proceeds, the links between countries are becoming closer, and problems of one country or region can rapidly spread to other countries and regions, such as environmental issues, epidemics, regional clashes and wars, and terrorist attacks. Global security issues become prominent.

1.2.3.2 Globalization intensifies risks.

Not only does globalization have a double effect, it also increases or intensifies possible risks a country may encounter in the process of development. Thus, developing countries face more uncertainties and instability. As a historical process, globalization is accompanied by risks in the modern sense, and with globalization becoming a main feature of the current age (a global age), risks turn to be a basic character of the society.[1]

---

[1] Yang Xuedong, "Risk Society in the Context of Economic Globalization", *Study Times*, 2005-01-17.

Ulrich Beck, a German scholar, thinks that mankind has entered a world risk society in the current age, where non-Western society and Western society share not only the same space and time, and more importantly, also share the basic challenges of the second modernity.[1]

Why does globalization co-exist with risks? There are at least three causes.

One cause is that globalization speeds up the spread of risks and crises. Economic globalization has profoundly changed the operational environment of world economy and the world market turns to be more open, with keener competition. The cross-border flow of production factors such as capital, technology, information and personnel are facilitated. The means of contact of world economy has turned from mainly international trade in the past to cross-border flow of capital. While economic contacts are getting closer, all kinds of other contacts are becoming closer, too. The closeness of contact has provided channels and routes for the transfer and spreading of various risks and crises in the global scope, and as a result, the spreading speed of risks and crises is increased.

Secondly, globalization amplifies the influence of risks and potential outcomes. The progress of globalization makes the emergence of risk society become a possibility, and the outcomes of risks of globalization go beyond political-geographical boundaries, and the interdependence of world risks is deepening. The most outstanding example is, as financial globalization proceeds, financial crisis spreads at a faster pace and its scope expands. Domino effect of financial crisis is increasing, and financial crisis in one country may cause financial instability and turbulence in other countries or even the whole world within a short time. At the same time, advanced information and communication technologies enable more people to be aware of the potential outcome of risks, and people tend to get panic due to incomplete or imbalanced information. What is worth noting is that in the context of economic globalization, international contacts are increasing, so are contacts between economic departments and sectors of industries. As a

---

[1] Ulrich Beck, *World Risk Society*, pp 2-3, Nanjing: Nanjing University Press, 2004.

result, a certain risk or crisis may well trigger other risks or crises, resulting in a more complex risk or crisis. Preventing risks and handling crisis has become a tougher job.

Thirdly, globalization enhances not only exchanges but also interdependence trend. But the asymmetry of power between developing countries and developed countries in interdependence process causes greater sensitivity and vulnerability in developing countries, who are facing more unpredictable and uncontrollable risks or crises. As a result, there is no doubt that developing countries face much greater risks compared with developed countries.[1] At present, as limited by human resources, adequate material strength and finances, developing countries lack capabilities to prevent existing risks and respond to them, and even developed countries do not have a sound system of preventing risks and handling crisis.[2]

The basic thinking of maintaining and promoting the smooth operation of world economy and the sustainable development of the international society is to understand the uncertainties of the impact of economic globalization, to establish strategies of development in accordance with national conditions, to improve crisis management mechanisms, and to strengthen international collaboration.

1.3 The Impact of Globalization on Politics in the Contemporary World

One of the important outcomes of globalization is that different economies are closely linked and their interdependence are greatly enhanced.

---

[1] Robert Keohane and Joseph Nay realized the asymmetry in interdependence and proposed to analyze two variables of interdependence: sensitivity and vulnerability. Sensitivity refers to the degree of response of a policy framework. How fast is the change in one country resulting in change with cost in another country? How much is the cost? Vulnerability refers to the degree of loss suffered from cost imposed by external events (or change of policies). See Robert Keohane, Joseph Nay, *Power and Interdependence*, 3rd ed., pp 9-20, Beijing: Peking University Press, 2002.

[2] Jiang Yong, "On the Uncertainties of World Economy", *Qiushi Monthly*, 2003 (15).

Against the backdrop of globalization, economic interests of different nations is intermingled, and countries are sharing both interests and disadvantages, and all these bring major influences on international politics.

1.3.1 Rapid progress of globalization has strengthened the trend of international politics becoming more focused on economy.

Firstly, in the context of globalization, each and every nation has put economic issues in a very important position when handling international relationships. During the Cold War, there were quite a number of countries that had raised political and ideological factors to key positions in handling their international relationships. Since 1990s with the rapid progress of globalization, countries have adjusted their international strategies and have put economic issues to central position, thus foreign affairs and exchanges are monitored to serve economic development. Through international exchanges, governments have endeavored to attract foreign investment (or expand foreign investment), to develop overseas market, to improve international relations, to create a peaceful and secure environment, and to provide the latest technological and economic information, thus all these aimed at economic development task. Economic interests of countries contain the confrontations in political systems and ideology, but relations between countries generally form a mainstream trend of peace and development.[1] At the same time clashes and conflicts between countries take new forms, and competition of overall national strength—mainly economic and technological spheres—has become what great powers are competing for. After the Cold War, conflicts between developed countries, between developing and developed countries, or between members of regional alliances are almost mainly centered on economy. Maximizing economic interests has become the fundamental choice for foreign strategies of each country. The battlefield of confrontation has shifted to the economic sectors, capturing market shares, in particular the market share of newly emerging economies and

---

[1] Li Jingzhi as chief compiler, *Economy and Politics in the Contemporary World*, p 72.

new and high technological products which have become key area in terms of national security. Today's trade negotiations carry the same significance as those armament control negotiations in the Cold War, and maintaining technological superiority is deemed as important as controlling geographic strategic areas. Contending for human resources is not less sharp than contending for material resources. Economic powers and interest groups are increasingly becoming main players in international competition, and international economic organizations and multinational corporations have attained growing roles.

Secondly, with their economic power and dominance in the world economy, great powers increasingly use economic means for purpose of political ends. As economic globalization proceeds, international relations and foreign policies of each nation focus on achieving economic interests. It has become more common to solve political problems through economic means, and economic activities have become important means for countries to promote their diplomatic strategies and achieve their goals in the international political arena.[1] Since after the dramatic changes in the former Soviet Union and Eastern European countries, aiming to expand their power and seek world hegemony, Western countries led by the United States have generally lured these paralyzed countries by economic aids, and at the same time imposed them western political terms with economic aid carrot to follow orders and join in pro-Western front. Treating political issues from economic perspective and applying economic means for political ends have become usual tactics instrumentalized by Western countries. In international conflicts, confrontational measures aiming at economic threat are more frequently adopted.[2] Take the United States after the Cold War as an example: When an international crisis takes place, the first reaction of the US government is always to announce economic sanctions on the target country, and she had

---

[1] Zhu Qinjun, "Ten Influences of Economic Globalization on International Politics", *World Economic Research*, 2001 (5).

[2] Liu Xuelian, "Globalization and the New Development of International Relationship", *Social Sciences Journal of Jilin University*, 2001 (6).

economically sanctioned Iraq, Iran and Cuba. Moreover, when any economic issue threats its interest, the United States regards those issues from a view of political stakes and forces them to surrender. In trade relations between some large and small or medium-sized countries, there also exists such a tendency. It needs to be made clear that using economic means to political end will not only harm economic interest of the weak countries, but also affect that of great powers negatively.

Thirdly, against the backdrop of globalization, economic, political and cultural relations intermingle, and rapid spreading pace of economic risks has greatly increased the impact of economic factors on international relations. In the context of economic globalization, risks surfacing in any corner of the world will probably evolve into a crisis effecting the whole world. Risks and crises of a single country will rapidly spread to other parts of the world, thus risks and crises of a single country pose a potential risk for other countries, thus the possibility of each country to face a crisis has greatly increased. To control and manage economic risks, handle economic fluctuations and crises in the international markets will exert great positive influence on international political relations.

1.3.2 Globalization causes changes in actors and their ways of behavior in international relationship.

Over a rather long period of time, international relations are relationships between countries, and sovereign nations were the only actors in international relations. With the rising of international organizations, in particular the founding of the United Nations and other organizations since the Second World War, they exert increasing influences and take important roles in international relations. They are entitled to sign treaties and agreements with countries or other international organizations; officials of these organizations enjoy similar privileges and immunity like diplomatic representatives of sovereign nations. Playing special roles different from those of sovereign nations, many international organizations are endowed with the status of subjects in international relationship.[1] Since the end of Cold War, a new trend—countries establishing various international organizations for enhanced coordination and cooperation among themselves—becomes more apparent, i.e. NAFTA, ASEAN, etc. Today more and more actors appear in the international scenes which are not sovereign states, and they deepen interdependence between states and the progress of globalization. On the other hand, the progress of globalization also strengthens contacts and collaboration between countries in various sectors and promotes the establishment of different types of international organizations. As a result, today's actors in international relations include both sovereign nations and non-sovereign actors. Non-sovereign actors mainly include international governmental level organizations and non-governmental organizations, as well as multinational corporations. As a matter of fact, although the roles of international organizations in international relations have increased, sovereign states remain the most influential actors in the international community, and keep a key position in international relations.

At the same time, the behaviors of actors in international relations are changing, too. Globalization has integrated the world markets in a deeper level and increased the interdependence of actors in international political system, which objectively has resulted in the erosion and weakening of state governance, and made it impossible for a state to protect its own economy without facing pressure from outside. Furthermore, it is impossible for a state to limit economic, social and cultural processes since these factors have already transcended national borders, gained freedom, become self-perpetuating and cannot be managed within national borders.[2]

With the progress of globalization, not only economic interdependence, but political interdependence between countries is intensifying. What is worth noting is that, against the backdrop of globalization, political interdependence

---

[1] Liu Xuelian, "Globalization and the New Development of International Relationship", *Social Sciences Journal of Jilin University*, 2001 (6).

[2] Yuri Shishkov, "Economic Globalization: The Result of the Industrialization and Informatization of Society", *Social Sciences*, 2002, Vol. 33, Issue 3.

is no longer simply result in reciprocality; i.e., when a state's policy changes toward another that will not necessarily cause the latter to change her policies reciprocally. More often in international politics, multilateral interdependence has replaced bilateral interdependence. That is to say, international politics become increasingly dependent on multilateral negotiations and practices, not just on bilateral exchanges. As globalization has brought about a strengthening trend of interdependence, countries opt more for collaboration and coordination in dealing with international affairs. Against the backdrop of globalization, the rules of international relations no longer appear to be a traditional zero-sum game, but more often as "win-win" or "all-win" deal. As a result, to a certain extent the security of a nation no longer presupposes the insecurity of another country as the prerequisite, and a country seeking power and prosperity does not need to bet on the weakness of others. Mark Beeson and Alex J. Bellamy believe that, "sustainable security would seem to require approaches that go beyond traditional militarism and the zero-sum logic of neo-realistic policy making….the most powerful military apparatus ever assembled is incapable of protecting its citizens from attack like in 2001, it is hardly radical to question its efficiency or the appropriateness of any strategic doctrine that underpins this reality."[1] In the age of globalization, cooperation should be strengthened and effective international cooperation mechanisms should be established. Besides, it should be well understood that effective international cooperation is based on reasonable compromise, since adequate compromise and concession is the prerequisite for the most effective cooperation. With such a view, the ways of cooperation and compromise will increase, and confrontations and life-and-death struggles will gradually decrease.

In the process of globalization, a series of global issues have become outstanding, such as biological deterioration, environmental pollution, food shortage, swelling population, refuges, drug issues, etc., which raise new demands for international cooperation. With the progress of economic

---

[1] Mark Beeson, Alex J. Bellamy, "Globalization, Security and International Order after 11 September", *Australian Journal of Politics & History*, Sep. 2003, Vol. 49, Issue 3.

globalization, penetration, infiltration and interdependence between nations in economic, political, social and cultural spheres are deepening, and common global issues are growing in number. So-called global issues are issues or phenomena involving many or all countries in the world (not just one or a few countries), and solving them can not depend only on one or a few countries.[1] These global issues are related to the future and destiny of mankind, and disturb interests of all nations and regions. They can not be solved by one or just a few countries. On the contrary, they require concerted action by the international community. The increasing number of global issues has drawn people's concern on global interest idea, and encouraged world peoples to handle global issues with the idea of common interest of mankind which breeds as a new value. The emergence of such global issues has made it imperative to establish international systems, to intensify mechanisms of international coordination, negotiation as well as collaboration, and to apply global governance to global issues.

With the progress of globalization, the actors in international relations employ cultural means to achieve their purposes more frequently as ever, supplementing political and economic means. Against the backdrop of globalization, while different cultures meet or merge with each other in the global scope, it is inevitable that they may conflict or clash with each other. As the quintessence of spiritual wealth of mankind, culture is featured with both distinctive diversity and national character. Conflicts and clashes of different cultures reflect differences on factors such as political system, values, literature and arts, customs, philosophies, ethics, history and tradition, religious belief and national characters, both at theoretical and psychological levels. The exclusivity of these factors is one of the underlying reasons for current international conflicts. After the Cold War, it has become an important instrument for some countries to promote their foreign strategies and realize their political purpose through cultural infiltration. The developed Western countries promote Western values and their political system in other parts of

---

[1] Shi Xinghe, "A Probe into Contemporary Global Issues", *World Economics and Politics*, 2002 (3).

the world with an intention to seek hegemony. In the process of economic globalization, the political charm of cultural systems is once more enhanced, and cultural spheres tend to become a special battlefield of international politics.

1.3.3 Globalization erodes state sovereignty.

Sovereignty is the supreme power of a nation to deal with its domestic and foreign affairs independently. It has features including two aspects. One is that it is supreme domestically, and the other is that it is independent internationally.[1] Sovereignty is the foundation for the basic rights of a nation, which is not dependent or affiliated to any other right, domestically or internationally. Globalization has resulted in a deepening interdependence between countries in the world, which in turn brings about interwoven connections or restrictions between countries, or between countries and international organizations. Accompanying the interdependence, globalization erodes continuously state sovereignty, and erosion comes from three different directions.

The first is the erosion of state sovereignty by international organizations. Globalization has encouraged the international community to form various common interests, and pursuing these common interests requires countries to transcend national boundaries and to give away or share part of the sovereignty to facilitate cooperation. International cooperation may require that some rights, as part of state sovereignty, be given to international organizations, including part of macro-policy decision-making, customs tariff decision-making, resources management, foreign policies on economy, and industrial decision-making. As a result, each nation can no longer enjoy full sovereignty in domestic and foreign affairs, or even military affairs, in an absolute or supreme way as claimed by the classic sovereignty theory. Some nongovernmental organizations such as religious organizations, party alliances and trade unions, will exert influence on some sovereign nations. With a better understanding of the interdependence of mankind and common

---

[1] Zhou Gengsheng, *International Law*, Vol. 1, Beijing: Commerce Press House, 1976.

threats faced, more countries start to recognize—from a global perspective—and balance the relationship between maintaining state sovereignty and allowing a sphere for operations of international organizations aiming at coordination and cooperation. They have realized that a part of sovereignty needs to be given away and effective international mechanisms should be established in order to protect both the national interest and the interest of the international community. German scholar Ernst Benda believes that, "the 'de-boundary' phenomenon brought about by globalization puts all countries in a position whereby they would rather take action under the restrictions of the reality of globalization than be free to make any decisions on the basis of absolute state sovereignty. Global issues have to be solved within a global framework, which requires a partial transfer of state sovereignty. In nature, the signing of international treaties or agreements is a concrete manifestation of the partial transfer of state sovereignty"[1].

The second is the impact of multinational corporations. As economic globalization proceeds, multinational corporations, the main carriers of economic globalization, have grown both in number and size. In 1996, the number of multinational corporations reached 445 million in the world, and the number of subsidiaries controlled by them was 2.8 billion, and worldwide employees of multinational corporations reached more than 70 million. These multinational corporations control 40% of world production, 50%-60% of international trade, 60%-70% of international technological trade, and 90% of foreign direct investment. The existence and development of multinational corporations have greatly influenced the world economy and to some extent challenge state sovereignty. The volume of internal trade of multinational corporations realizes one third of the total trade volume in the world, which has an impact on the ways international trade being conducted and its future trends, and challenges the sovereignty of states. Meanwhile, innovation and transfer of production technologies are tightly controlled by multinational corporations. The top 500 largest multinational corporations in

---

[1] Ernst Benda, "State Sovereignty in the Era of Globalization", *World Economics and Politics*, 2004 (2).

developed countries control 90% of production technology of these countries, and technological transfer within the multinational corporations accounts for 80% of the world total. With their enormous strength, multinational corporations challenge state sovereignty by influencing government policies and their social welfare arrangements, in order to gain maximum interest. In addition, with their economic power and transnational network, multinational corporations can free themselves from the control of their host or parent countries, and exert direct pressure or seek for or train lobbyists in order to influence their decisions. Thus, the traditional state sovereignty is challenged.

The third is the challenge on developing nations' sovereignty by developed countries. Globalization is dominated by developed countries led by the United States, and they take advantage of their powerful positions in economic globalization to intervene or control domestic and foreign affairs of developing countries with various pretexts, and even exert military interference. Developed countries take advantage of globalization to erode state sovereignty, and try their best to advocate that state sovereignty is outdated and should perish, and negate or criticize state sovereignty from the perspective of globalization. Some believe that in the era of globalization, "state sovereignty is no longer sacred and inviolable". Some revise the concept of sovereignty in the period of Westphalia system and claim that there is a need to reevaluate the function of sovereignty in international relation theories. Thus arise many misconceptions in the concept.[1] At the same time, in the political circles in the West some people assert that the traditional principles of international relations should be revised, and propose a series of views negating state sovereignty and center their views on the idea advocating " human right value is superior than state sovereignty". Former Secretary General of the United Nations Kofi Annan also suggests: in the face of the pressure of globalization and international cooperation, state sovereignty is to be redefined in its most basic sense.[2] It is inevitable

---

[1] Andreas Osiander, "Sovereignty, International Relations, and the Westphalia Myth", *International Organization*, Spring 2001, Vol. 55, No. 2.

[2] Kofi Annan, "International: Two Concepts of Sovereignty", *The Economist*, Sep. 18, 1999.

that state sovereignty is to be partly diminished, eroded or weakened under the impact of globalization, thus limited to a certain scope. But, state sovereignty under the current conditions or in the near future will possibly not disappear.[1]

1.3.4 The rapid progress of globalization has increased the prospects of peaceful development in the world.

Firstly, the expansion of common interest of mankind and the deepening interdependence of countries brought about by globalization are favorable for maintaining world peace and security. The progress of globalization has resulted in a situation that, in political, economic, cultural and many other areas, countries are closely connected and what happens in one country, positive or negative, affects others. The development of any country or region is possible only through constant exchanges with other countries or regions. At the same time, with the growing number of global issues and emerging of world risk society, all countries have grown into a community sharing both pleasure and misery. Against a backdrop of globalization, national interest is linked to international interest, and collaborations and exchanges between countries are enhanced. Members of the international community should adopt a spirit of sharing responsibilities and risks to maintain world peace and stability, and promote peaceful, healthy and sustained development of the world.

Secondly, a global civil society is emerging, favorable to the world peace and stability. Global civil institutions play growing roles in national as well as international sphere. Over the past decades, these institutions have emerged with the progress of globalization and have to a large extent displayed the power of globalization.[2] Civil society actors are non-state, state-transcending

---

[1] Xiong Guangqing, "On the Opportunities of Maintaining State Sovereignty by Developing Nations in the Era of Globalization", *Capital Normal University Journal* (Social Sciences Edition), 2002 (4).

[2] Joseph S. Nye, John D. Donahue, *Governance in a Globalizing World*, p 242, Beijing: World Affairs Press, 2003.

or citizen social groups.[1] To be specific, global civil society is composed of non-governmental organizations, religious groups, trade unions, native ethnic communities, philanthropic institutions, community organizations and private foundations. It is an important force appeared in the field of international development over the past two decades. Democratic governance and the rapid progress of globalization expand the scale, scope and abilities of global civil society. American scholar David Brown and his colleagues have noted: "Civil society institutions are playing increasingly important role in many international domains and in many countries. Over the past decades, the rise of civil society institutions has been linked to the force of globalization, and partly promoted by the latter."[2] At present, global civil society develops rapidly. Reports indicate that in 1999, the number of international NGOs have increased to 26,000. Civil society institutions have become an important player in global development aids. Reports of OECD indicate that, in 2003, international aids provided by civil society institutions have reached at least 12 billion US dollars. Over the past 20 years, civil society institutions have started to acquire abilities in influencing and forming global public policies, and their vigor in public sphere has won them supporters from all over the world. For example, they have put forward proposals regarding ban on landmines, debt relief and environmental protection. The vigor of global civil society is proven recently by the 2005 World Social Forum, held in Porto Alegre, Brazil, with 155,000 registered participants. Fairer and more sustained options were proposed in line with the current pattern of economic globalization during the forum. Global civil society has its internal rationale and is endowed with unique and functional features: one is that it seeks the unanimity of behaviors of multiple actors and builds a global ethic as coordination and cooperation; secondly, it criticizes the conflict between the limitless expansion of global free market and the limited capacity of nation

---

[1] Akiyoshi Hoshino, *World Politics in the Age of Globalization: The Actors and Structures of World Politics*, p 177, Beijing: Social Sciences Academic Press, 2004.

[2] David Brown, "Globalization, NGOs and Multi-Sectoral Relations", *Globalization and Civil Society*, edited by Li Huibin, pp 142-157, Guilin: Guangxi Normal University Press, 2003.

states, and explores a solution for a reasonable tension; thirdly, it advocates an effective governance of global public issues, and seeks for a practical bridge between global public order and collective behaviors.[1]

Thirdly, the progress of globalization has radically changed the strategic environment of hegemonic great powers in the world system, thus reduced the likelihood of a world war. Observing the international situation, multi-polarity is facing serious challenges but still making progress despite all the difficulties, which is favorable to maintaining world peace. On the one hand, the strongest opponent of the United States during four decades of Cold War disappeared suddenly with the dissolution of the former Soviet Union, and the United States remains as the sole superpower. On the other hand, the configuration of forces in today's world pattern has become rather complicated. American scholar Joseph S. Nye notes that: in the global information age, power configuration displays a pattern that resembles a complex three-dimensional chess game. On the top chessboard, military power is largely uni-polar. The United States is the only country, possessing both intercontinental nuclear weapons and large state-of-the-art air, naval and ground forces capable of global deployment. But on the middle chessboard, economic power is multi-polar, with the United States, Europe and Japan producing two-thirds of world products. With its rapid growth, China is likely to become the fourth big player. On this economic board, the United States is not hegemonic, and must often bargain with Europe. The bottom chessboard is the realm of transnational relations that transcend government controls. On this bottom board, power is widely dispersed, and it makes no sense to speak of uni-polarity, multi-polarity or hegemony.[2]

Conceiving the current world situation is closely linked with correct assessing the position of United States. There is no doubt that the United

---

[1] Yuan Zushe, "The Formation of Global Civil Society and Its Cultural Significance, the Implication of 'Personality' of World Citizen and the Awareness of Global 'Public Value'", *Peking University Journal* (Philosophy and Social Sciences Edition), 2004 (4).

[2] Joseph S. Nye, "The New Rome Meets the New Barbarians", *The Economist*, 3/23/2002, Vol. 362, Issue 8265.

States is the sole superpower in the world and positions itself as hegemonic in the world system. But, her status is challenged by various powers, thus her power is limited. Joseph S. Nye argues that, although the United States remains the world's leading power, it cannot act alone to solve global problems such as transnational terrorism, the proliferation of weapons of mass destruction and global warming. Although the United States is the only country in a position to take the lead in protecting "global public goods", such as open international economic system and international stability, she can maintain leadership only if she can succeed an international consensus on issues of global importance.[1] According to Samuel P. Huntington, contemporary international politics does not fit to any of these three models of uni-polar, multi-polar or non-polar. Instead it is a strange hybrid, and a uni-multi-polar system with one superpower and several great powers. The settlement of key international issues requires actions of the superpower, but always need combined efforts of other powers; the single superpower can, however, employ veto action on key issues by the support of other states.[2] After the Cold War, the strategic environment of the United States has dramatically changed. Paul Kennedy notes in his essay, "… vulnerable to mass destruction arms, the unmatchable economic advantage eroded, and international system becoming even more multi-polar: these are the three aspects of the largest change of the American grand strategy since the 1940s."[3] At the same time, the limitation of the power of the United States makes her to trade off or choose the composing parts of various factors in balancing its strength. If it cannot handle the trade-off appropriately, she will lose her power. Jin Chanrong, a Chinese scholar, believes that at the beginning of the new century, the promoting effect of new economy on the rapid economic growth of the United States has diminished, the intensity of her ideological attack has eased, and will be threatened by terrorism for a long term. As a result, dominance of the United States in the world will

[1] Joseph S. Nye, "The American National Interest and Global Public Goods", *International Affairs*, April 2002, Vol. 78, Issue 2.

[2] Samuel P. Huntington, "The Lonely Superpower", *Foreign Affairs*, Mar./Apr. 1999, Vol. 78, Issue 2.

[3] Paul Kennedy, *Grand Strategies in War and Peace*, p 176, Beijing: World Affairs Press, 2005.

be decreased.[1] Cal Jillson, an American scholar, suggests that the United States needs to maintain on the one hand its global advantage of economic competitiveness, on the other hand her superior military power. To balance the two is a paradox.[2] It shows that, despite being a superpower, the United States is not powerful enough to do anything out of its own will.

Meanwhile, the United States is the key driving force of globalization, receiving the biggest benefit from globalization. In the process of globalization, the United States has obtained enormous economic benefits and she can coach the world via economic means replacing military means. The possibility for any country to resort to military means is lowered if she realizes that the cost of war is larger than the profit it brings. If the United States can keep those interests, she will no doubt continue to maintain the present system, instead of waging a war to change the current world system or world order. Shi Yinhong holds that the basic principle of smoothing or circumventing conflicts through mutual respect, tolerance and compromise is not only a rule vital to world political prospects in the new century, but also an existing trend strongly supported by economic, political, military and cultural realities. Among these factors, the value of war as an effective tool is rapidly diminishing, and the new trend enhances this principle.[3] We should also note that in a context when global power configuration loses its balance, a world war can only be initiated by the United States, and the United States still possesses a strong desire to solve international conflicts through military power. But the possibility of waging a mass war is greatly reduced, and the possibility of a world war is very dim.

[1] Jin Chanrong, "On the United States' International Position from a Perspective of Internal Balancing Mechanism", *Modern International Relations*, 2004 (3).

[2] Cal Jillson, *American Government: Political Change and Institutional Development*, Belmont, CA: Thomson/Wadsworth, 2005, p 439.

[3] Shi Yinhong, *New Trend, New Pattern and New Norms*, p 421, Beijing: Law Press House, 2000.

Chapter 2

Globalization and Capitalism in the Post-Cold War Era

Globalization is the outcome of the long-term development of capitalism and at the same time exerts important influence on the development of capitalism. Developed capitalist countries remain to be the dominant force in the process of globalization, on the other hand capitalist system causes many drawbacks in the process of globalization. Globalization has promoted the global expansion of capitalism but at the same time raises new challenges to capitalism. Against the backdrop of globalization, the development of capitalism displays a relatively strong vitality, and compared with socialism, capitalism holds a more advantageous position.

2.1 The Role of Contemporary Capitalism in Globalization

2.1.1 Globalization is the outcome of the long-term development of capitalism.

Up till now, globalization is priorly and foremost an economic globalization. In terms of the facts of world historical evolution, globalization is directly connected with the development of capitalism. In the status of natural economy times, production activities of mankind were quite discrete. But capitalist commodity production and the market economy nurtured later in history and had enabled mankind's production activities to grow in a continuous expansion, that is, seeking for profit to meet the pursuit of value increase of capital. The sprout of globalization was indeed nurtured in the early period of capitalist development. In *The Communist Manifesto*, Marx and Engels noted, "The discovery of America and the voyages round Africa provided fresh new territories for the rise of bourgeoisie." "Modern industry has established the world-market, for which the discovery of America paved the way. This market has given an immense development to commerce, to navigation, to communication by land. This development has, in its time, reacted on the extension of industry."[1] "The need of a constantly expanding market for its products chases the bourgeoisie over the whole surface of the globe. It must nestle everywhere, settle everywhere, establish connections everywhere." "The bourgeoisie has through its exploitation of the world-market has given a cosmopolitan character to production and consumption in every country."[2] Economic activities of mankind were extensively inter-connected for the first time due to the appearance of the world market, and economic globalization had first grown in international trade. Economic globalization not only means that production activities transcend the boundary of a certain nation, but more importantly, means the expansion of production relationships, the globalization of capital movement and the international circulation of capital. But economic globalization has experienced a rather long period of development from the first sprout to today's actual form. From geographical discoveries and industrial revolution to colonialism wave, capitalism developed through embryonic stage, liberal capitalism, monopoly capitalism and state monopoly capitalism stages. Capital has broken through fetters of geographical boundaries, and transcended the limits of national states to

---

[1] *Selected Works of Marx and Engels*, 2nd Edition, Vol. 1, p 273, Beijing: People's Press, 1995.
[2] *Ibid*, p 276.

greater scopes.

After the Second World War, led by the large-scale transnational movement of industrial capital, advanced capitalist countries have formed international circulation of capital and since then capital has started its movement of accumulation in a rapid and comprehensive way. The large-scale transnational movement of capital and the establishment of mechanisms for the circulation of capital internationally have eventually formed the world economic system of capitalism, and thus capitalist production has become a worldwide production in its true sense. Hence the world economy has started to transit to the stage of all-round globalization. After the Second World War, worldwide flow of commodities and resources has remarkably grown. Western capital has flowed out of national boundaries and been invested to overseas market on a large scale. A global production system has been established. Between the 1960s and the 1980s, the growth of overseas production of Western countries is 1.5 times of that of gross domestic production, and overseas investment and production have become an important new sphere of economic growth. According to the statistics of Conference on Trade and Development of the UN, international direct investment was 40 billion US dollars in 1970, which grew to 170 billion US dollars in 1980, 315 billion US dollars in 1995, and 700 billion US dollars in 2000. In the process of direct investment movement in the world, multinational corporations have played key roles. Many famous corporations have taken it as part of their development strategy to shift their production overseas and set up overseas production bases. Take Panasonic Electronics of Japan as an example. In 1986, Panasonic had 138,000 local employees in Japan, and 44,000 employees abroad; in 1996, Panasonic had 158,000 domestic employees and 108,000 overseas employees. Overseas employees have made up over 40% of the total number of employees. At present, companies having global operations in the United States make up 60% of the total number of companies in this country. Multinational corporations are having increasingly prominent position in the world economy. In the process of globalization, multinational corporations have gained the most rapid development, and globalization is more embodied within multinational corporations. Capital, information, wealth and power are increasingly clustered in multinational corporations. International trade has gained unprecedented growth. After the Second World War, in 1950, world export volume was only 61 billion US dollars, which increased to 315 billion US dollars in 1970, and exceeded 600 billion US dollars in 1997. Capital, goods, people, service and even knowledge, all have started cross-border flow on a large scale.

Globalization is the outcome of long-term development and evolution of capitalism. The large-scale cross-border movement of Western capital after the Second World War has resulted in an intensive expansion of capitalist production. International capital re-produces and circulates globally, and forms a true international cycle of capital, which expresses the all-round progress of economic globalization. Due to the organic nature of social development, economic globalization inevitably causes a series of chain reactions in other social domains, and further promotes globalization to evolve in greater depth and width.

2.1.2 Capitalism: the driving force of the current globalization

The wave of globalization sweeping the modern world is the outcome of capitalist long-term development. In addition, capitalist countries, in particular, the United States and other developed Western countries, are the most active advocators and the major promoters of the current wave of globalization. It is foreseeable that for a long time in the future, globalization will remain to be dominated by capitalism.

Before the October Revolution in Russia, the world economy was a capitalist one, social system and ideology were either capitalist or dominated by capitalism. After the October Revolution, two different social systems had co-existed in the world, but taken as a whole, capitalism was enjoying a dominating position in various aspects such as economy, technology, politics and social life. Globalization proceeds under the dominance of capitalism. In terms of economic sphere, the world economy is led by capitalism, or to be more exact, by a small number of advanced capitalist economies. Statistics show that, the GDP of the United States, some European countries and Japan accounts for over 70% of GDP in the world, and export volume and foreign direct investment of these countries account for 70% and 90% of the world total respectively. In terms of political system, capitalist democracy has matured and kept improving within several centuries of evolution and constant reforms. Capitalism has a strong capability of self-renewal and self-adjustment which was rare in history. In terms of ideology, since capitalist system had won over feudalism, capitalist ideology has controlled the commanding heights of world thought and cultural sphere. This was even true even after the surging of socialism after the Second World War. In terms of human social life, capitalist lifestyle is admired with excitement and penetrates every corner of the globe.

Since the 1980s, globalization became prominent first in economic sphere, and the development of the world economy has witnessed several major changes, which had basically originated in developed capitalist countries and controlled and led by these countries. Among these changes, the first was the trend and feature of adapting information technology and web technology in the economy. This remarkable trend had two results: information and web have become part of the economy, with the appearance of information industry and web economy. On the other hand, with the rapid popularity of computers and other information technological equipment, the Internet has rapidly connected the whole world and global economic activities. During the whole process of applying information technology and web technology, Western developed nations have actively promoted and played a leading role. Secondly, countries and regions in the world have been more rapidly included into the world market, and the outline of the world market which is global and all-inclusive has turned to be clearer. Since the mid-1980s, many developing countries have adopted economic reforms with market orientation, and opened to the world market. Since the dramatic change in the former Soviet Union and Eastern European countries, they have also vigorously developed the market economy and have joined the world market. Thirdly, advocated and promoted by the United States, economic liberalization has gained a strong momentum. Since the Second World War, aiming to expand in the world markets, capitalist countries, especially the United States, have made great endeavors to promote policies and institutions for economic liberalization, and requested other countries to reduce or cancel trade barriers, to loosen or give up financial controls, and to adopt free flow of goods and capital. The United States is the biggest economic power and beneficiary of a free world economy. For this very reason, it spares no efforts in advocating a free world economy.

Developed countries are strong in technological resources with advanced high-tech industries and high-tech contents of products. Multinational corporations of these countries hold enormous advantages in the world production and world markets, which enables them to take a leading position in the wave of globalization. The establishment of computer networks and global information highways has connected televisions, telephones and computers, and the whole world has become a "global village". Who controls the resources in the world? According to some documents, the top 500 multinational corporations in the world own 90% of the new technologies and realize 75% of technological trade volume in the world. Among the states, U.S.A ranks No.1 in terms of high-tech. The development of science and technology and knowledge economy in the United States is closely linked to the process of economic globalization. Taking advantage of its strength in science and technology, knowledge economy and high value-added technology, the United States exchanges its knowledge economy products by unequal trade with the Third World and buys low value-added raw materials and labor-intensive goods from them. Thus large amount of economic surplus is transferred to the United States. The achievements and advantages of the modern capitalist economy are mainly obtained by the progress of science and technology as well as knowledge innovation (R&D). Statistics show that 70%-80% of economic growth since the Second World War in developed countries in the West mainly came from the progress of science and technology. With the rapid development of science and technology, the tertiary industry, which mainly includes finance, information and other services, has been booming and accounts for 2/3 in the national economy of developed nations in the West. Correspondingly, labor market structure of modern capitalist countries has undergone major changes. Agricultural laborers only account for 5%-6% of labor force in developed countries in the West, and less than 3% in the United States. The number of industrial workers in the traditional sense has dropped sharply and the proportion in labor force is less than 30% in most of developed countries. On the contrary, the number workers in the tertiary industry and its production has increased year on year and accounts for 60%-70% in the total number of gross production.[1] Labor force shows a new trend of having more knowledge, using more mental ability, creating more white-collar jobs, and more segmented by different skill levels. The overall level of technology and cultural quality is increasingly improving. At the same time, the new technological revolution has created a great amount of new products, new technologies and labor services, expanded the space of international trade, caused the internationalization of production, operations and capital flows, and promoted the trend of economic globalization. As the carrier of internationalization of production and capital, multinational corporations have sharply grown both in number and size. Multinational corporations in developed capitalist countries have made up the major proportion of international trade, finance, investment, production and operation. In the information age, service industry creates the most wealth; and its main products are software, not the hardware. Take cell phones for example. Cell phone is a low-priced product in the developed countries, and what earns money is the rich service contents provided on those phones. Some big companies have no production lines but have generated sales income of 10 billion US dollars each year, with values created by their network and sales systems. This high sales turnover volumes are created by innovative software. As a result, the values created by the

---

[1] Doroth Riddle, *Service-Led Growth*, New York: Praeger, 1986, pp7-9; William J Baumol etc., *Productive Power and American Leadership*, Cambridge, Massachusetts: MIT Press, 1989, pp 145-150.

traditional industries are decreasing and getting smaller. Developed capitalist countries holding commanding of advanced technology have inevitably been advantageously positioned in the age of globalization.

Developed capitalist countries are playing dominating roles in various international organizations, in particular, economic organizations. Most of the basic regulations of international economic and political relations are laid and decided by developed capitalist countries. They are both players and referees. Globalization has provided an unprecedented opportunity for the global expansion of capital. But the anarchy in the global markets is as horrible as the anarchy of markets in the early period of capitalism. As the inter-connection of countries and regions gets closer, a turmoil in a country or a region usually affects other countries or even the whole world. This will naturally require strengthened coordination and cooperation between countries in the world, in order to join efforts in addressing problems of common concern. To avoid or reduce to the largest possible extent the harm of global anarchy to capital expansion and to grab the largest possible interest, developed capitalist countries have become the advocates and promoters of collaboration and cooperation. Their purpose is to exert the largest possible influence on mechanisms and rules, including WTO and its predecessor GATT, the World Bank and IMF.

2.1.3 Many drawbacks exposed are originated in the system of capitalism.

Globalization is the outcome of the constant expansion of capitalism and is dominated by capitalism with a clear mark of capitalism in it. Globalization has many major drawbacks existing in or accompanying capital expansion. It is not an idyllic and romantic process. Actually economic globalization has globalized many negative aspects in market economy, including pollution, immigration, epidemics, biological destruction and spreading drug problems. Globalization itself also causes many chaos and disharmonies. The process of globalization in the political and military domain more often expresses a naked nature of hegemony politics.

First of all, with the deepening of globalization, the gap between poor and rich nations is not narrowing, but widening. Statistics show that two centuries ago, per capita income in the richest nation was 5 times of that in the poorest nation. In the 1970s, the gap was more than 50 times, and by the end of the 20th century, the gap exceeded 500 times. In the 1960s, GDP per capita in the richest nation was 30 times of that in the poorest nation, which exceeded 70 times by the end of the 20th century. According to the Human Development Report 1999 of the United Nations Development Program, number of countries which benefited from globalization were less than 20. More than 80 countries still had per capita incomes lower than that they had a decade or more ago. The world's 200 richest people had more wealth than 41% of the world population. They doubled their wealth in four years to more than 1 trillion US dollars. But there were nearly 1.3 billion people in the world with less than 1 dollar income every day. By the late 1990s one fifth of the world's people living in the highest-income countries had 86% of world GDP, 82% of world export markets, 68% of foreign direct investment, 74% of world telephone lines, and the bottom one fifth had just about 1% of all these items. In this sense, some critics sharply point out that, globalization is America's globalization, or at the least it is developed nations' globalization, and developing nations were just drawn into it passively. At the same time, globalization has increased another trend of widening gap between the rich and the poor. That is, the poor and jobless continue to increase in rich countries, but in poor countries there appear some rich people having equal wealth with their counterparts in the rich countries. The worsened gap between the rich and the poor brings greater inequality, which is a prominent issue facing this era of globalization, and a major challenge posted by globalization for mankind.

Secondly, the economic and political order in the world is not reasonable. UN's Human Development Report 2000 pointed out that, global economic decision is made on the basis of extremely unequal economic powers. The poor countries and developed countries have great disparity in strength but face the same rules of competition which mainly represent the interests of developed nations. The poor countries are taking part in this decision process with a great inequality. WTO and GATT, representing the realities of globalization process, provide the best example. WTO stresses to create free and fair trade environment through negotiations. But as a matter of fact, for more than five decades since the establishment of the former GATT in 1947, WTO is rather, an organization controlled by a few great powers. Due to the disparity of the conditions of economic development, the foothold of negotiations is not a fair one. Take the WTO Ministerial Conference, Seattle, as an example. The US delegation had as many as 200 people, and the EU had nearly 600. Their strong lineups of negotiation could not be matched by other member states, most of which were developing nations. Developing countries rarely have any practical opportunities to take part in negotiations and almost all the important decisions are made by a few great powers. Because of this, WTO multilateral trade negation system claiming fair principle and free trade has long been regarded as the most unfair negotiations by many trade experts. Quite a number of developing countries directly criticize that WTO is boosting the arrogance of developed nations, and is just a tool used by developed countries to implement neo-colonialism. In the political domain, the problems exposed by the process of globalization are more outstanding. At present, while economic globalization is proceeding, political exchanges and cooperation are increasingly growing, and national egoism, national hegemony, ethnic separatism, ethnic exclusion, hegemonic policies of capitalist imperialism, war threats or acts of neo-interventionism are increasingly escalating, too. On the one hand, Western capitalist countries wantonly intervene or openly trample on the sovereignty of other countries, under the disguise of slogans of political globalization such as "global citizen rights", "global society" and "human right values higher than sovereignty value". On the other hand, they are taking advantage of unreasonable regulations and logic of globalization to play tricks and implement double standard over many issues. The United States gives the loudest voice in advocating globalization and criticizing other countries for market protectionism. But her domestic market is not fully open and employs various measures for protection. Other developed countries are no worse than the United States in trade protectionism. They also adopt double standards in the domain of political democracy, human rights, disarmament and environmental protection issues. Once they face any rules or mechanisms unfavorable to them, they either distort facts and thus justify their own needs, or wantonly choose to reject, or press for immediate revision in line with their interests. They even openly break their own promises, ignoring social conventions or rules. George W. Bush—soon after his inauguration as the American President—had stated that the United States would not ratify Kyoto Protocol. Kyoto Protocol aiming to protect the earth and mankind, is an international agreement to reduce greenhouse gases and save the earth that mankind lives on. It was signed in December 1997 by 149 countries in Kyoto, Japan. This treaty is an agreement reached after painstaking negotiations and bargaining among developed nations, between developed and developing nations. George W. Bush had defended his position, saying: "It is not fair and not in accordance with American interest." Mahathir Mohammad, Prime Minister of Malaysia, has sharply criticized the undisguised egoism of developed countries including the United States in the process of globalization: "Western countries ask for greater opening of Asian countries but disguise or never doubt on their own brand of global capitalism. It is high time to break the taboos and discuss them openly."[1]

Thirdly, the risks for global crises are growing. The basic contradiction between socialization of capitalist production and the private ownership of means of production display many new features in the age of global economy, such as contradiction between the adjustable and planned national economy and the anarchy and quasi-anarchy of global economy, the contradiction between the precise organization, scientific management and the bare-knuckle expansion and chaos of world market, the contradiction between the extreme expansion of world production and severe conflicts between monopolistic multinational corporations. The sharpening of these

---

[1] Mahathir Mohamad, *A New Deal for Asia*, Malaysia: Pelanduk Publications, 1999, p 9.

contradictions inevitably cause structural asymmetry between aggregate supply and aggregate demand in world markets, and uneven development between various economic departments and territories, thus lead to turmoil and crises in world economy. In the age of globalization, one of the important features of world economic crisis is the constant turbulence of the financial sector. The financial markets seem more like a horse freed to run wild, with an uncontrollable instinct of natural expansion. International financial capital is highly virtual, liquid and mobile, and its extreme risky, speculative character by no doubt increase the possibility of a global economic crisis. Till the legendary financial crocodile Mr. Soros attacked Southeast Asian monetary system in 1997, no one could ever guess a possibility that a single individual could destroy such huge banks. At present, what dominates global trade are no longer commodities like steel, automobile or wheat, but stocks, securities and currency deals. Since the 1990s, financial turmoil and crises have become the most important and main content of world economic crisis. The collapse of the bubble economy in Japan and its long-term weakness ever since, the constant fluctuations of the European monetary system in 1992, 1993 and 1995, financial crisis of Mexico in 1994, Southeast Asia in 1997, in Russia in 1998, and in Brazil in 1999, all had rapidly caused repercussions in other parts of the world and had thus fired economic and political panic on a global scope. The scale and speed of global financial crises far exceeds the reach of authorities or capabilities of any state or international financial institution, and their impact can rapidly spread to any remote corner of the world. Globalization spreads economic prosperity as well as economic recession.

2.2 Impact of Globalization on the Evolution of Contemporary Capitalism

2.2.1 Taken as a whole, globalization promotes the global expansion of capitalism.

As early as 150 years ago, when revealing the nature of the expansion of capitalism, Marx had noted, "Different from any other old modes of production, capitalism cannot exist without constantly revolutionizing the instruments of production, and thereby the relations of production, and with them the whole relations of society."[1] The unlimited desire of expansion is the nature of capital, with an ever increasing demand and expanding markets. The need of a constantly expanding market for its products chases the capitalist over the whole surface of the globe. It must nestle everywhere, settle everywhere, and establish connections everywhere. And every physical breakthrough in the market will bring a new opportunity for the development of capitalism. Emerging of national states and the unification of domestic markets, then the reduction of tariff barriers between countries and establishment of tariff alliances, the exploration of colonial markets and the surging of cross-national trusts to the lengthy GATT talks and the appearance of global multinational corporations, capitalism grew rapidly as a result of the development of market space and potential. The final and necessary consequence of globalization will inevitably lead to the generation of a world market as described by Marx, and a unified world market will in turn directly provide an unprecedented space for the global mobility of capital. The predictions in *The Communist Manifesto* has fully turned into reality: "The bourgeoisie keeps more and more doing away with the scattered state of the population, of the means of production, and of property. It has agglomerated population, centralized the means of production, and concentrated property in a few hands." "Independent but loosely connected provinces, with separate interests, laws, governments, and systems of taxation, became lumped together into one nation, with **one** government, **one** code of law, **one** national class-interest, **one** frontier, and **one** customs-tariff."[2] Globalization on a comprehensive scope has generated large-scale capital movement across borders and international circulation of capital. Consequently, the global expansion of capitalism is speeded up, economic system of the capitalist world is matured, and capitalist means of production became the means of

---

[1] *Selected Works of Marx and Engels,* 2th Edition, Vol. 1 p 275.

[2] *Selected Works of Marx and Engels*, 2nd Edition, Vol. 1, p 277.

production for the whole world in its true sense.

Globalization is increasingly eroding various trade barriers and even national boundaries. After the Cold War, even some of the most closed economies started to open up, though slowly. In the age of globalization, a world factory in its true sense has appeared. World factory used to refer only for the distribution sector, but today's world factory is true to its name. With the appearance of multinational corporations, the "nationality" of products increasingly becomes fuzzier. This not only means that products labeled "made in one country" are usually not made in this country, but also the raw materials, sophisticated processes and the final products are always produced and delivered by different countries. It is likely that in the near future "made in one country" will gradually disappear, replaced by "made by one 'multinational' corporation", such as "made by Motorola", "made by Panasonic", or "made by Samsung". Multinational operation is decided by the intrinsic nature of capital expansion. As early as in the Middle Ages, trade across national borders was under way. In the early 20th century, cross-border flow of goods, capital and personnel became very active. And, since the Second World War, cross-border business operations between Western countries came back as a trend, and trade and finance liberalization were revived. After the Cold War, pushed by the wave of globalization, cross-border business operations as well as trade and finance liberalization witnessed unprecedented growth. At present, among the top 100 largest economic entities, more than half are not nations but enterprises. The pursuit for profits chases the capitalists over the whole surface of the globe. In the age of globalization, the traditional boundaries of sovereign nations are transcended, and traditional national cultures are being impacted. Political system and principles, culture, ideology and lifestyle of capitalism are spreading to the whole globe in an unprecedented manner and unprecedented scale.

2.2.2 The impact of globalization on developed countries and developing countries displays huge differences.

Globalization enhances the coordination and cooperation between countries and regions, which is beneficial to alleviating or overcoming difficulties in the development of countries. Undertaking major development programs usually cannot be completed by one single country or a number of countries. Economic globalization also implies the possibility of allocating resources effectively in the global scope, favoring complementary competitiveness of different economies, professional coordination on a global scale, and the competitive advantage of scale economy of each nation. Global cooperation and coordination in political and military domains is indeed favorable to eliminate national hostilities, enhancing understanding and avoiding conflicts. The extensive cultural exchanges and infiltration of lifestyles is favorable to drawing on others' strong points to offset one's own weaknesses, and increasing common social and cultural prosperity for all nations. On the whole, countries and the human society could likely gain a better and healthier development. However, this positive effect of globalization is "true" only at a highly abstract theoretical and logical level. Viewed realistically, globalization effect, on the development of countries, is much complicated. In terms of the impact of globalization on capitalist countries alone, different advanced countries are gaining much different benefits from globalization, too.

At the present stage of globalization, a small number of developed capitalist countries are the biggest beneficiaries of globalization. Globalization has penetrated different regions in the world. The interaction between multinational corporations based in the West and geographical, political and economic entities in the former Southern nations, the peripheral countries, and the Third World, and the differentiation of the Southern nations, and the peripheral countries, the Third World, as well as the success achieved by multinational corporations not based in the West have made up a global economy true to the name. However, the center and driving force of globalization remain in the West and other economically and socially advanced regions. The theme of globalization is a globalization led by corporation (capital), enhanced by technology, initiated by market, and supported by governments. A small number of developed capitalist countries have strong economic power, manipulate the global market, and control or dominate most of international organizations and institutions. They are the regulator and beneficiary of the existing international rules. They are not only strong in international trade, international finance, technology and in national scale but also are home countries to the majority of multinational corporations. The above-mentioned facts have enabled these countries to occupy the commanding heights of development when the wave of globalization first surged and hence they have taken initiative in the process of globalization. As a result, they are likely to gain the most benefits in the process.

Most developing countries are passively involved in the process of globalization, though generally they are not against globalization. Almost all the governments of developing nations are eager to join in the tide of globalization on an equal footing. They have all realized that a country will not be able to develop and prosper in a closed manner. The ways for developing countries to catch up are to take part in the process of globalization, to seize the opportunity of globalization and give full play to "late-comer effect", find appropriate solutions for the inherent defects of capital accumulation and strive more initiative for choices of technology and market. New comers can also create an opportunity from the industry transfer started by developed countries—which aim to climb higher ladders of industrial hierarchy—and thus speed up industrialization and modernization. To actively take part in globalization does not necessarily mean to be "westernized" or fall into "a pitfall". As a matter of fact, some developing countries, with less strength than developed countries, have surprisingly seized opportunity or the space provided by globalization at certain stage of development and have gained great benefits. Some developing countries won the opportunity and have joined the newly industrialized nations. It must be noticed that, since the developing nations are generally weaker, and disadvantaged in the world economy, they are facing greater risks in the waves of economic globalization. In addition, the unreasonable regulations existing in the process of globalization, as well as the hypocrisy of all-round market freedom of developed countries challenge them with a great deal of sufferings. Politically, these countries are not strong and prone to be attached to other powers, democracy practice usually has started later and their internal social integration is yet poor, all these negative factors position them as passive/guided actors. The financial crisis in 1997 which swept East Asian developing countries fully revealed the vulnerability of victimized countries in handling risks of globalization. In the process of globalization, underdeveloped countries are always faced with various unfair phenomena such as sovereignty being intervened, or turning into appendage of or being looted by developed countries. In addition, globalization is likely to speed up the differentiation among developing countries and result in "the Fourth World". The reason is that the progress of globalization has caused greater Matthew effect in social development. Rich countries, due to the advantages and resources they possess are naturally like fish in water, but quite a number of developing countries are staggering because of various disadvantages. According to statistics of the World Bank, most of the least underdeveloped countries are more and more "marginalized" in the process of globalization, becoming poorer and more backward. They cannot benefit from globalization, but further lag behind. Under the impact of globalization, the biggest issue facing developing countries is how to win the opportunity provided by globalization to develop, eliminating disadvantages and improving the advantages.

2.2.3 Globalization also poses new challenges to capitalism.

As globalization proceeds, many global social problems have surfaced and pose new challenges to modern capitalism. These problems include the widening gap between the rich and the poor globally, the de-regulation of traditional labor protection system and the collapse of welfare system being pushed by multinational corporations, the global deterioration of environment, tension between the rapid progress of economic globalization and political state powers, the conflict between economic globalization and regional integration, unfair world economic and political order, etc.

The imbalances in political and economic development in the world is the absolute law of capitalism. The polarization of the rich and the poor and a large number of poor population are the intrinsic phenomena of capitalism and the inevitable outcome of the law of capital accumulation. As globalization proceeds, the polarization between the rich and the poor is not eased but grows in intensity. The polarization between the rich and the poor on a global scale is a recurrence of the law: imbalanced world economic development. In essence, it is the outcome of the turbo expansion of few developed capitalist countries and their monopolies, taking advantage of globalization. Moreover, the distribution of polarization of the rich and the poor on a global scale tends to be more complicated than before. Firstly, in the world there are many people living in poverty, and the disparity between the richest and the poorest is widening. Secondly, in the broad context of economic globalization, the economic development in different countries is uneven and the disparity between the rich and the poor is growing more obvious. Thus the gap between the rich Northern countries and the less developed Southern countries tends to grow. Thirdly, along with the progress of globalization, the disparity between the rich and the poor within many countries is rapidly increasing. In a small number of developed countries, the wages of many workers can hardly support a family of a smallest size, and in the large number of developing countries or even some poor countries, a batch of rapidly emerged rich people taking the opportunities offered by globalization have possessed as much wealth as the richest in developed world. Fourthly, another negative sequence of globalization is that it widens the inequality between the educated and less educated people, and intensifies the income disparity between urban and rural areas. Individuals with higher education can move freely in the developed countries to seek higher remuneration, especially in sectors such as information technology and the Internet. The less educated ones lack mobility and are unable to seek for a higher income.

The increasing global disparity between the rich and the poor standing out in the process of globalization is attracting widespread concern. People not only start to question the existing political and economic order in the world, but start to criticize globalization itself. Since the mid and late 1990s, the surging anti-globalization waves have pin-pointed the issue of increasing global disparity between the rich and the poor. Same as in the early period of capitalism when disparity between the rich and the poor caused a series of social miseries and in turn resulted in long-term and large-scale social conflicts and turmoil, in the age of global capitalism, whether or not capitalism can effectively solve the issue of increasing global disparity between the rich and the poor is fundamental and directly related to the existence of the system.

Due to the progress of globalization and the accompanying global expansion of multinational corporations, labor protection and welfare systems established through efforts of several generations since the 20th century, have been collapsing, and they are either weakened, paralyzed, or dismantled. Against the backdrop of globalization, a great number of workers are facing a complicated situation of "starting from the beginning" to secure basic human rights in a totally new context. Under the constant impact of the waves of globalization, because countries have successively accepted market rules and reduced functions of government and public sectors, the traditional welfare systems face frequent attacks. They are squeezed and contained, and are being criticized as "exploiting" tax payers' money. Or they are targeted to be reversely reformed, being criticized as inefficient, or even abolished as claimed to be conflicting with the rules of free trade. Global expansion of multinational corporations even directly threatens the traditional system of basic labor protection. Driven by their basic interests of seizing unlimited profit, multinational corporations seek for the cheapest labor force in the global scope and try their best to avoid any restraints on labor protection. Take the Walt Disney Company as an example. Shops selling Disney commodities can be found almost in every major city in the world, and the factories producing toys or textiles are mostly located in underdeveloped countries such as Haiti and Myanmar, because these countries have cheap labor and weaker protection of labor rights. When encountering resistance or protest from the workers, Disney will not clash with the workers as the capitalists did in the 19th century or seek compromise with the workers. Disney, rather leaves one location and move to another rapidly. And the new location it moves to has usually worse working conditions, incomplete labor protection and undeveloped trade unions. Protection of labor rights has become another new topic faced by capitalism in the age of globalization. If this problem is not duly solved, by the deepening of globalization and further development of multinational corporations, sooner or later it will explode like the workers movement in the 19th century. Over the recent years, the consumers' global anti-Disney movement have rung an alarm in a special way.

Another major challenge posed by globalization to modern capitalism is how to handle the tension and conflict between the rapid progress of economic globalization and the rights of nation states. In the process of globalization, economic sector witnesses the most rapid progress and raises many new requests for countries with traditional political practices or mentality. The increasing liquidity of international capital, market globalization, the expanding functions of international economic organizations and the increasing international competition have brought about huge impact on the system, and challenges political leaderships, political super structures, social infrastructure, policy system, values and cultures of all countries. The role of traditional national state is weakened, and every country (including developed countries) has to adapt to the increasingly globalized world market through reforms. In the past, even countries faced with civil wars domestically, it was regarded as an internal affair and could not be intervened. Nowadays, in case of a financial crisis, usually an appointed official from International Monetary Fund will be dispatched to tell a country what policies to be implemented. In such cases tension between economic globalization and those countries governed by traditional politics is openly reflected. In the first place developed capitalist countries face this challenge, and later other capitalist countries take their turn to face those tensions when they seek to participate or get involved in the process of globalization. But the complexity of the problem lies in that developed capitalist countries make use of international organizations under their control to exert various pressures to developing countries with an aim to intervene the internal affairs of other countries. As a result, the tension between economic globalization and the rights of national states not only creates a conflict between transfer of sovereignty and nationalism, but also creates conflicts shaped as hegemony and anti-hegemony and intervention and anti-intervention, between developed and developing nations. The global expansion of multinational corporations directly impacts and erodes the functions of nation states. Multinational corporations are the most important carrier and leading players in globalization. They direct their investment opportunities to places with lowest labor cost and least restrictions on working conditions. They make their own decisions on where to invest, make production, to pay tax or reside. They usually make production in one country, pay tax in another country, and yet ask the government of another third country to build an appropriate infrastructure for them. As a result, governments operating in traditional sense lose control over taxation. Globalization has enabled multinational corporations to increasingly become independent kingdoms transcending national boundaries and by-passing their governments. The problem lies in how to and who should regulate behaviors of multinational corporations which in reality by-pass the rights of nation states. In addition, some multinational corporations are trying to mask their images in the process of development and merge into local communities by sponsoring cultural or sport events, which no doubt produces another challenge and another aspect for the administrative rights and civil society of the host countries. Furthermore, another form of tension between economic globalization and national political sovereignty is the anarchy in world market and each country's right to choose her own economic development pattern or mode.

In the process of globalization, developed capitalist countries try their best to maintain the existing world political and economic order which is not reasonable and fair. However, voices for change will definitely grow stronger. With the evolvement of globalization, world order as dominated by developed capitalist powers will face ever greater pressures and challenges. In the long term, the dominance of developed capitalist countries will be gradually weakened. Though developing nations are relatively disadvantaged and face greater risks, some of them will move forward quicker and more newly industrialized countries will emerge. As a result, the position of developing countries as a whole in the world economy will gradually be improved, and the position of developed countries will be lowered correspondingly. The old balance of power will be bygone; and the world order will inevitably be reshaped. The pressure and challenge faced by developed capitalist powers in maintaining the old world political and economic order is also a pressure and a challenge against the capitalist system. How to react to this challenge and avoid the pressure and challenge evolving into a threat to the system and the order of capitalism is one of the difficult issues faced by modern capitalism.

Moreover, how to handle effectively the increasingly serious global environmental issues, how to solve the conflict between globalization and regionalization, how to ease many regional conflicts and maintain a sustained world peace, and how to respond to criticisms on capitalism from various left-wing social movements, in particular socialist movements, are all constitute strong challenges for modern capitalism, especially the developed capitalist powers.

2.3 The Overall Situation of the Evolution of Capitalism in the Post-Cold War Era

2.3.1 Capitalism "won without fighting" in the long-term confrontation with the Soviet Union and Eastern European countries.

After the Second World War, the Yalta pattern gradually came into being with two social systems, two ideologies and two confrontational military groups standing up quite equally against each other. This is also known as Cold War pattern. It was a confrontation between two superpowers, the United States of America and the Soviet Union, resulting in the Cold War pattern in Europe and the whole world. The Cold War pattern emerged in the international politics of Europe starting with the split of Germany. Eastern Europe and Western Europe political division came into being accompanying the division of East Germany and West Germany. Militarily, North Atlantic Treaty Organization and Warsaw Treaty Organization were two opposing military groups with escalating arms race, especially nuclear arms race. Each of the two groups stationed a few hundred thousands of soldiers respectively in Western and Eastern Europe. The boundary of their armies was the division of East and West Germany. Economically, the Western countries were closely allied and they blocked or embargoed socialist countries at varying degrees. The Soviet Union and Eastern European countries with the Council for Mutual Economic Assistance (COMECON) as the center had their own economic integration and had also kept solid economic relations with some socialist countries in Asia. The two types of economy grew in parallel with little connections between them, which was "the collapse of a unified and inclusive world market" as noted by Stalin, and "two parallel and confrontational world markets have appeared"[1]. Taken as a whole, the Cold War polarization after the Second World War remained relatively stable until the late 1980s and early 1990s.

In the late 1980s and early 1990s, the Eastern European countries changed dramatically, the Soviet Union collapsed, and the Cold War pattern which lasted for over five decades has terminated. Dramatic changes first took place in Poland. In February 1988, the Polish government sharply raised the prices of daily necessities including food and gasoline, causing the explosion of its people's indignation, dissatisfaction and large-scale strikes. Trade Union named Solidarity took this chance for its political aims, stirred up the masses, and brought chaos and crisis to the country. The 10th Plenary Session of the 10th Central Party Committee of the Polish United Workers' Party held at the end of 1988 and early 1989 established the political system of separation of powers of legislative, executive and judicial branches, and the principle of pluralization in political and trade union activities. In June

---

[1] *Selected Works of Stalin*, 2nd Vol., p 561, Beijing: People's Press, 1979.

1989, the 10th period parliament and senate were elected, the United Workers' Party was defeated and Trade Union Solidarity won a landslide victory. In the direct election of president in December 1990, Walesa, leader of Trade Union Solidarity, was elected as the President of Polish Republic.

In May 1989, a "Reform Club" was formed by the radicals within the Communist Party in Hungary. Together with Hungarian Democratic Forum established by the national opposition, a strong force was formed behind the changes in Hungary. During June and September, a national round table, consisting of representatives of Socialist Workers' Party, opposition groups and different social groups, met to discuss ways of transition to multiparty system. In October, the Socialist Workers' Party convened its 14th (Extraordinary) Congress, and re-established itself as Hungarian Socialist Party. The new ideological guideline and constitutional chapters of Socialist Party were passed, which revised the goal of the party as democratic socialism. In March and April 1990, Hungary held its first free election under the multiparty system, and the Hungary Democratic Forum opposition won the parliamentary election, and formed a coalition government with the Independent Peasant Party and the Christian Democratic People's Party. Socialist Party was reduced to be the opposition.

Upon the year 1989, demonstrations in Czechoslovakia surged. In December, the Communist Party reached an understanding with the opposition groups to form a multi-party political system and a governmental coalition. But the Communist Party had become the minority in the coalition government and its seats in the Federal Assembly were reduced to less than a half. In the extraordinary congress of the Communist Party convened in December, the action guideline on adopting democratic socialism was passed and the nature of the party was fundamentally altered. By the end of December, the Federal Assembly elected Havel, the leading figure of the opposition organization, Civic Forum, as the President of the republic. In March 1990, the Federal Parliament passed on the resolution to change the previous name of "Czechoslovakia Socialist Republic" to "Czechoslovakia Federal Republic", and soon in April it was changed to "Czech and Slovak

Federal Republic". In November 1992, the Federal Assembly passed Constitution Act 541 and agreed to the dissolution of Czechoslovakian state. And on January 1, 1993, Czechoslovakia was split into two independent countries of Czech Republic and Slovakia Republic.

In December 1989, demonstrations appeared in Timişoara, Romania and soon swept the whole country. The demonstrators in the capital surrounded the Presidential Office. The Patriotic Guards had refused the order of Ceauşescu to shoot the demonstrators and turned mutinous. Mr. and Mrs. Ceauşescu fled. They were arrested and soon executed. Romanian Save the Country Frontier Committee took over the political power and announced multi-party administration, separation of powers of legislative, executive and judicial branches, and free elections. It also announced that Romania would be built as a socialist democratic country, and the name of the Socialist Republic of Romania was changed to Romania.

In 1989, Bulgaria witnessed a turmoil caused by ethnic issues, and soon after many opposition organizations appeared and formed a Democratic Forces Coalition, challenging the Communist Party. In February 1990, the 14th Congress of the Bulgarian Communist Party approved the Statement of Democratic Socialism of Bulgaria, announcing to adopt the multi-party system and parliamentary democracy. In April, the Communist Party was renamed Socialist Party of Bulgaria. In June, the Socialist Party won the parliamentary election and formed the government. But the opposition parties continued fighting for power both inside and outside the parliament. The Socialist Party eventually gave up the presidency and the right of forming cabinet and became a party out of office.

In May 1989, Hungary demolished the border watch between herself and Austria, and a big number of citizens from the Democratic Germany fled to Federal Germany via Hungary and Austria. In October, Socialist Democratic Party—opposing to the old regime—was founded and various other opposition groups were formed. As a result, demonstrations became frequent. The ruling United Socialist Party was split up. On November 9, the border between the Democratic Germany and the Federal Germany was fully opened, and the Berlin Wall had collapsed instantly and masses of citizens from the Democratic Germany marched into the Federal Germany. In December, the United Socialist Party held an extraordinary congress to rename itself German United Socialist Party-Democratic Socialist Party, and later to Democratic Socialist Party soon after. In March 1990, the first multi-party parliamentary election was held in the Democratic Germany and the Democratic Socialist Party became the party out of office. The political upheaval in the Democratic Germany promoted the unification process of the Democratic and Federal Germany. On October 3, 1990, the Democratic Germany officially became part of the Federal Germany.

Under the impact of the situation in Eastern Europe, in 1990, Albania also experienced political turmoil. At the end of June and in the beginning of July, mass demonstrations had exploded. In December, the plenary session of the central committee of the ruling Labor Party decided to adopt the multiparty system. In March 1991, the first multiparty parliamentary election was held in Albania. The Labor Party won the majority in the parliament, and the opponent Democratic Party became the second largest party. In June, the 10th congress of the Labor Party renamed itself as Socialist Party and announced to follow the road of democratic socialism. In March 1992, the second parliamentary election was held and the Democratic Party won a landslide victory.

The dramatic change of Yugoslavia started with ethnic splits. In October 1989, the plenary meeting of the Central Committee of League of Communists of Yugoslavia passed the Outline of Political System Reform and decided to establish a multiparty system. In January 1990, the 14th extraordinary congress meeting was decided, but many representatives refused to attend the congress. Then the congress decided to terminate the Central Committee of League of Communists and its Secretariat. The individual republics successively started to change their names and sought for independence. In July, the Federal Assembly passed the Political Associations/Parties Act and thenceforth emerged various political groups. When the individual republics organized their multiparty elections after 1990, the communist parties mostly failed to win the re-elections except Serbia and Montenegro provinces. The parliaments of other four republics were won by the opposition. In June 1991, Croatia and Slovenia announced independence from Yugoslavia; Macedonia and Bosnia also became independent states in November 1991 and March 1992. In April 1992, Serbia and Montenegro announced a new (state) League of Yugoslavia but each of these two republics became independent in February 2003.

Like the Domino chain reaction, the dramatic changes in Eastern European countries—though with slightly different characteristics—had born the same nature. First of all, the nature of the party in power was altered. Not only the name was changed from the Communist Party to the Socialist Party, but the nature, guideline, organizational principles and goals were all changed. Secondly, the nature of political power was changed. After the dramatic changes, the parties that came into office were either the opposition parties aiming to demolish Communist Party, or Socialist Parties born as a result of revising the original Communist Party. Thirdly, after the dramatic change, all these countries ruptured the Soviet Union model with no exception, and were transformed to market economy and political democracy. They no longer insisted on the direction of socialism, and the institutional reforms implemented were not aimed at improving and developing socialist system.

On the other side, firstly, the dramatic collapse of the Soviet Union mainly consists of several complex processes related to each other. One is that the Communist Party had lost office and was eventually dissolved. The second is that the 15 union republics forming the Union of Soviet Socialist Republics had split apart and become independent countries. After the 19th Representative Meeting of the Communist Party of the Soviet Union in June 1988, many non-governmental organizations had appeared. In October 1990, the Supreme Soviet passed the Act on Associations (Parties), allowing a multiparty system. On August 19, 1991, some leaders of the Soviet Union attempted a political coup to topple Gorbachev on August 24, but had failed. Gorbachev announced his resignation as the Party

Secretary of the Communist Party of the Soviet Union, and asked the Party Central Committee to dissolve itself totally, and halt all the activities of the Communist Party in the army and other governmental offices. Meanwhile, communist parties of other union republics had also faced heavy blows. They were either banned, announced illegal, dissolved, or renamed. The properties of the Communist Party of the Soviet Union were confiscated, and its newspapers and other publications were banned, and the Party was no longer in existence.

Secondly, the process of the dramatic change was also a process in which the Soviet Union style socialist road was gradually abandoned. Politically, since the 19th Representatives' Meeting of the Communist Party of the Soviet Union in 1988, the state's political form was changed to a parliamentary system. In January 1990, in his speech delivered in Lithuania, Gorbachev had advocated a multi-party political system in the Soviet Union, and the 28th Congress of the Communist Party of the Soviet Union had officially announced the decision to allow for the multi-party system. In the Plenary Session of the Party Central Committee meeting in February 1990, Gorbachev politically maneuvered to by-pass the Communist Party mired in crisis by adopting a system of presidency and had succeeded. In March, he was elected the first president of the Soviet Union. The Presidential Committee under Gorbachev ensued to take charge of domestic policies, replacing authority of the Communist Party of the Soviet Union. In the economic sphere, under the impact of radical shock type—privatizations and market reforms—economic reform of the Soviet Union had lost its direction; in other words, it had lost its aim. In fact no successful economic reform in the true sense could be achieved under those conditions of grave political turmoil. The state economy was soon controlled by the bureaucratic social class with special powers, and socialist state ownership was transformed into a chaotic "private ownership". In July 1991, the Supreme Soviet ruling organ passed the Act of Privatization which legitimated illegal privatization and erosion of state properties. After the dissolution of the Soviet Union, Russia had adopted a "Shock Therapy" and implemented measures as follows: promoted and allowed operation of non-state ownership enterprises, abolished the planned price system and allowed markets to decide the prices and tightened the monetary supply. As a result, the basic characteristics of planned economy and state ownership of the Union of Soviet Socialist Republics had perished.

Thirdly, the dramatic change was a process of the dissolution of the union republics. During February and March, 1990, three Baltic republics announced themselves independent. In June, the Supreme Soviet of Russian Soviet Federative Socialist Republic (SFSR) declared Russia's independent sovereignty. Then Moldavia, Ukraine, Belarus and five Middle Asian states had all declared independent sovereignty. Though still acknowledging the Soviet Union, they emphasized that the union republics were sovereign countries with independent economic and cultural rights, and their respective constitutions were the supreme law. Gorbachev—in panic and confusion—had offered a New Union Treaty of former Soviet nations as an attempt to preserve the Union. On the other hand, the August Coup on August 19, 1991 had speeded up the collapse of the Union. Boris Yeltsin, the President of Russian SFSR crashed the coup and came out as a hero, taking over the power of the Central Committee of the Party, the military and administrative power, and had captured media tools of the Party and state. He then dissolved many organizations of the Party and transferred its institutions, buildings and other properties to the Russian government. On December 1, 1991, a referendum was held in Ukraine to decide on her independence. Soon after, Yeltsin acknowledged Ukraine's sovereignty. On December 8, 1991, without the participation of Gorbachev, the presidents of Russia, Ukraine and Belarus signed the Belavezha Accords in the suburb of Minsk, which declared the dissolution of the Soviet Union and established in principle the Commonwealth of Independent States (CIS) which would replace the former state. On December 13, leaders from Kazakhstan, Kyrgyzstan, Uzbekistan, Turkmenistan and Tajikistan issued a statement in support of the Belavezha Accords. On December 21, 1991, representatives from all Soviet republics except Georgia, including those republics that had signed the Belavezha

Accords, signed the Alma-Ata Protocol, which confirmed the dismemberment and consequential extinction of the USSR and re-stated the direction for the establishment of the CIS. On December 25, 1991, Gorbachev yielding to the inevitable situation, resigned as the President of the USSR. The following day, the Supreme Soviet organ, convened its last meeting, acknowledged the bankruptcy and collapse of the Soviet Union and dissolved the Soviet Union as a functioning state. Two days later Yeltsin replaced his position, assuming the presidency.

The dramatic changes in Eastern Europe and the Soviet Union marked the end of the Cold War pattern. First of all, Germany reunified and the Soviet army withdrew from East Germany. The most prominent mark of the Cold War pattern, the separation of Germany, no longer existed. Secondly, Warsaw Treaty and the Council for Mutual Economic Assistance were dissolved and the two military and economic bloc organizations in Europe became extinct. Thirdly, due to the dramatic changes in Eastern European Countries and the collapse of the Soviet Union, the political and ideological confrontation between these countries and the West had disappeared. The Cold War had ended with the collapse of the socialist alignment of the Soviet Union and Eastern European countries, and Western capitalist alignment had won them over without battles and rifle smoke.

2.3.2 The constant adaptation and renewal of capitalism has enhanced its capability of responding to risks.

The 20th century was a century when capitalism and socialism had co-existed, learned from each other, and also rivaled and fought with each other. As a matter of fact, not only socialism learns from capitalism during its developing process, but capitalism also draws on the practices of socialism in addition to its countering polices, as strangling, containment and "promoting peaceful transformation". Such learning can be examined from two aspects: one is the socialist elements emerging within the capitalist system, such as the pressure from workers' and socialist movements and partial absorption of socialist ideas. The second effect is sourced outside the capitalist system, as the inspirations reflected from the successful operations of the socialist system, such as the planned nature of economy and the state's regulations and interference to optimize the market operations. For capitalism, the purpose of learning from socialism is to maintain its development, and generally that purpose is effectively achieved.

Passed through the test of the two world wars and several rounds of severe economic, political and social crises, and on the basis of drawing upon lessons and elements of the successful experiences of socialism, capitalism has adapted, adjusted and renewed itself to a large extent, and remarkably increased its capability of responding to risks. Economically, advanced capitalist countries have implemented major adjustments to a certain degree as allowed by capitalist production relationships, such as the development of stock (type) companies—backed by several million individual stock-holders—transnational type corporations, and state's interference in the whole social-economic operation of the society, those which have all broken through the limit of private ownership. The expanding and deepening of the state's macro-adjustment has greatly lessened the anarchy of production in free market conditions. The welfare security system covering the entire society has guaranteed the rights of the working class and labor force, curbing to a certain extent the vicious development of the gap between the rich and the poor. The coordination between labor and management, labor protection laws, stock ownership of laborers and participation of laborers in the management all have eased social and class conflicts to a high degree. Politically, history of the political system of capitalism shows that every major social or economic turbulence had caused a great turmoil to political system, and in turn, political system was obliged to respond to the new demands of the environment, i.e. demands of the era, and hence was pushed to re-structure, adjust and seek renewal. Through several such adjustments, capitalism was able to maintain its vigor and energy. If there was no adjustment, it would not be able to cope with the destructive catastrophes such as the two world wars, and even the frequent economic crises and a political turmoil could perish capitalist power and capitalist system. For instance, for countries in the world, it has become a general trend to strengthen the administrative power and decrease the power of the parliaments. In response to this trend, the parliaments of capitalist countries compromise— aiming to protect their rights—and transfer part of their powers, on the other hand thus follow the trend of the era. They recognize the centralized administrative power, but choose to retain their power of constraining the excessive use of administrative power. Opposite to the administrative power is the trend of gradual expansion of the rights of citizens, which has also become a common phenomenon. With the process of modernization and socio-economic, political and cultural progress, citizens' awareness of participation in political affairs is growing, and it becomes imperative to give more democratic rights to the citizens. States have started adapting to those new phenomena either in form or in practice at various paces, including revising the constitutions. The growing rights of citizens' participation in political affairs express a contradictory trend to the centralization of administrative power. The expansion of the conflicting tendencies has helped the parliamentary democratic political system complete its change in adapting to the new environment. On the other hand, the expansion of participation of the citizens in political affairs is to certain extent, expresses a remedy effect to the centralization of administrative power. By the early 20th century, the progressive evolution of parties and party politics was another major change in the development of capitalist parliamentary system and has played a consolidating effect on the parliamentary democracy, and at the same time caused renewal of the functions of the parliamentary system. In the early period of party politics, the change of parties in office had always caused the alteration of (assigned) cabinet level high officials. This system had not only caused cyclical political unrest, but had facilitated structural political corruption. The socio-economic development has called for more mature party politics, and a modern civil high-officials' assignment system is emerging to cope with the demands of the era. The civil official system separates administration from the political (executive) function sphere. Thus, politics and high-level administration are separated, which is a remedy to the defects of party politics. The alternate development of civil official system and that of party politics is thus another reform in the parliamentary system, which stabilizes and consolidates it to a greater extent.

The continuous development of capitalism is propelled to a large degree by its "awareness of crises" mood, and its active response needs practice to the frequent cyclical crises. Capitalism has adopted various approaches to overcome or circumvent various crises. It employs major adjustment for major crises and minor adjustment for minor crises. These adjustments or reforms cannot solve the inherent problems of capitalism, but it improves the political and economic system of capitalism. In contrast to capitalism, most of socialist countries fail to recognize the shortcomings of socialism, but think that just the establishment of socialist system has displayed—eternally—the vanguard nature of the system as compared to capitalism. They generally have weaker crisis awareness, lack motivation for reforms or spirit of innovation. In these countries, phenomena of glossing over errors and putting on a false show of prosperity exit. As a result, serious social conflicts keep accumulating. The dramatic changes of Eastern European countries and the Soviet Union were explosions of all the crises accumulated in these countries.

Developed capitalist countries have experienced continuous self-adjustment. Taking advantage of the power of globalization and the overall strength accumulated from the long-term development, they have initiated the offensive of "promoting peaceful transformation" targeting socialist countries with unprecedented magnitude. Hence, achieved a major progress by promoting the dramatic changes in Eastern Europe and the collapse of the Soviet Union, and greatly expanded the space of capitalism globally. Though the goal of capitalist countries to destroy all socialist countries could not be achieved, and they continue to have their own social and economic problems, capitalism enjoys a superior strength and advantage over socialism in the post-Cold War period.

2.3.3 The advantageous position of global capitalism in the post-Cold War period

It was in the middle of the 19th century that the initial socialist sparkling of a few philosophers developed into majestic social movements with sweeping momentum, though with countless difficulties, setbacks and failures. The birth of scientific socialism merged socialist movement with workers' movement, and ideology had eventually turned to a physical force transforming the world and formed a movement sweeping almost the whole globe. In the 20th century, with the rumble of gunfire, a brand new system of socialism was born, which triumphed over hunger, blockade, domestic turbulence, civil war and foreign invasion, and grew from political infancy into a big power. After the Second World War, more than one socialist country were established and geographically connected, and a strong system of socialism in the world came into being, leading 1/3 of the population and 1/4 of the land in the world. Ideologically, these countries were guided by Marxism and Leninism, and the political power of these countries was mastered by the people as led by the Communist Party. Militarily, bilateral or multilateral treaties[1] were reached to form common defensive alliances. Economically, a socialist world market was established through bilateral and multilateral treaties.[2] In the 1960s, Cuba in Latin America had embarked on the road of socialism. In 1975, after winning the war against America on the Indochinese Peninsula, Vietnam, Cambodia and Laos also took the socialist road. The number of socialist countries led by the Communist Parties had reached 16 at that peak point. In the developed capitalist countries in Europe, many socialist parties won elections and became ruling parties. They followed the principle of (social) democratic socialism and reformed to a great extent political, economic and cultural system in those countries. Their reformist practice had led to many positive results, and the Swedish

---

[1] Before 1962, China dispatched observers to take part in the meetings of the Warsaw Treaty.

[2] After the Council for Mutual Economic Assistance was founded, Albania, the German Democratic Republic, Mongolia, Cuba and Vietnam joined. As observers, China, Yugoslavia, Laos and the Democratic People's Republic of Korea took part in some regular meetings.

Model was particularly encouraging. Socialist parties—in some developing countries—which attempted to practice (social) democratic socialism also scored remarkable achievements both in theory and in practice. In addition, after the Second World War, the nationalist parties of many newly independent countries raised banners of socialism, and implemented socialist policies. The socialist movement in the world once posed victorious momentum. In the confrontation of the two systems during this period, capitalism still had more strength, but socialism was full of vigor and had very bright prospects.

However, after the dramatic changes in Eastern Europe and the collapse of the Soviet Union, socialist and communist movements in the world have encountered unprecedented setbacks. Thence after, socialism turned from strong offensive to defensive and capitalism showed a most strong momentum.

Firstly, developed capitalist countries have utilized the advantage of the comparatively mature market economy and mature democratic politics, later promoted the advent of new industrial revolution and revolutionized their productive forces power through large degree of self-adjustment and renewal, developed in an all-round manner micro-electronic technology, laser technology, advanced materials technology, aerospace engineering, marine engineering, biological engineering, and thus brought about major changes in all sectors of the society and thus exhibited the shiny aspect—the vigor and attractiveness of capitalist system—over socialist countries.

Secondly, driven by the new technological revolution and supported by the waves of globalization, capitalism takes the initiative of globalization and holds the strategic commanding in economic sphere. It pursues to label the world economic globalization with capitalism, and agitates that globalization equals capitalism. Capitalism strives to restrict the space of existence and development of socialist countries by making use of its advantageous position.

Thirdly, the dramatic changes in Eastern Europe and the collapse of the Soviet Union announced the bankruptcy of previous two parallel world markets theory. The advanced capitalist countries have utilized the opportunity of their victory: the "peaceful transformation" in Eastern Europe and Soviet Union, in order to win a controlling position, to promote cultural hegemony; and have boosted their "victory" through media propaganda aiming to surrender yet surviving socialist countries and resisting socialist forces. Noisy theories such as almighty liberalism, winning without fighting, the end of history, grand failure, etc., all have exerted strong ideological pressure to socialist forces and countries.

Taken as a whole, capitalism has shown a strong momentum of global expansion in the post-Cold War period, which is represented not only by its geographical expansion, but also by the positive effects brought along by its capability of self-adjustment. The effects include the revolutions in leading technologies, continuous and steady economic development, relatively better living standards and social welfare system, and democratic rights for the people. The advantages of capitalist system have been enhanced, and socialist system established on backward economic and cultural basis has proven to be a disadvantage. In political, economic, military and ideological aspects, capitalism in the post-Cold War period enjoys an advantageous position and poses enormous challenges to socialist system.

Chapter **3**

Globalization and Socialism in the Post-Cold War Era

Globalization is both an opportunity and a challenge for the development of socialism. It provides opportunities for socialist countries to develop by utilizing foreign capital, advanced technology and management expertise, to speed up domestic industrial restructuring and modernization and promote the development of socialist politics. At the same time, globalization poses challenges for economic, political and cultural security of socialist countries. In the age of globalization, the world of socialism has a broad space to grow and develop. In the post-Cold War period, the basic situation of the development of socialist movement in the world is as follows: on the one side there is partial revitalization and on the other an overall low tide. Besides a moderate development trend in the major setback trend, the extension of socialist movement has narrowed but her intension had deepened and improved in quality. When the socialist movement in the world is at the low tide, there surge several new waves of socialist developments.

3.1 Opportunities for the Development of Socialism in the Process of Globalization

Globalization enables the free flow and optimized allocation of production factors on a global scale, accelerates the inter-connection of mankind, enhances interdependence of countries and provides valuable opportunity for the rapid development of socialist countries by utilizing resources of other countries.

3.1.1 Globalization provides opportunities for socialist countries.

The accelerating globalization implies the quickening flow of capital, technology and knowledge wealth globally, which in turn provides important opportunities for socialist countries to develop by utilizing foreign capital, advanced technology and management expertise. For instance, transnational corporations producing and operating in socialist countries are growing in number, and these socialist countries are able to get large amount of foreign capital, technology and management expertise. Transnational investments and in particular "creative investment packages", the inflow of a bundle of factors such as mindset of market mechanisms, technology, management, marketing network resulted from the inflow of capital, enhances the growth of high-tech industries and facilitate structural optimization of export commodities. Globalization is favorable for socialist countries to gain more from global division of labor, advanced management expertise and production technology. The experiences of China merging into the world economy through reform and opening up since 1979 have indicated that globalization is the source for developing countries to speed up their economic growth.[1]

As economic globalization proceeds, the global transfer and cross-

---

[1] Paul M. Augimeri, "The Effects of Globalization on China, a Developing, Newly Industrialized Economy", *Ecodate*, March 2001, Vol. 15, Issue 1.

border research and development of science and technology have become important ways of assimilating advanced technology for developing countries, including socialist countries. As displayed by international experiences, assimilating advanced technology from other countries is one of the important measures for developing countries to speed up modernization. Science and technology research, both theoretical and technical, poses a highly difficult problem. A large-scale science and technological project cannot be completed with the capacity of a single enterprise or industry, and it has become a trend to join efforts for research and development. Enterprises, universities and research institutes within a country collaborate, and regional and international collaborations can be conducted, too. A wave of joint-international research and development of science and technology is surging and transnational corporations in Western countries have played remarkable roles in transferring and transmitting advanced technology. They own most of the technological inventions and innovations and almost control the technological trade in the world. Statistics show that the top 500 transnational corporations in developed capitalist countries control 90% of technological production and 75% of technological trade of these countries.[1] In pursuit of maximum profit, transnational corporations need to make use of the competitive advantages of different countries and regions in technological development, productive forces, natural resources and cost of productive power, to allocate different links of production to different locations and assemble final products competitive both in quality and price.[2] Previously, the most advanced products and technologies developed by transnational corporations were only utilized in their own countries, which later were transferred to developing countries only when they turned mature or obsolete. If developing countries only rely on foreign technologies, they will remain in a backward stage. This is the core of the traditional theory of technological

---

[1] Niu Jianguo, "Transnational Corporations and Economic Globalization", *Journal of China's Economy and Trade*, 2003 (9).

[2] Long Yongtu, "Actively Participate in Economic Globalization and Seize Opportunities for Development", *Journal of Zhejiang Wanli College*, 2004 (4).

transfer. Since the mid-1990s, economic globalization has been accelerated, global production and supply chains has formed rapidly, and some changes occurred: First, due to the rapid technological development, investment of R&D and manufacturing depreciates at a quicker rate, and new technology developed at a high cost by enterprises must be utilized fully within a short period of time in order to match investment costs and satisfy the capital owner. Second, in some important sectors, division of labor is changing from the vertical integration to horizontal one, and enterprises with horizontal integration need global market more than those with vertical integration in order to share R&D expenses and maintain the scale of the enterprises. Third, the number of enterprises at the same technological level is increasing, and competition is getting harsher. Those with quicker speed and larger scale win the competition. For the above three reasons, once new technologies are invented, today's enterprises will try to have these technologies rapidly utilized and manufactured. Today, the technology importer countries may not possess the leading core technologies, but are able to utilize them rapidly within their countries.[1]

3.1.2 Globalization provides opportunities for socialist countries to speed up industrial restructuring and modernization.

Economic globalization and world industrial restructuring, both inevitable result of the development of productive forces, are interconnected and mutually enhancing. World industrial restructuring and transfer of industries are closely linked to economic globalization. In a closed economy, it is much harder to adjust and upgrade country's industrial structure while trying to import advanced foreign industries. Today the upgrading industrial structure in a country is propelled by the increasing intensive international competition and is closely linked with the deepening economic globalization.

After the Second World War, world industrial restructuring and transfer

---

[1] Jiang Xiaojuan, "Take the Opportunities Provided by Economic Globalization and Develop China's Economy", *Journal of Shanxi University of Finance and Economics*, 2004 (1).

have gone through four stages:

The first stage (1945-1960) saw the first upgrading of industrial structure in Western countries including the United States. Production technology moved toward capital-intensive sectors, and labor-intensive sectors such as textile industry were quickly transferred to Asian, African or Latin American countries.

At the second stage (1961-1971), industrial structure in developed countries including the United States and Japan was upgraded, and labor-intensive products were transferred to developing countries, such as the Four Asian Tigers. This stage was marked by the National Income Multiplication Plan focusing on heavy industry policies implemented by Japan in 1961. In the 1960s, countries such as the United States and Japan developed vigorously capital-intensive industries such as steel, chemicals, automobile and machinery driven by technological revolution, and at the same time technology- and capital-intensive industries with high added value were developed, including robotics, electronic and aerospace industries. Labor-intensive textile and light industries including textiles, garment and shoe making, heavy chemical industries with high energy consumption and high pollution, were transferred to developing countries, especially East Asian countries. The Four Asian Tigers and other countries seized opportunities of expanding labor-intensive products processing and exporting and started to transform their economy from import substitution model to export oriented models, and gradually grew into newly industrialized countries.

At the third stage (1972-1986), the industrial structure of developed countries in the West had the second upgrading and new industries such as nuclear energy, space technology and computer industry were extensively developed. At the same time, the newly industrialized countries and regions entered a period of developing heavy chemical industries, and a large amount of traditional industries were transferred to other developing countries in Asia, Africa and Latin America. The economic crisis on a global scale in 1973-1975 caused by oil crisis dealt a heavy blow on the heavy chemical industries of developed countries in the West, and forced them to speed up industrial structural adjustment and to develop knowledge and technology intensive industries with less consumption of resources and energy, chiefly focusing on microelectronic technology. Capital-intensive industries such as automobile, steel and shipbuilding were transferred to newly industrialized countries and developing countries, and the level of industrial structure was improved. At the same time, newly industrialized countries or regions in Asia seized the opportunity of industrial adjustment and industrial transfer provided by international economy. They adjusted their industrial structure in a timely manner, and imported and introduced into their countries some capital-intensive industries, and transferred labor-intensive industries to other ASEAN countries. In this way, they had upgraded their industrial structures.

At the fourth stage (since 1986), due to the sharp fall of the price of oil and primary products, international economy was greatly affected, and trade frictions between developed countries had increased. In order to establish new international division of labor, international trade pattern, as well as economic structure in line with international economy, another wave of industrial restructuring and transfer wave had emerged. During this period, the economies of newly industrialized Asian countries gained remarkable growth, their traditional industrialization was basically completed, and they transferred labor-intensive industries to other developing countries. The industrial structure in the United States was upgraded for the third time, and information industry gained tremendous growth with a great number of high-tech enterprises booming and created a "new economy" miracle in the 1990s. At present, high technology and related industries have a growing influence on the overall national strength, and knowledge innovates at a quicker pace. The cycle and time gap for science and technological research knowledge transforming into productive force becomes shorter, and the original innovations increasingly grow to be the commanding heights for the contemporary technological competition. Many cutting edge technologies are brewing major breakthroughs and a new economic pattern based on knowledge is emerging. Developed countries in the West as represented by OECD members have entered a period of knowledge economy, known also as the new economy. With knowledge economy gradually turning into an economic pattern in reality, the global economic system faces changes in the international division of labor, and a new round of industrial restructuring in the world is inevitable. In the international division of labor, new features such as deepening "division of product differentiation" and "division of production process" appear. Taken as a whole, the United States takes a leading role in the international division of labor, and engages in the production of high value-added production by giving play to its advantage of innovation in new technologies and products. Japan and other countries in West Europe also engage in high value-added production by giving play to their advantage in technological development. Developing countries have lower technological level and mainly engage in general industrial production with lower added value.

By the whole process of industrial restructuring in the 20th century in the world, it seems that the restructuring is a gradual substitution of the dominant industries in certain developed countries, and a transfer them to developing countries, which in turn results in the changes of industrial structures like waves moving forward. Along with the progress of technological and economic globalization, especially with the deepening of cross-border company mergers, acquisitions and restructurings, the industrial structure of developing countries has been integrated into the industrial structure of the world as a whole. As globalization proceeds, the new round of world industrial restructuring and transferring will exert profound influence on socialist countries and offer great opportunities for the upgrading of their industrial structure.

3.1.3 Globalization will promote political development of socialist countries.

Implying the adjustment and reform of political relations, political development is one important aspect of social development and accompanies mankind's political life. But political development is not just the adjustment and reform of political relations in its general sense. It is a process changing from less developed to advanced political system, and it also includes positive political changes taking place in political territory when a traditional society develops into modern society. Li Jingzhi, a Chinese scholar, notes that, "Political development refers to a process of renewal of political ideas, improving of political structure and system as well as progressing of political behaviors."[1] For socialist countries, it is an important task to promote political development, which is inevitable for the development of socialist democracy and for displaying the superiority of socialist democracy. Currently, globalization has quite a role in promoting the political development of socialist countries.

Globalization is not a pure economic phenomenon but will greatly influence political and cultural spheres and social life. The process of economic globalization is always accompanied with cultural infiltration, changes of value and system transplantations. Globalization is not only a tendency of growth of culture and civilization of countries, but also a tendency of growth of social and political life of countries.[2] Economically, the development of globalization is displayed as the global expansion of market economic system. Along with the development of economic globalization, especially the globalization of market economy, it becomes imperative for political ideas in line with market economy to be transmitted globally, and political system in line with market economy to be improved gradually. When a country is seeking to merge with global capital markets, and to attract more direct foreign investment, advanced technology and expertise to a greater extent, the pressure of improving its institutional and political administration and abiding by laws and regulations will greatly increase.[3]

At the same time, globalization is changing political ideas of people,

---

[1] Li Jingzhi, et al, *Political Development and System Innovation in Contemporary China*, p1, Beijing: Peking University Press, 2006.

[2] Elena Safronova, "Globalization from the Perspective of the PRC and Developing Countries", *Far Eastern Affairs*, 2003, Vol. 31, Issue 4.

[3] Jean Pierre Lehmann, "Developing Economies and the Demographic and Democratic Imperatives of Globalization", *International Affairs*, January 2001, Vol. 77.

and hence the criteria of judgment of citizens on their country's political system and government. Developed countries are leading globalization, and the expansion of their ideas and values of democracy and their institutional practices exert pressure on developing countries in terms of system. Anthony Giddens, a British sociologist, notes that, "Globalization is transcending national borders to promote the communication of thoughts and ideas, which results in more active citizens in many regions of the world."[1] In the process of globalization, the diversified criteria and values will require brand new values and moral standards and cause a series of changes in values, mentality and orientation of values.

At the time when economic exchanges are growing between countries with different social systems, political and cultural exchanges are growing, too. On the one hand, it benefits socialist countries in absorbing fine cultures of mankind and improving themselves; on the other hand, it causes conflicts of ideologies between the East and the West, especially the conflict between planned intentional infiltration and natural influence. This is true both for Western and socialist ideologies. Instead of diminishing or weakening, the conflicts, mainly conflicts of ideology or political values, become more outstanding in the process of globalization, which in turn brings heavy pressure on the political development of socialist countries. If the pressure is effectively turned into a motivation, it may drive and disturb the political development of socialist countries. On the whole, globalization could play a positive role in promoting the transformation of political culture as well as political development of socialist countries.

3.2 Globalization Brings Serious Challenges to Socialism

Globalization brings opportunities for the development of socialism, but it also brings huge challenges. In the process of globalization, socialist

---

[1] Anthony Giddes, *Sociology*, p 542, Beijing: Peking University Press, 2003.

countries face many challenges in economic security, political development and cultural security. At the same time, capitalist countries increase pressures and attacks on socialist countries by taking the opportunities brought by economic, political, and cultural exchanges.

3.2.1 Challenges of globalization to economic security of socialist countries

First, economic globalization and industrial security. Industrial restructuring in a global scope brings both opportunities and challenges to developing countries. The basic pattern of industrial restructuring and transferring in the world is as follows: developed countries vigorously develop high-tech industries such as information industry, advanced materials industry and biological engineering industry, and at the same time export secondary technologies and import more primary products and traditional products. As a result, developing countries update their industrial structure at a lower level. Countries with higher level of economic development and R&D capacity, such as newly industrialized countries and regions in Asia and South America, have their industrial structure further improved by introducing new and high technologies, and continue to transfer labor- and capital-intensive manufacturing industries to other less developed countries. Developing countries with lower level of economic development absorb manufacturing industries from the newly industrialized countries and regions and speed up their process of industrialization.[1] As a result, industrial restructuring and transfers bring about vertical division of labor with developed countries having higher level of industries. The industrial structure in developing countries has a low level and a single form, and is in a subordinate position. In terms of industrial structure, a flying geese pattern has been repetitively seen, that is, developed countries take the leading role, and developing countries follow suit and receive the lower level industries from developed countries. The existing socialist countries are all developing

---

[1] Xiong Guangqing, "Challenges of Economic Globalization to Developing New and High-Tech Industries in China", *Journal of Science, Technology and Management*, 2003 (2).

countries and their industrial structures are at a lower level. While these countries join in the world economic system, they face huge pressure in adjusting their industrial structure. Take China as an example, it is both imperative and necessary for China, the largest developing country, to take part in economic globalization. Since the 1980s, China has gained a strong momentum in economic growth, with the average annual GDP growth rate over 9%. But China remains at a lower level in the overall layout of industrial restructuring, and the upgrading of her industrial structure faces severe challenges. If right strategies and measures cannot be taken to speed up industrial restructuring and development, the momentum of economic growth in China will weaken.

In the process of economic globalization, many traditional industries in socialist countries are disadvantaged and lack competitiveness in international market, and their new industries and high-tech industries also encounter many difficulties. Socialist countries lag behind developed countries in many areas and thus face industrial insecurity. Industrial insecurity refers to a status that the pillar industries and leading industries in a country are not able to follow the will of its political government or fulfill the requirements of sustainable development in its economy, or not to be implemented or controlled by its national capital. A typical form of industrial insecurity emerges by the behaviors of transnational corporations and foreign capital ignoring national boundaries. For instance, the host country's industries are monopolized by foreign capital through company mergers and acquisitions; the control of the host country's economy and industrial policies are impacted and she can implement no effective control on its own economic development or industrial structure in the host country is maturing but its pillar industries are manipulated by the will of foreign capital. With the development of information industry, the industrialized countries reconstruct and upgrade their industries and large amount of traditional industries are transferred to developing countries. Developed countries keep control of core and key technologies, and developing countries become their manufacturing bases; thus industrial benefits in developing countries vanish to a great extent. Through internationalization of transactions, transnational corporations import their own machineries at high prices and export products at lower prices and cause great loss of industrial benefits in the host countries. Limited resources are controlled or explored in a destructive manner. The uneven input of foreign capital in different sectors results in the flow of human resources to foreign investment enterprises.[1] These have become outstanding problems and phenomena in some socialist countries and should be paid much attention.

Second, economic globalization and financial security. Finance is the core of modern economy and the most sensitive and fragile "nerve" in the development of national economy. The level of globalization of the financial sector presents the highest hidden risk in the process of economic globalization. As experiences show, the largest risk in the development of national economy of a country is always a financial crisis, which will cause chain reaction in all sectors of social life and have major or even destructive impact on economic development, social stability and the life of its people. A scholar believes that modern finance is the crossroads of paradise and hell.[2]

Under financial globalization, the speed of international capital flow greatly increases, so does the speed of the transmission of financial risk and crisis internationally. Financial security becomes a general concern for countries in the world. In merging into the process of financial globalization, socialist countries have a greater possibility of encountering financial crisis due to their limited experiences and deficiencies of the system. International capital flow refers to the flow of capital from one country or region to another country or region, which has intrinsic difference from the flow of currency resulting from commodities trade or the import and export of labors. The latter causes the transfer of the ownership rights. But international capital does not cause the transfer of the right of ownership, but only the right

---

[1] Hu Guoliang, "Globalization and Protection of Economic Security", *Journal of China Statistics*, 2002 (11).

[2] Wu Xiaoqiu, "Modern Finance, the Crossroads of Paradise and Hell", *Journal of Wuhan Finance*, 2005 (1).

of its use. As economic globalization proceeds, international capital flow becomes more frequent on a larger scale. Many countries have to loosen financial controls, and financial liberalization becomes an irreversible trend. In particular, since the 1990s, the speed of expansion of financial assets has exceeded that of economic and trade growth. Normally the natural base of international financial transactions is international trade, but speculative currency capital is able to detach from industry capital and business capital movement and may grow to unimaginable huge volumes, and make much higher profits than the production and distribution of commodities. Such kind of capital has become a special tool for pursuing super profits. Thousands of billions dollars of speculative money capital is invested in stock, bond, foreign exchanges and gold market. To some extent, speculative capital can promote economic development, but is easily affected by non-economic factors, short-term speculations, or psychological expectations. Currency capital has derailed from the base of commodity production, and the growth rate of virtual economy far exceeds that of physical economy. Potential financial risks exist and may possibly evolve into financial crises. International expansion of financial crisis can not only exert major influence on economic development and economic order, but also result in political turmoil in some countries, directly or indirectly, which in turn has impact on regional or world politics. Financial risk is an issue that must be carefully addressed by socialist countries in the process of economic globalization.

Third, economic globalization and global spread of economic risks. Economic globalization provides channels and holes for global spread of economic risks. Economic globalization has profoundly changed the operational environment of the world economy, and the world market becomes more open, with keener competition. The cross-border flow of capital, technology, information and personnel is more facilitated. Close connection has provided channels and holes for and increased free movement of various risks and crises on a global scale. The spread of financial risks can serve as an example. As financial globalization proceeds, with the growing speed and scope of the expansion of financial crisis, the

Domino effect increases and a financial crisis of one country may rapidly spread to many other countries and cause regional or global crisis. In this context, any country is faced with increasing financial risks from outside. Socialist countries, while opening up to the world, face higher possibility of having problems due to inappropriate financial system and risk prevention mechanisms, as well as limited capabilities of controlling financial risks, and need to take effective measures to solve these problems. Now with many financial institutions entering Chinese financial market, China's banking, stock and insurance industries face serious challenges. The conditions and mechanisms of forming financial risks, as well as the features of financial risks are becoming more complicated. Intrinsic reasonable risks may turn into high risks under the interaction of internal and external conditions. As a result, possibility of financial risks grows remarkably.

3.2.2 The challenge of globalization to political development of socialist countries

In the context of economic globalization, political development of a country is not only influenced by various social factors in this country, but it is also closely linked to international environment.

Firstly, in the progress of economic globalization, the waves of democracy in the world find more channels to spread, and in particular, the third wave of democracy has produced huge influence, taking advantage of economic globalization. Samuel P. Huntington divides democratization in the world into three waves. The first wave of democracy, starting from the long wave of democratization in the early 19th century till 1920, won in about 30 countries and monarchs had to leave. Renewed authoritarianism and the rise of fascism in the 1920s and 1930s had reduced the number of democratic states in the world to about 12 by 1942. The second wave, the democratic short wave increased the number of democratic states to over 30 after the Second World War, though later some democratic regimes collapsed. Since 1974, the third wave saw a far greater speed and scale, as compared with the previous two waves. In the two decades between the 1970s and 1990s, the third wave of democratization has swept the whole world. Its start was marked in South Europe in 1974 by the dismantling of military dictatorship and the establishing of democratic regime in Portugal. Greece and Spain soon swept military dictatorships and established democratic regimes. Huntington noted, "The third wave of democratization that Portugal initiated, literally created the age of democracy."[1] After since, the wave of democratization swept developing countries in Asia, Africa and Latin America. In the 1980s, most of the military regimes in Latin America were replaced by civil governments and representative democracies were established. In the late 1980s and early 1990s, this wave of capitalist democratization, featured by multi-party system and the separation of powers of legislation, jurisdiction and administration, rapidly influenced the former Soviet Union and Eastern European countries. Under the impact of democratization wave, these countries had chosen the capitalist road. In the 1990s, 40 out of 47 African countries, under the impact of democratization, abolished one-party political system, adopted multi-party system and held multi-party elections, and some military regimes turned into civil governments.

In Asia, in the 1980s and 1990s, more than 10 countries, such as the Philippines, Korea, Pakistan, Bangladesh, Thailand, Indonesia, Mongolia, transformed from authoritarian to democratic regimes. Statistics show that about 2/3 of developing countries have been impacted by the third wave of democratization, and nearly 40 of them turned from authoritarian politics to democratic politics, established democratic regimes and embarked on the road of political democratization. As Samuel Huntington notes, "Two decades ago, less than 30 percent of the countries in the world were democratic; now more than 60 percent have governments produced by some form of open, fair and competitive elections. A quarter-century ago, authoritarian governments (military coup, dictatorship regime) seemed to be dominating. Today, hundreds of millions of people who previously suffered under tyrants live in freedom." "The rapid growth of democratic system within such a short

---

[1] Samuel P. Huntington, *The Third Wave: Democratization in the Late Twentieth Century*, Preface, p 2, Shanghai: SDX Joint Publishing Company, 1998.

period of time was no doubt the most magnificent and significant political change."[1]

The third wave of democratization is strong and sweeps the whole globe, with sophisticated and profound impact. The wave has not ceased and a fourth wave of democratization will possibly surge. In nature, it is a process of capitalist democratization, and most developing countries follow the West. They take establishing Western democratic system as their basic goal of political democratization, and follow the path of capitalism. Though some developing countries had already entered the capitalist road long time ago, democratic system such as capitalist multi-party system and the separation of legislation, jurisdiction and administration was adopted later. In the process of political system improvement, socialist countries should continue to explore their own ways of political development and stick to socialism.

Secondly, globalization facilitates the "promoting peaceful transformation" strategy of Western countries aiming at socialist countries. As two opposing social systems, socialism and capitalism are inevitably confrontational. As long as the two systems co-exist, the confrontation will not cease. But under some conditions, changes will occur in the methods of confrontation between the two systems. As globalization proceeds, Western countries speed up in promoting the "promoting peaceful transformation" strategy. Peaceful transformation refers to the cultural and ideological infiltration into socialist countries by Western capitalist countries, taking advantage of their advanced strength in economy, technology, military power and culture, in order to cause changes within socialist countries favorable to capitalism, and eventually promote fundamental changes of the political system of socialist countries and start a reverse evolution towards capitalism, and thus capitalism can win without battles. During the existence of the Soviet Union and Eastern European socialist countries, Western capitalist countries deployed various means, political, economic, technological, even religious, nationalistic or cultural, to penetrate into socialist countries. They

---

[1] Samuel P. Huntington, *The Third Wave: Democratization in the Late Twentieth Century*, Preface, pp 2-3.

promoted Western lifestyles and values, supported nationalism in Eastern European countries, incited them against the Soviet Union and encouraged them to split from the socialist bloc led by the Soviet Union. As a result, the Soviet Union and Eastern European socialist countries were coached toward capitalist system.

In the context of economic globalization, socialism and capitalism are interdependent, but their confrontation remains and is fundamentally irreconcilable. The intention of capitalist countries to reverse socialism has not changed. They take advantage of the favorable conditions provided by globalization and attempt to enforce their economic and political system on developing countries, and in particular, they constantly promote "peaceful evolution" strategy aiming at socialist countries. Deng Xiaoping had asserted, "Capitalism intends to win the war against socialism. In the past it used weapons, such as atomic bomb and hydrogen bomb, which encountered resistance from people in the world. Now it deploys peaceful evolution strategy."[1] "Western countries are fighting the Third World War without causing smoke of gunpowder."[2] War with no smoke of gunpowder means "peaceful evolution" of socialist countries. Between socialism and capitalism, struggles of infiltration and anti-infiltration, subversion and anti-subversion will exist for a long time to come. As a result, in the process of political development, socialism will inevitably face choices as to what direction it goes, as well as pressure from international environment.

Thirdly, the imbalance between the power of socialism and capitalism in the world has resulted in great pressure for political development of socialist countries. In the late 1980s and early 1990s, the dramatic upheaval in Soviet Union and Eastern European countries had reduced the number of socialist countries from fifteen to five, and socialist movement in the world was seriously reversed. The collapse of the Soviet Union did not terminate the tendency of polarization but brought about structural changes in the world pattern. After those dramatic changes, some people had believed

[1] *Selected Works of Deng Xiaoping*, First Edition, Vol. 3, p 326, Beijing: People's Press, 1993.
[2] *Ibid*, p 344.

that socialism which emerged in the 20th century would also die out in the same century. Francis Fukuyama, an American scholar, asserted that, free democratic system may be "the termination of ideological development of human beings" and "the last form of rule of human beings", and thus cause "the end of history"[1]. The dramatic changes in the Soviet Union and Eastern European countries caused unfavorable changes of world political power for socialism, and socialism faces greater pressure in sticking to its own political path. The political development and ideological safety of socialist countries face severe tests and challenges.

The imbalance between the power of socialism and capitalism in the world has resulted in great pressure and enormous impact on political development of socialist countries, which can be seen from the political development of China. After the dramatic changes in the Soviet Union and Eastern European countries, the change in the power of socialism and capitalism caused greater pressure for socialist China. Since the mid-1980s, Chinese leaders had started to realize that the fundamental drawbacks, or the evil roots of China's political system was the high concentration of power, in particular, the high concentration of the leaders' individual power. In the early period of reforming the political system, including the 13th Congress of the Communist Party of China, the political reform had focused on eliminating this fundamental drawback. But due to the dramatic changes in the Soviet Union and Eastern European countries, the focus of political reform in China was shifted from assaulting the fortified position and addressing those fundamental drawbacks was delayed. Thus political reform was reduced to address peripheral issues, such as reforming governmental organizations. It is fair to say such a shift was reasonable at that time. However, the reform of economic system cannot stand on its own for a long term, and the reform of political system cannot only focus on peripheral spheres of the system. In sum, in a world with increasing interdependence and close connection, the imbalance of power between socialism and capitalism has exerted great

---

[1] Francis Fukuyama, *The End of History and the Last Man*, Foreword, p1, Beijing: China Academy of Social Sciences Press, 2003.

influence on political development of socialist countries.

3.2.3 The challenge of globalization to cultural security of socialist countries

The progress of globalization has both positive and negative influences. On the one hand, it enhances economic, political, and cultural exchanges between nations and countries, and fine fruits created by human culture can be shared. On the other hand, as globalization proceeds, countries in the world face cultural clashes, conflicts and frictions, that is, the issue of cultural security.[1] In the process of globalization, powerful, big and rich countries, as represented by developed countries in the West, and weak, small and poor countries in the Third World are not positioned on an equal footing. Taking advantage of their economic strength, developed countries control more resources, play a dominating role in the world, and become culture imperialists as defined by the American scholar Edward W. Said.[2] They offer models not only in economy, but in culture, ideas or lifestyles. They take a leading role in establishing cultural hegemony. As a result, in the process of globalization, socialist countries inevitably face problems of cultural development or cultural security, challenged by the strong cultural position of the West.

Firstly, the strong cultural position of the West, along with the rapid expansion of globalization, will narrow the space of national cultural development. Nation, representing a cultural group, is a social community formed over history, with common language, common territory, common economic life, as well as common psychological qualities represented by common culture. National culture composes the culture and value system of the common behavior pattern of a nation. Culture will have to be national before it becomes international. Against the backdrop of globalization, maintaining cultural diversity is closely linked to maintaining national

---

[1] Li Jinqi, "Globalization and Cultural Security of China", *Journal of Philosophy Research*, 2005 (1).

[2] Edward W. Said, *Culture and Imperialism*, Beijing: SDX Joint Publishing Company, 2003.

independence. One of the basic characteristics of culture is that it is national, and it is the cornerstone for a nation to stand among the many nations in the world. If a nation fully negates its cultural tradition, will lose the national confidence, and willingly accept the assimilation of other nations, thus it will start to go extinct. National culture is the label of existence of a nation. When any culture loses its characteristic of being national, it will no longer exist as an independent culture. Globalization of culture is led by American culture, and the nature of it is to promote cultural hegemony. This is a typical cultural imperialism.[1] Globalization, led by Western countries, strengthens the leading position of Western culture and limits the space of national cultural development. Some folk cultures or ethnic cultures may well go extinct. Some Western scholars have asserted that, in the process of globalization, "world capitalism is always equaled by westernization. It controls not only the economic territories, but also culture and lifestyle in the non-West world."[2] The strong position of Western culture will have great impact on the value systems of national cultures. Globalization has involved almost all countries and nations into the process of modernization, but from the very start, this process is based on the inequality between developed and developing countries in terms of national power. Developed countries, economically dominating in the process of globalization, promote their cultural products and implement unequal cultural hegemony and aggression in the form of cultural exchanges, supported by their strong economic power. Cultural development of socialist countries is restrained and squeezed. Taken as a whole, despite the pressure from globalization they are facing, developed countries are beneficiaries of globalization. Taking an active position, their cultural spirit and values are expanded. But the national cultures of developing countries are pushed to the edge, and even face the danger of losing independence.[3]

[1] Yu Pei, "Anti-Cultural Globalization—Thoughts on Cultural Diversity in the Context of Economic Globalization", *Research of History Theories*, 2004 (4).

[2] Rhoda E. Howard-Hassman, "Culture, Human Rights, and the Politics of Resentment in the Era of Globalization", *Human Rights Review*, Oct. /Dec. 2004, Vol. 6, Issue 1.

[3] Dai Lu, "A Few Thoughts on Cultural Globalization", *China Youth Daily*, 2001-12-06.

Secondly, in the context of globalization, Western culture may possibly gradually erode the roots of traditional cultures of socialist countries. The strong position of Western culture not only poses threats to cultural security of socialist countries, but also squeezes space for the development of the national culture in socialist countries. Some reactionary trends and spiritual trashes in Western culture will have negative influence on socialist culture when being introduced to socialist countries, and pose severe challenges to building socialist culture. The mass cultural products in Western countries are deceitful in that they conceal the existing social conflicts and splits by means of showing leisurely, recreational and cozy life. Along with globalization, mass cultural products are diffused to the whole world, including socialist countries and the Third World. They wear down the will and resolution of the general public, and erode the root of traditional culture of other countries. Therefore, in the process of globalization, the cultural development of socialist countries is facing severe challenges, which is an important issue that should not be overlooked.

Thirdly, the political culture of socialist countries is facing challenges, too. To a great extent, globalization is the expansion of the growth pattern of capitalist countries. In such a system, developing countries, in particular socialist countries, are being dominated or impacted due to their weakness in power and strength. Covered by the economic, political, military and cultural strategies of developed capitalist countries on a global scale, the cultural security of socialist countries is facing a grim situation.[1] After the Cold War, the progress of globalization had accelerated, and the position of economic and technological factors in international politics had become predominant, but the ideological offensive by capitalism on socialism had not stopped. Capitalist countries, the United States in particular, cannot hold back their ideological urges, and take various measures to promote the democratic system, values and lifestyles of capitalist countries, to speed up infiltration into socialist countries in terms of ideology and cause immense threats to

---

[1] Li Jinqi, "Globalization and Cultural Security in China", *Journal of Philosophy Research*, 2005 (1).

the development of political culture of socialist countries. In the context of globalization, socialist countries are conducting reforms on economic and political system, and the previously dominating ideology and values are greatly impacted.[1] As a result, the cultural development of socialist countries face a double pressure, which also threats the political and cultural security of socialist countries.

3.3 The Overall Situation of the Evolution of Socialism in the World in the Post-Cold War Era

After the dramatic changes in the Soviet Union and Eastern European countries, socialist movement in the world had suffered a major setback and subsided. This is viewed from three aspects, namely, the development of further resisting socialist countries, the development of communist parties in non-socialist countries—due to changes in the socialist bloc—and thirdly the development of different schools of socialism. At the same time, in the overall low tide of socialist movement in the world, several new waves and tides of socialist development surge.[2] Yet, socialism has a bright future for development in the long term.

3.3.1 The development of the existing socialist countries.

In the late 1980s and early 1990s, dramatic upheaval took place in the Soviet Union and Eastern European countries, socialist movement in the world suffered major setback, and there were only five socialist countries left in the world. At that time, Deng Xiaoping had noted, "Grave twists appeared in some countries, and it seems that socialism is weakened. But like being put into a melting pot, people are made stronger through trials and draw lessons from the dramatic changes, which will promote the development of socialism

---

[1] Ren Junying, "The Strategic Direction of Socialist Development in the Context of Globalization", *Journal of Henan Normal University* (Philosophy and Social Sciences Edition), 2001 (6).

[2] Xiao Feng, "The Current Situation of Socialist Movement in the World", *Journal of Party Building*, 2000 (10).

toward a healthier direction."[1] Deng Xiaoping's prediction has been proven correct, as shown by the development of socialism in the world in only over ten years after those dramatic changes.

After the dramatic changes in the Soviet Union and Eastern European countries, socialist countries enjoyed a healthy development. Before the changes, socialist countries were in an abnormal state of development, but after the changes, they gradually embark on a path of a healthy development. It can be shown in the following aspects: In terms of international situation, it was strongly believed that the main trend of the age was war and revolution, whereas today peace and development constitute the main trend; politically, the high concentration of power has changed to the remarkable progress of political democracy; economic growth has taken the path of balanced development; cultural freedom has notably increased; international relations have been enhanced, different from the previous closed or semi-closed status.[2] In particular in China, the new theory of the scientific outlook on development has been proposed, which stresses all-round, balanced and sustainable development and acknowledges the ultimate goal of development is to develop the ability of the people and to achieve the all-round development of the people and the individuals.

In terms of theoretical innovation, after the dramatic upheaval in the Soviet Union and Eastern European countries, socialist countries have emancipated their thinking modes and achieved many breakthroughs in that sphere. The existing five socialist countries have revised their views on socialism to varying extent, and broken the fetters of the traditional Soviet model. Major ideological change has taken place in terms of the basic theoretical issue of what socialism is and how to build socialism. For instance, the perspective on the phases and future of socialist development becomes more practical, and the expectations have turned from high to low, from idealistic to practical; in terms of guideline and model of development,

---

[1] *Selected Works of Deng Xiaoping*, 1st Edition, Vol. 3, p383.

[2] Xiong Guangqing, "The Current Situation of Socialist Development in the World", *Qiushi Monthly*, 2004 (10).

the emphasis is put on exploring a way of development suitable for the practical, real conditions of the country; the nature of socialism is better understood, with more emphasis on the emancipation and development of productive forces; it is realized that socialist and market economy is not contradictory.

In terms of practice, the existing socialist countries have safeguarded their position, and stood up to the impact of the dramatic changes of the Soviet Union and Eastern European countries. They stick to the basic system and the direction of socialism, explore ways suitable for their national conditions and have scored remarkable achievements in social development. The five socialist countries basically all show favorable momentum of development, with political stability, growing economy and improving living standards of the people. Through reform, China has succeeded in finding the correct path to build socialism with Chinese characteristics, and achieved great accomplishments in material, political and ethical progress that have caught attention of the whole world. Since the Sixth Party Congress of the Communist Party of Vietnam in 1986, Vietnam adopted economic renovation and opening up, replaced planning mechanism with market mechanism, and implemented policies of all-round opening up. In 2001, the Ninth Party Congress of the Communist Party of Vietnam resolved that the development mode of economic system is market economy with socialist orientation, and setting advanced socialist democracy as one of the ideal goals of socialism in Vietnam. Between 1991 and 2001, GDP in Vietnam reached an annual average growth rate of 7.6%; political reform and democratization of social and political life have been promoted in an active and stable manner; and legal system was improved. The People's Revolutionary Party of Laos adopted a series of measures in a resolute manner after the dramatic changes of the Soviet Union and Eastern European countries; it consolidated domestic stability and resisted the attack of peaceful evolution from the West. Over a decade, the renovation and opening up of Laos has obtained huge achievements. It has growing economic strength and further opens to the outside world.

DPRK and Cuba also stick to the path of socialism, though they have fewer achievements in reform and opening up, which is closely related to the extremely unfavorable international environment they are facing. After the Cold War, they have not enjoyed an improved international environment, but rather faced greater pressures from the superpower. It is shown by the nuclear crises in DPRK that the root of the crises is the remnants of Cold War world political configuration, or the continuation of Cold War in Northeast Asia. The nuclear crisis in DPRK is largely a result of direct or indirect policies aimed at her by the United States against the backdrop of globalization. Since the 1990s, the nuclear issue on the Korean Peninsula has gradually intensified. In the early 1990s, with the influence of her victory "won without battles", the United States had strongly desired to establish a new political and economic order in the world. But the several new developments around the Korean Peninsula made the United States think that the region would run out of her control. At that time the situation on the Peninsula was easing, and DPRK and Japan were improving relations, and South and North Korean dialogue had achieved some positive progress. In this background, DPRK nuclear crisis broke out on a massive scale, and the South and North relation on the Peninsula was changed into the relation between the United States and DPRK. In appearance, the first wave of nuclear crisis in October 2002 was caused after Mr. Kelly's visit—envoy of President Bush—to DPRK. But it was actually a result of the deep-rooted hostile policies of the Bush administration toward DPRK.[1] Since Bush took office, he had believed that policies of the Clinton administration were too mild and ineffective. Bush and most of his advisers thought that Clinton was too soft toward DPRK and too hard toward Japan and ROK, allies of the US.[2] It is generally fair to say that DPRK's tough attitude toward the US is a strong reflection of the hostile attitude of the US toward DPRK.

---

[1]　Pu Guoliang, "The Origin and Nature of the Nuclear Crisis on the Korean Peninsula", *Research of Socialism of Chinese Characteristics*, 2003 (5).

[2]　Iov H. Daalder, James M. Lindsay, *America Unbound: The Bush Revolution in Foreign Policy*, p 237, Beijing: Xinhua Press, 2004.

Cuba is the only socialist country on the west hemisphere of the globe, in close proximity of the United States. Since the Cuban revolution in 1959, the United States has adopted hostile policies to Cuba and the relation between the two countries has always been confrontational. After the dramatic changes in the Soviet Union and Eastern Europe, the United States intensified its embargo on Cuba and applied greater pressure on Cuba to promote possible changes. Thus the confrontation between the US and Cuba had sharpened. In 1990, TV Martí was established in the US to attack and conduct subversive propaganda on Cuba. The Cuban Democracy Act, also known as Torricelli Act, was passed in 1992, which prohibits the overseas branches of American companies to do business with Cuba, and prohibits American citizens to travel to Cuba, and prohibits Cubans in the US to transfer money to relatives in Cuba. Around 1994, the US also encouraged Cubans to flee from Cuba, and immigration surged. In March 1996, Clinton signed Helms-Burton Act and intensified embargo on Cuba to a greater extent. Since 1998, American-Cuban relation has been relatively eased, though the prospects are not optimistic.[1] After the dramatic changes, same as DPRK, Cuba showed intentions to reform and open up and has obtained remarkable achievements in economic and social development, though no big steps have been taken due to the hostile and containment policies followed by United States. By the opening of the 21st century, the revival of Cuban economy took place at the same time with "the battle of thinking", a social revolution in the revolutionary process. Cuba has initiated 150 plans with reasonable goals in the spheres of education, health, culture and caring for her vulnerable citizens, and scored important achievements. These plans benefited all the families in Cuba and provided equal chance to everyone. In 2004, Cuba had obtained positive and encouraging results. Despite difficulties brought about by natural disasters, electric power shortages and intensified embargo, Cuba's economy had grown 5%. Tourism grew annually 10% and became the most vigorous sector in Cuba. The number of foreign

---

[1] Cui Guitian, "On American-Cuban Relation and the Characteristics of Cuban Socialism", *Contemporary World and Socialism*, 2003 (1).

tourists had exceeded two million for the first time in history. Nickel industry and bio-technology industry have witnessed remarkable leaps. In terms of social life, two results were glorious: registered college students has reached a record high of 380,000, and infant mortality rate was reduced to 5.9‰, one of the lowest countries in the world (compared to 6.8 in the United States).[1] According to the UN, the life expectancy in Cuba is 78.3 years (76.2 for males and 80.4 for females). This ranks Cuba 37th in the world and 3rd in the Americas, behind only Canada and Chile, and just ahead of the United States.

3.3.2 The development of communist parties in non-socialist countries after the dramatic changes in the Soviet Union and Eastern Europe

The dramatic changes in the Soviet Union and Eastern Europe had imposed a huge impact on communist parties in many countries. The most direct result was the communist parties in several countries were dissolved, or the names were changed due to pressure or other reasons. The number of communist parties was reduced, and the ideologies of some communist parties fell into chaos. Resisting this severe reverse situation, many communist parties have tided over the difficulties through theoretical reflections and organizational and policy adjustments. They have recorded some positive and important changes over recent years. Several communist parties and left-wing forces of the former Soviet Union and Eastern European countries have restored themselves and started to played important roles in domestic politics; communist parties in major capitalist countries have taken a stronger foot hold, adhered to their positions and witnessed new developments; communist parties in the Third World endeavored to get rid of crisis and embarked on new path of development. On the whole, the turbulence and shock period opened after of the dramatic changes has basically ended, and the world socialist movement once again entered into a relatively stable period of progress and revival despite several difficulties and

[1] Alberto Rodriguez Arufe, "Current Situation in Cuba", *Journal of Latin America Research*, 2005 (2).

complications.[1]

3.3.2.1 Revival of communist parties in the former Soviet Union and Eastern European countries

After the dramatic changes, countries in this region have started to adopt capitalist system after the Soviet model of socialism had failed. But as an ideology and movement, socialism has not disappeared. With adjustments over ten years, communist parties in this region regained some strength and the Communist Party in Russian Federation, Ukraine, Tajikistan and Party of Communists of Kyrgyzstan became major parties in these countries. Leaders of these parties won positions in the governments or parliaments. Communist parties of Armenia, Azerbaijan and Georgia also have won important positions in the parliament.

After the dissolution of the Soviet Union, the Communist Party of Russia was prohibited to have any activities by Yeltsin administration in November 1991. It soon resumed its legal status through great endeavors. It was reestablished in December 1993 and won 12.35% votes in that year's parliamentary election, becoming the third largest party in the State Duma. In December 1995, it won 22.3% votes in the parliamentary elections and became the biggest party. During the presidential elections in June and July 1996, Zyuganov won 32.04% votes in the first round of election and 40.3% in the second round. In the Duma election in December 1999, the Communist Party of Russia won 113 seats as the largest party in Duma. But since 2001 the power of this party was frustrated. On July 3, the party had split apart and held separate 10th Party Congress, led by party chairman Zyuganov and Vladimir Tikhonov the chairman of People's Patriotic Union of Russia, an umbrella organization. Two new leading organs were elected. The Duma seats of the party were soon reduced. It is yet hard to tell what the future will bring for this party.

The Communist Party of Ukraine resumed its legal status in October

---

[1] Gao Fang, Li Jingzhi and Pu Guoliang as compilers, *Theories and Practices of Scientific Socialism*, 4th Edition, p 244, Beijing: China Renmin University Press, 2005.

1993 and gained a remarkable development. In the election of the new parliament of Ukraine in March 1994, the Communist Party won 89 seats out of 338 and became the largest party in the parliament. It formed coalition with left-wing Social Party and Peasants' Party and nominated the chairman of Social Party as the first vice-chairman. Together with other supporters, the three-party coalition halted the plans for privatization. At present, the party led by Tymoshenko has 41 seats out of 450 in the parliament, Party of the Regions led by Yanukovich has 50 seats and the Communist Party has 56 seats. The largest party, People's Union Our Ukraine led by Yushenko, has 96 seats. The Communist Party of Ukraine still plays an important role in the political fate of Ukraine.

There are some new communist organizations emerging in the former Soviet Union region. Though most of them have small number of members, and social and political influence, they signal the bright future of socialist development in these countries. In particular, the Party of Communists of Moldova has succeeded outstanding achievements. Moldova is a small country with a population of only 4 million, while the party members amount to more than 100,000. In the parliamentary election in 1998, the Party of Communists of Moldova became the largest party in the parliament. In 2001, the Party of Communists of Moldova won the parliamentary elections, and the chairman of the party Vladimir Voronin was elected the president of the country. The Party of Communists of Moldova is the first Communist Party that had won the elections and become the ruling party after the dramatic changes in the former Soviet Union and Eastern Europe, and its rise stands as exceptional at the low tide of socialist movement in the world. As the ruling party, it maintains social stability, promotes reform policies and enjoys the support of the majority of Moldovian people. Its position as the ruling party has been consolidated. In March 2005, it won the parliamentary election again and Vladimir Voronin was re-elected as the president for the second term. In addition, the communist parties of some other countries of the Commonwealth of Independent States have developed to varying degree and some have won government seats sharing the ruling powers.

There are also communist organizations being re-established in some

Eastern European countries, including Communist Alliance "Proletariat" in Poland, Socialist Workers' Party in Hungary, Communist Party of Albania, Czech- Bohemian Moravian Communist Party, etc. They stick to Marxism and Leninism as the guiding ideology and continue to take communist cause as their goal of endeavors. In particular, Czech-Bohemian Moravia Communist Party has scored most remarkable achievements. It is a party with the most members and most disciplined organizational structure in Czech Republic. Since 1996, it has won growing support in the parliamentary election and in the 2003 election it became the third largest party in the parliament. It now has about 120,000 party members and 5,000 grass root units.[1]

3.3.2.2 Communist parties in major capitalist countries have gained new development.

After the impact of the dramatic changes in the former Soviet Union and Eastern European countries, there are 12 communist parties and communist organizations in West Europe that have resisted the adverse trends. They were severely oppressed, and urged to halt their activities or were faced the danger of dissolving; these challenges had occurred both from inside and outside of the party and the state. They managed to hold their ground, continued struggling and survived indomitably and have kept their old names and ultimate goals have remained unchanged. But they have revised the political routes and strategies of the party adapting to the major changes that have occurred in domestic and international situation. They have also progressed despite of all these difficulties.

Over the recent years, communist parties in West Europe have succeeded to reverse the tendency of losing party members and votes. Some have progressed in terms of gaining new members and votes in elections and have expanded their political influence. Communist organizations in some countries were rebuilt. With over a decade of struggle and adjustment,

---

[1] Cai Wu, "Current Situation and Characteristics of Socialist Movement in the World", *Journal of Teaching and Research*, 2004 (1).

communist parties in West Europe grew to more than 20 in number, with about 500,000 party members. Those with strength and influence are the Communist Party of France, the Communist Party of Portugal, the Communist Party of Spain, the Communist Party of Greece, and the Re-Foundation Communist Party of Italy. The Communist Party of France, as one of the leading communist parties in developed nations in the West, has more than 80 years of history and more than 200,000 party members. In 2001 the CPF took part in the left-wing coalition government led by the social party (Socialists), including Greens, and four leaders from the Communist Party were cabinet ministers. Sticking to Marxist theoretical foundation and the goal of Communism, the communist parties in West Europe continuously upgrade their ideas and adjust their action strategies to adapt to situational changes and to pursue development.

The Communist Party of the United States of America was established in 1919 and once was a party of the working class with the most power and influence in the West. The dramatic changes in the former Soviet Union and Eastern Europe caused immense pressure for the Communist Party of the United States of America. The number of party members was sharply reduced and the party's influence had diminished. But the backbone of the party was preserved and the party has gained some development over recent years. But on the whole, its power is weak, and the estimate number of party members is between 7,000 and 10,000 with 3,000 regularly taking part in activities. Yet it remains as a left-wing party in the United States with the most members and largest influence. The Japanese Communist Party had in the past reflected on some of its extremely left stances and had adopted a more practical line with flexible principles and policies, built a more open image of itself and shown new momentum of development. In the 1996 general election, the seats of the Communist Party jumped from 15 to 26, and the votes it won increased from 4.83 million in the last election to 7.27 million. In local parliaments, members of local parliament of the Communist Party were 4,049, overtaking Liberal Democratic Party as the largest party. There were 150 autonomous municipalities that this Communist Party had ruling seats, in which 76 were ruled only by the Communist Party. In 2000, the Communist Party of Japan had 20 seats in both the House and the Senate. In January 2006, the 24th Congress of the Japanese Communist Party was held with about 1,000 representatives attending. The congress elected the new Central Committee with Shii Kazuo as the Chairperson of the Executive Committee and Ichida Tadayoshi as the Head of the Secretariat. Over 21 parties from 17 countries, including China, sent their representatives to the congress at the invitation of the Japanese Communist Party. The Japanese Communist Party is playing growing role in social and political life of Japan.

3.3.2.3 Communist parties in the Third World countries in Asia, Africa and Latin America

Apart from a few communist parties that collapsed or changed names, the communist parties in most countries in the Third World have kept their flags and some have embarked on a new road of development. In Asia, the development of Communist parties in South Asian countries maintains a positive momentum. In 1990 and 1991, the Communist Party of India (Marxist) had issued many statements and resolutions to criticize "the distortion and betrayal of socialist principles" by the Soviet Union and Eastern European countries. After the dramatic changes, the number of its members increased sharply from 465,000 in 1988 to 630,000 in 1995, and it became the third largest party in India. The left front led by the Communist Party of India (Marxist) has ruled in the state of West Bengal for nearly 30 years. In the general election of May 2004, the left-wing front won 62 seats out of 543 seats in the House of the People, the lower house of the parliament, in which the Communist Party of India (Marxist) held 43. In the 14th election of the House of the People in 2004, the leader of the party, Somnath Chatterjee was elected the speaker of the House of the People and was sworn in on June 2 the same year. He was the first communist elected as the speaker in the history of Indian parliament. The Communist Party of India—original—also had a remarkable performance. It has about 467,000 party members and increased its seats in the parliament from three to six after the dramatic changes in the Soviet Union and Eastern European countries. She had participated governments both in central and the local levels. After she participated in the coalition government of India, several of its members had retained positions in the cabinet. Now it has 560,000 party members, more than 6.8 million members in mass organizations, 10 seats in the House of the People and seven in the Council of States. It jointly runs in two states including the state of West Bengal. The Communist Party of Nepal-M-L won the parliamentary election and became the ruling party in November 1994. Though it was attacked jointly by the conservative forces and had to resign in less than a year, it nevertheless attracted broad attention of the international community in the doldrums of socialist movement in the world. Since then, the Communist Party of Nepal adjusted its lines of principle and formed a new government together with other parties in March 1997. The Communist Party of the island country of Sri Lanka had also resisted the pressure from the dramatic changes in the Soviet Union and Eastern European countries, with members growing from 5,000 to more than 10,000, and the parliamentary seats from just one to four in 1994.

In Africa, South African Communist Party is the most influential socialist party. It has fought for the cause of justice of the people of South Africa for nearly 70 years and gained legal status in 1990. In December 1991, South African Communist Party held the eighth congress which stressed it would stick to the principles of the party and issued the statement of "establishing the working class' political power in the democratic change". In the general elections in April 1994, South African Communist Party struggled under the banner of African National Congress and won over 50 seats in the 400 seats of the National Parliament. She has two ministers and three vice-ministers in the tripartite alliance government. Her reputation grows and members had increased sharply from over 2,000 in 1990 to 80,000. The party has established grass root organizations in nine provinces. South African Communist Party adopts a strategy of cooperating with the governing party African National Congress, and has become one of the important parties running the country with seven party members holding positions as ministers or vice-ministers of the central government. Recently it has 80 of the 400 seats in the parliament, accounting for 1/5. In addition, in Indian ocean islands an autonomous part of France, the Reunionese Communist Party with 10,000 members is the largest ruling party in the government of this island country. The Communist Party of Lesotho grows to be an influential opposition party in the country. Communist parties of both Senegal and Benin have become parties with legal status in their countries.

The communist parties in Latin America, except for the Communist Party of Cuba, were greatly impacted by the collapse of the Soviet Union and most of them were split apart and their power was greatly weakened. After a period of turbulence, many of them have managed to hold their grounds and turned for the better. Now there are over 30 communist parties and about 400,000 members in that continent. Comparatively the communist parties of Brazil and Chili have more forces. Since 1990, communist parties of Latin America have held several regional meetings which emphasize that they will stick to socialist causes, and all this facts display that socialism is still full of vigor and remains to be the hope of mankind.

3.3.3 The development of other schools of socialism

After the dramatic upheaval in the Soviet Union and Eastern European countries, socialism entered a phase of reflections and explorations and appeared various new ideas and schools of socialism. Many scholars have taken the collapse of the socialist system in Soviet Union and Eastern European countries as an opportunity to reflect upon and re-examine the nature and future of socialism, taking into account the new characteristics of the current age and the developments in contemporary capitalism. Different schools of socialist thought and movements surge and support each other, forming a remarkable landscape of socialist movement in spite of the overall doldrums.

3.3.3.1 Democratic socialism of the socialist party

After the dramatic changes in the Soviet Union and Eastern European countries, (social) democratic socialism entered a new phase of development.

Although it had chosen reformist thinking and strategy, it shares origins with the scientific socialism. After a long evolution, most of the (social) democratic socialist in developed countries in the West have given up the guideline of Marxism and formed their basic values of freedom, democracy, justice, equality, solidarity, etc. Politically, they distance themselves from or even become confrontational with the communist parties. However, under the current conditions of contemporary capitalism, (social) democratic socialism, although being reformist, represents the interests of a large number of voters and is more advanced compared with liberalism and conservatism.

In 1980s, (social) democratic socialist movement had encountered a serious crisis for the following reasons; the impact of dramatic changes in the Soviet Union and Eastern European countries was also very important at a later stage; the structural changes in the society entering the post-industrial era in Western countries was a challenge; blue-collar segment of the working class had decreased substantially; and a recession had occurred in traditional movement of workers and the left-wing trade unions had lost many members. In such a context, since the 1990s, (social) democratic socialist parties have readjusted social democracy for the third time in history and further replaced socialist ideas with the values of equality, freedom, democracy and solidarity. The role of the state in political and social life has been re-examined and was further emphasized. While the reverse conservative reforms attacking welfare system had speeded up, modernization of social democratic parties was promoted. These parties have internationally supported peaceful methods and objected war and war-like policies. After efforts these parties have created a new image and another important phase of the social democratic parties returning to the political arena was initiated.[1] Thomas Mayer, a theorist and a member of the Basic Values Commission of German Social Democratic Party has since 1991 reiterated in his works such as *Introduction to Democratic Socialism—Social Democracy* and *What Is Left From Socialism?* many new perspectives. He had asserted that, in

---

[1] Yang Shuang, "The Basic Features of Ruling Social Democratic Parties", *Research of Marxism*, 2005 (3).

face of the new situation after the dramatic changes in the Soviet Union and Eastern European countries, (social) democratic socialist parties should give up the concept and terming "democratic socialism", but once again return to use "social democracy" to express their theories and policies. In face of the grim reality of losing their traditional social bases in the society after the re-adjustments of capitalism, (social) democratic socialist parties have changed their long existing policies, which had mainly relied on industrial workers and chose a new direction to for an alliance and cooperation with the middle class stratums in the society, and tried to get the support of all societal forces supporting peace and progress in the world. They have expanded joint struggles with various new social movements, in order to expand their social bases and have as many supporters as possible. At the same time, in face of the increasing conservative pressure against social welfare policies these parties have revised their ideas on the state's welfare policies and have made new adjustments. The basic idea behind their adjustment was to reduce the excessive social welfare budgets and pay more attention to the role of market competition, including labor markets. The Labour Party of the United Kingdom proposed to change the previous policies of "high income taxes, high welfare spending and high social expenditure" and had proposed the following ideas: Fairness and social justice, liberty and equality of opportunity, solidarity and responsibility to others—these values are timeless. Social democracy will never sacrifice them. To make these values relevant to today's world requires realistic and forward-looking policies capable of meeting the challenges of the 21st century. Modernization is about adapting to conditions that have objectively changed, and not reacting to polls. She proposed financial and monetary policies replacing taxes, aiming to increase government expenditures and at the same increase pace of economic growth, and plan the expenditures according to state income. With Tony Blair, Prime Minister of the U.K and Gerhard Schroeder, German Chancellor, as the representatives, social democracy had started a new round of reforms. Under Blair's leadership, British Labor Party had created trendy slogans such as "New Labor Party", "Innovation", "New Politics" and "New Welfare", and achieved her goal of transforming Labor Party, ideologically and organizationally. In practice, she combined social democracy with liberalism further and chose a new term with a tint of ideology: "the Third Way". In particular, after Blair and Schroeder's declaration of the British Third Way and the German New Middle in June 1996, "the Third Way" gained great reputation and became the new mainstream of social democracy in Europe and had become an international phenomenon.

After a few years of adjustments, social democratic parties had once again risen in Europe. Since the mid-1990s, (social) democratic socialist parties have gradually transcended their crisis and silence after the dramatic changes of the Soviet Union and Eastern European countries. Left wing or middle-left wing governments once again appeared in West Europe and Middle and Eastern Europe. Europe then had appeared pink and rosy. In 1997, British Labour Party, under the leadership of Blair had won and ruled for 18 years, and Blair became the youngest Prime Minister in the history of Labour Party governments. He changed the image of Labour Party of being in a state of inertia and his political achievements were acknowledged by the British people. He was re-elected for the second term in the general election in 2001. In May 2005, Labour Party won the election again, and Blair continued his office as the Prime Minister, he was the first Prime Minister in office for three terms in the history of Labour Party. On September 27, 1998, in the 14th election of federal parliament in Germany, Social Democratic Party and Green Party (Bund 90/The Green) formed the red-green coalition, and won the election receiving 47.5% of the votes (Social Democratic Party had won 41% of the votes). On October 20, the Red-Green Alliance signed the agreement of terms for the new government short term program. In 2002, Social Democratic Party and Green Party allied and won victory again and ran the government till 2006 defeat. Social Democratic Party of Sweden was established in 1889, and had entered the cabinet for the first time in 1917, had formed the one-party government for the first time in March 1920. She took the office again in 1932 and had been the governing party for more than 70 years. She is the party with the longest history of running the governments in Sweden, and the Social Democratic Party with the longest history of governing in the world. She had established the Sweden Model (democratic socialism) that is admired by the whole world.

There are over 40 (social) democratic socialist parties in Latin America and over 20 in Africa. A decade ago, there were very only few numbers of social democratic parties in Asia but now they have grown remarkably. The influence of social democratic parties is displayed in their organizational strength and ideological theories. Aiming to win the government post or offering a constructive opposition is also the basic method for them to demonstrate their strength.

3.3.3.2 Trotskyite socialism

Trotskyite socialism has gained notable development, either organizationally or theoretically, since the dramatic changes in the Soviet Union and Eastern European countries. The Fourth International of Trotskyite socialism has experienced zigzagging and painstaking development since its foundation. After the dramatic changes, Trotskyite socialism has entered a new phase and has expanded its organizations. The extreme left wing tendency in her socialist theories has been reduced and their policies have become more practical, and many of its analyses and ideas are more in line with the current realities and provide guidance for socialist movement in developed countries in the West.

Trotskyite organizations have displayed a growth after the dramatic changes. Organizations of the Fourth International cover about 50 countries and regions in the world with about 50,000 members. There are also usually different Trotskyite factions with varying names in every country. For example, in France there are Revolutionary Communist Front, International Communist Front, Lutte Ouvrière, League of Marxist Revolution; and in UK there are Socialist Workers Party, Workers Revolutionary Party, International Marxist Group; in the U.S there are Socialist Workers Party, Spartacus League; and there are International Marxist Group, International Communist Group in Germany, and S. A. V. Group also in Germany, Communist Revolutionary Group and Red Flag Group in Italy, Labour Revolutionary League and Revolutionary Workers Party in Belgium, Revolutionary Workers

League and Laborers Socialist Group in Canada, Revolutionary Communist League in Japan, and Equal Social Party in Sri Lanka. There are over 40 Trotskyite organizations in more than 10 Latin American countries, as well as organizations in Australia and New Zealand.

Since the 1990s, Trotskyite organizations have become more active and Trotskyite socialist theories have been innovated and developed. As a world-wide renowned socialist theorist, a revolutionary and a Marxist economist, Ernest Mandel has made significant contributions. He has published several important articles including *Power and Money: A Marxist Theory of Bureaucracy, From Capitalism to Socialism*, and *Marxism and the Fourth International*, which all have exerted a huge influence. In his works, he has criticized the bureaucratic class of the bureaucratized workers' states, analyzed the deficiencies of capitalism, and had debated on Marxist theories, also discussed the strategies of socialist movement and the future of socialism. After the dramatic changes, Mandel gave a new explanation for the nature of the former Soviet society. He had noted that, different from capitalism and feudalism, the Soviet society was a transitional society. He had asserted that such a transitional society had demonstrated intrinsic instability, and it might return to capitalism or march forward into genuine socialism. In line with the transitional character of the Soviet society, the workers' bureaucracy had double facets and was contradictory, which were clearly demonstrated in the relation between administrative power and monetary wealth. "The non-capitalist nature of bureaucratic class is represented by a fact, which is the rule of the bureaucratic class was not established through the possession of monetary wealth, but established a monopoly over political power. On the other hand, non-socialist nature of the bureaucratic class was expressed in that it could not get rid of the influence of money and monetary wealth."[1] The bureaucratic class was a new social class that had seized the administrative functions and working class was hindered to form self-government organs. The process of bureaucratization had a prerequisite, that is, the working class had lost the control of its organizations and of the

---

[1] Ernest Mandel, *Money and Power: A Marxist Theory of Bureaucracy*, p8, Beijing: Central Compilation and Translation Press, 2002.

workers' state. Mandel had asserted that, "To be exact and from a long-term perspective, the bureaucratic class promotes the comeback of capitalism."[1] He had further suggested, "The failure of Gorbachev's reform of the Soviet bureaucratic political power proves that the self-reform intention of the bureaucratic class is unlikely to succeed." "Gorbachev was not overthrown by the opposing masses, or by external imperialist attack or a domestic capitalist force. He was just overthrown by a political wing led by Yeltsin, socially based in the bureaucratic class."[2] By Mandel's studies, it becomes easier to understand the restoration of capitalism in the Soviet Union.

Mandel has revealed the new contradictions and their reflection forms occurred in late period of capitalism. He noted, "The huge imbalance causing stock market collapses and the third universal world recession occurred in the 1970s, has implied new basic contradictions of 'late capitalism' as part a of the 'long wave of recession of capitalism'. These contradictions have appeared in the growth period of the last phase."[3] According to Mandel, the huge debt of the developing countries is linked to the survival of capitalist system in a structural pattern. Extreme accumulation of these debts transcends the demands of the "normal" capitalist accumulation. As a result, in the future the normalization of production accumulation will be very difficult or impossible. Since the 1970s, the new contradictions express themselves as follows: the global attack of capital on laboring classes, broad masses of the Third World face more suffering and poverty, the gap between the rich and the poor in the world widens, the global spread of new epidemics, the destructiveness of free and liberal market economy increases, etc.[4] He has concluded that the sins of capitalism are increasingly exposed and the boarding line for capitalism is approaching—where capitalism will lose its adaptation capabilities.

Mandel proposes new strategies for the key tasks of contemporary

---

[1] Ernest Mandel, *Marxism and the Fourth International*, p211, Hong Kong: October Books, 1996.

[2] Ernest Mandel, *From Capitalism to Socialism*, p151, p155, Hong Kong: October Books, 1997.

[3] *Ibid*, p14.

[4] Ernest Mandel, "Socialism or Neo-Liberalism", *Research of Theories from Overseas*, 2002 (12).

socialists and socialist movement. To solve the worldwide belief crisis on the future of socialism, socialists should shoulder three key tasks: to unconditionally and firmly safeguard the demands of all the peoples of the world, addressing their genuine needs; to conduct basic socialist education and publicity; to align socialism ideal with freedom ideal.[1] Mandel did no way to give up Trotskyite idea of "permanent revolution", but has raised more practical revolutionary strategies. According to him, neither the two classes of capitalist society, bourgeois and proletarian, can achieve a final victory. So, in the current age, the struggle of the working class should be defensive. "On the immediate agenda, it is not the task that the working class strives to seize political power through a revolution; instead both the West and the Eastern working class should resist unemployment with radical means and struggles, and the people of the South should fight unemployment vigorously."[2]

Mandel has also expressed his thoughts on future socialist society. He believed that in the socialist society of the future, the fundamental deficiencies of the capitalist society will be eliminated and class type society in any form will be buried; the goal of socialists is to build a society with no exploitation, oppression, power or injustice, and with no human group being discriminated; future socialism should be a society not motivated by the desire of competition, rivalry or individual wealth, but motivated by social behaviors: cooperation and solidarity. To abolish private ownership of the main means of productions and also the means of exchange and to adopt a planned economy is the necessary prerequisite, though not sufficient to achieve these goals.[3]

3.3.3.3 Ecological socialism

Ecological socialism is a unique trend of thought which dates back to 1980s in the green movement of develo ped countries in the West. From the perspective of the reality that the environment in which human beings

---

[1] Ernest Mandel, "Socialism or Neo-Liberalism", *Research of Theories from Overseas*, 2002 (12).

[2] Ernest Mandel, *Marxism and the Fourth International*, p236, Hong Kong: October Books, 1996.

[3] Ernest Mandel, *The Status and Future of Socialism*; Gorbachev, Brant, *The Future Socialism*, pp 132-171, Beijing: Central Compilation and Translation Press, 1994.

live is facing serious crises, ecological socialism has re- examined the issue of capitalism and socialism relations, the root of the ecological crisis and the ways to eliminate it. It offers a unique set ideas as component parts of a socialist theory.[1] Since the 1990s, ecological socialism has formed a set of systematic ideas in a perspective enriching criticisms on capitalism, thoughts on driving social forces for transformation of the society and the route of this transformation, and new ideas for a better future society. Thus it has become a new school of thought in the socialist movement of the world. Some scholars predict that it will become the most vigorous socialist thinking in the 21st century.

Theoretically, ecological socialism has gained a new development since the 1990s and its theoretical system has become more mature, which is expressed in the following aspects. Firstly, its criticism on capitalism has deepened and become more complex. Generally, the ecological socialists have attributed the global ecological crisis to technology and industrialization, which indeed exaggerates the negative effects of technological development and attack the industrial system as the direct target for criticism. Since the 1990s, ecological socialists have pointed out accurately that the intrinsic contradiction of the means and methods, and/or values of capitalism are the fundamental reason for the ecological crisis. Secondly, their political theories were further developed. The important sign of theoretical maturity of ecological socialism is that a more completed and systematic set of political theories have been formed. Examining the leading and main active social forces in transformation, ecological socialists suggest that the role of workers' movement and trade unions should be paid more attention. In terms of the route of social transformation, they advocate not only the non-violence principle but also the role of class struggle. Thirdly, their economic theories have become more realistic. Since the 1990s, ecological socialists have started to question the "steady-state economic model" theories and re-approached to the idea that future socialist economies

---

[1] Wang Zhenya, "A Multi-Dimensional Analysis on the Values of Ecological Socialism", *Journal of Marxism Research*, 2003 (1).

should also attach importance to growth, but the growth should be proper and sustainable and aim at satisfying the limited material needs of the people, rejecting the profit orientation in economic activities. In addition, the growth in a socialist economy should be rational, at the same time compatible and harmonious with the ecological environment. They have started to oppose E. F. Schumacher's ideas and his motto suggesting "small is beautiful"; and have concluded that in face of economic globalization, issues such as mass unemployment, severe resource scarcity and population explosion exceed national boundaries and should be handled globally. Fourthly, in terms of value orientation, the ecological socialists have returned to human-centered positions. Before the 1990s, ecological socialism had basically advocated ecology-centered values with a coloring of post-modernism borrowed from the mainstream green parties. Their theoretical exploration on values had initially started from natural ecological system and emphasized the intrinsic value of nature and its ecological significance. The start point of its theoretical thinking has shifted from the pure natural ecological system to social ecological system, thus, social issues in the reality were more addressed.[1] Barry Pepper, a UK theorist of ecological socialism, asserts that ecological socialism is based on human centralism (not in the sense of capitalist technology centralism) and humanism. He also thinks that human beings should not give up the "human scale" while opposing ecological crisis and re-examine human attitudes toward nature.[2] Since the 1990s, ecological socialism has become more mature theoretically. It changed its practices of accepting the political guideline and social ideal of green political movement in its early period of development and as a result has overcome many theoretical shortcomings of its theories in the early period, such as the tendency of ecological centralism on the relation between man and nature,

---

[1]　Wang Zhenya, "A Multi-Dimensional Analysis on the Values of Ecological Socialism", *Journal of Marxism Research*, 2003 (1).

[2]　The above elaboration on the theoretical development of ecological socialism largely refers to *"Socialism" in the Age of Globalization*, with Yu Keping as the chief compiler, pp 229-245, Beijing: Central Compilation and Translation Press, 1998.

and unpractical socio-economic thoughts of E. F. Schumacher in socio-economic territory, steady-state model of economy and decentralization. This maturation is one of the important reasons that ecological socialism has increased its influence.

In terms of political practices, movement of ecological socialism has faced a political division since the 1990s. On the one hand, the end of Cold War provides has given greater opportunity and political space for green ecological movement, which has formed more extensive social foundation and shown stronger prospects of development. On the other hand, after the dramatic changes of the Soviet Union, Marxists, socialists and left-wing activists faced a painstaking task of re-examining the fate of socialism, so their eyes had turned to the mainstream of new social movements—green ecological movement. Therefore, the criticism offered by green ecological movement had shifted its focus more to political and cultural levels. There are other divisions or combinations inside the ecologist socialist movement, which shows complicated pattern. Since the 1990s, the ecological movement has turned away from the mingling of reds and greens. Before that development "red parties" (the Communist Party, Social Democratic Party, left-wings) had experienced a trend of borrowing "green" theories. But today the two different blocs as "red-green parties" and "green parties" has been formed. Red and green (Red-Greens) parties refer to parties which are theoretically based on socialism and also carry out ideas of ecological socialism. Their members include Marxists and (social) democratic socialists. On the other side Green parties refer to parties which are theoretically based on anarchism and carry out ideas of ecological centralism, including ecological fundamentalists, deep-ecology green parties, ecological anarchists and mainstream green parties.[1] Theorists of ecological socialism try to reform ecological movement with Marxism, to transcend global ecological crisis and to lead it to the direction of socialism. Some communist parties and social parties—left wing social democrats and right wing Christian democrat

---

[1] Xu Juezai, *The History of the Schools of Socialism*, p 485, Shanghai: Shanghai People's Press, 1999.

parties—in Europe adopt policies of allying with green movement and parties. After some communist parties were dissolved, many members had joined green organizations, and red had turned green. As a result, ecological socialists felt the need to reform ecological movement by applying Marxism and socialism.

Ecological socialism ponders over the impact, the roots and the solutions of ecological crisis that mankind faces. It advocates combining ecological movement with workers movement and socialist movement, demolishing capitalist system and hence the institutional roots of ecological crisis through social reform. It evokes a remarkable social influence and draws massive attention. But the mainstay of ecological socialism's intention to criticize and reform scientific socialism with the contents of anarchy is close to petty bourgeois socialism in 19th century European history and also close to contemporary (social) democratic socialism. Taken as a whole, ecological socialism is one of the non-Marxist socialist schools, which has indeed not provided a workable solution for relieving the global ecological crisis.[1]

3.3.3.4 Market socialism

Market socialism is a theory probing into combining public ownership of means of production with market economy system in order to realize socialism. Market socialism is dated back to the 1930s and was systematically set forth for the first time by Polish economist Oskar R. Lange during his American interlude between 1933 and 1945. Ever since, market socialism has raised its influence and there have been more profound researches. In the late 1980s and early 1990s, left-wing scholars in the West started a surge of research on theories of market socialism in the process of studying and exploring the failures of the Soviet Union and Eastern European socialist countries. Many models of market socialism have been reestablished or developed, and theories of market socialism have been improved. Amongst these models, the most influential are: pragmatic market socialism of James A. Yunker, co-operative model market socialism of David Leslie Miller,

---

[1] Han Zhaozhu, "Analysis on Ecological Socialism", *Academic Research*, 2004 (8).

bank-centered market socialism of John E. Roemer and economic democracy centered market socialism of David Schweickart. Advocates of these models have all reflected on the collapse of the socialist system in the Soviet Union and Eastern European countries, and also revealed the defects of capitalist system. They raise that experiences and lessons of economic development in today's world need to be summarized comprehensively and dialectically, and the blueprint of the future socialism shall be re-established in line with the principle of combining efficiency and justice.

After the collapse of the Soviet Union, market socialists reflected on the practices in real socialist countries and the lessons received from those practices and further enriched the ideas on the deficiencies of capitalist market economy. James Yunker has developed and improved his theories in line with pragmatic market socialism. He has suggested that it is yet too early to predict the demise and failure of socialism, though Soviet communism had failed. Among the reasons contributing to the fall and collapse of the Soviet communism, socialism may have not played its role to cure the defects of the Soviet communism using the advantages brought by public ownership of means of production in full.[1] Does socialism fail? Yunker's answer is explicit: socialism has not failed. In the 20th century, socialist ideology was one important factor that caused a series of violence and civil wars. But it was not socialism that contributed to the failure of the Soviet communism, but the non-democratic and centralized political system and the overly ambitious centrally planned economic system.[2] Therefore, the view that socialism has failed is too assertive and unreasonably simplified. The possibility of a democratic market socialism, which is not constrained by the hindrance and incompetency of communist-style socialism, has not been experimented yet. James Yunker also notes that the central problem faced by modern capitalism is that there exists a serious unequal distribution of income caused by capital

---

[1] James A. Yunker, *On the Political Economy of Market Socialism: Essays and Analyses*, Aldershot, Hampshire, England; Burlington; VT, USA: Ashgate Publishing Ltd, 2001, p 197.

[2] James A. Yunker, *Economic Justice: The Market Socialist Vision*, Lanham, Maryland: Rowman & Littlefield Publishers, 1997, pp 1-2.

benefits that are not generated by work. What capitalists gain as profits far exceeds their contribution in the economic process, and at the same time the majority of working class and middle class do not gain the benefits of their contribution.[1] Market socialism can take into account both economic justice and economic efficiency, which defends for the reasonableness of market socialism. David Schweickart asserts that, capitalism cannot defend itself neither by relying on the concept of "contribution", because investing capital or time is not a productive activity; nor can capitalism protect itself by relying on the concept of worker's "sacrifice", because many who are the winners do not sacrifice; capitalism cannot attribute to the concept of "risk", because the investment game of capitalism does not follow any rules. A kind of defense indeed derives from Nozick's Entitlement Theory, but this ethical theory is based on many unproven suppositions as grounds of its argument, so its conclusion lacks power.[2] Schweickart concludes that capitalism is not a reasonable social system and he proposes a model of economic and democratic market socialism and suggests that this model is far superior than capitalism.

After the dramatic changes in the Soviet Union and Eastern European countries, the new conception of the blueprint of market socialism becomes the theoretical pillar of establishing an ideal future socialism by many left-wing scholars in the West. Before the dramatic changes, market socialism theories explored the rational allocation of resources by market forces under the condition of public (or social) ownership. But after the dramatic changes, in face of the failure of realistic socialism practices, the renewed market socialism theories tried to argue the organic combination of market with public (social) ownership in terms of efficiency and equality, and in turn defended socialism. John E. Roemer notes that market socialism is beneficial to equality, and not only promotes social welfare, but also reduces public peril. James Yunker proposes pragmatic market socialist theory aiming at reforming modern capitalism and curing the evils of capitalism, achieving at

---

[1] James A. Yunker, *Economic Justice: The Market Socialist Vision*, Lanham, Maryland: Rowman & Littlefield Publishers, 1997, p 55.

[2] David Schweickart, *Against Capitalism*, pp 6-54, Beijing: China Renmin University Press, 2002.

the same time both economic justice and efficiency. Schweickart designs the blueprint of economic and democratic market socialism and compares it with capitalism, and he severely criticizes unrestrained freedom and the capitalism of today's neo-liberalism. He sufficiently testifies the superiority of economic and democratic market socialism. Many market socialists generally claim that in the global crisis of belief on future socialism, only market socialism has the genuine vitality and that it is the third choice for the people who combines the freedom and efficiency of the free economy with socialist humanity and equality.

Market socialists have strong confidence in the future of market socialism. John Roemer, claims that modern capitalism provides many possibilities for designing the next upsurge of socialist experiments.[1] Schweickart has worked carefully on the transitional schemes and plans leading to future—economic and democratic market socialism—society in developed capitalist countries, mandatory type socialist countries and in the less developed countries under neo-colonial rule. He believes that in certain ways these three types of countries can transit to economic democratic market socialism, which means that economic democratic market socialism is feasible.[2] From the perspective of sociology and political science, David Miller has established the model of co-operative market socialism in terms of economic, political and social relations. His model of co-operative market socialism has won extensive applause and exerted much influence on the economic creed of the British Labor Party.

Market socialism theorists have raised and reasoned in details various models of market socialism, differing from the Soviet Union and Eastern European socialist model and modern capitalist economic model, with the aim to establish a more efficient, impartial and democratic socio-economic system, as compared with modern capitalist society. The models of modern market socialism vary, yet with many features in common. In terms of ownership, the majority approve the public ownership of means of

---

[1]   John E. Roemer, *A Future for Socialism*, p114, Chongqing: Chongqing Press, 1997.

[2]   David Schweickart, *Against Capitalism*, pp 289-321.

production but allow the existence of minor private ownership; in terms of economic operational mechanism, all the models put the emphasis on the role of market; in terms of macro-adjustment, these models advocate that the state should intervene the economy with limitation; in terms of the pursuit of values, they stress efficiency, equality, democracy and freedom at the same time. While the world socialist movement is at the low tide, the in-depth research of market socialism theories by scholars in the West, and the rise and dissemination of the thought of market socialism in developed nations in the West have strengthened the confidence in socialism to a certain extent.

3.3.3.5 Western Marxist socialism

Western Marxist socialism is one of the important schools of Marxism in the modern times since 1920s. After the dramatic changes in the Soviet Union and Eastern European countries, the themes of Western Marxism researches have shifted from philosophical and cultural issues to political, economic and ecological ones, and the focus shifted from criticism on developed capitalist countries to reflections on "realistic socialism". Moreover, Marxists in the former Soviet Union and Eastern European countries and neo-Marxists show a tendency of joining the ranks of the Western Marxists. In such a context, Western Marxists reflect on and re-explore socialism once again.

First, reflections on the dramatic changes in the Soviet Union and Eastern European countries. Many Western Marxists stick to their position of insisting on Marxism after the dramatic changes, reflect on the roots and influence of the dramatic changes and raise a variety of new theories and views, which are inspiring and worth careful research. Jürgen Habermas is a renowned German philosopher and acclaimed representative of "Critical Theory" trend and Western Marxism. After the dramatic changes, as one of the main thinkers of the Frankfurt School and an outstanding representative of Western Marxism, Habermas faced up great pressure and continued his research and preaching of Marxism. How should the dramatic changes be viewed? Habermas' perspective was that the dramatic changes were a "rectifying revolution". On the one hand, he opposes the current model of capitalist development; on the other hand, he also opposes "state socialism" of the Soviet model. According to him, the dramatic changes were a revolutionary transition to a more rational society. It is not advisable for the peoples of the former Soviet Union and Eastern Europe to follow and adapt the current model of capitalist development, nor is it workable to resume the state socialism model of Stalin. He also believes that Marxism remains realistic and socialism has a broad prospect. However, with the progress of history, Marxism needs to grow and develop as well.[1] So Habermas thinks that the dramatic changes fit with the logics of historical civilization. István Mészáros enjoys high reputation in the academic circles of Western Marxism and is regarded as the important representative of Hegelianism and Marxism in the modern times. In the special context of the dramatic changes, Mészáros sticks to the viewpoints of Marxism in analyzing the reasons of the dramatic changes. In the same manner he has examined the contradictions of the capitalist world, and explored to raise an alternative solution for future socialism. He has asserted that the dissolution of the Soviet Union was a result of capital's universal power. Based on the analysis of the reason of the disastrous failure of the Soviet style system, as well as various experiments of reforming the system, he has asserted that, "Though under a totally different political form, the continued power of capital in the former Soviet system has been the reason for this failure."[2] He notes that the post-revolution development was consolidated under Stalin's period and a construction line—not conflicting—to the existing social and economic structure had been conducted. As a result, the development was maintained within the restrains and frame of capitalist system. Under the highly hierarchical division of labor, surplus labor was politically squeezed at the highest possible ratio, and the working people continued to be exploited and suppressed. The structural crisis thus caused had resulted in the dissolution of

---

[1] Jürgen Habermas, *Dramatic Changes of East Europe and Communist Manifesto*; Yu Keping, *Marxism in the Age of Globalization*, pp 36-43, Beijing: Central Compilation and Translation Press, 1998.

[2] István Mészáros, *Beyond Capital: Toward a Theory of Transition*, Vol. 1, pp14-15, Beijing: China Renmin University Press, 2003.

the Soviet Union.[1] Fredric Jameson, the most important contemporary critic and theorist of Marxism, is reputed in the Western world for his strong sense of historical responsibility toward Marxism. After the dramatic changes, he still holds a strong belief and cherishes a strong responsibility for Marxism. According to Jameson, the dissolution of the Soviet Union was a victory of communism, which is utterly different from any other view on the dissolution of the Soviet Union. He notes that the dissolution was not due to the Stalin style political system. The system enabled the Soviet Union to embark on the road of modernization and thus completed its historical mission. It was then natural for the system to collapse.[2] To a certain extent, reflections on the roots of the dramatic changes by the Western Marxists have insisted on applying the basic views of Marxism and have revealed the deep reasons of the dramatic changes. These reflections have a common feature, that is, they don't regard the dramatic changes as a failure of Marxism. Some even regard the changes as being positive to the healthy development of Marxism and remain confident in Marxism and socialism. Some of their views may not be agreeable but they indeed provide certain clues for studying the reasons of the dramatic changes in the Soviet Union and Eastern Europe.

Second, reflections on the realistic significance of Marxism. Is Marxism out of date and without any value of existence after the dramatic changes? This is an important proposition that needs to be pondered over, answered and solved by the Western Marxists. They attempt to prove that it is not reasonable to equalize the failure of socialism in the Soviet Union and Eastern Europe with the "bankruptcy" of Marxism. What went into bankruptcy was only a deformed model of socialism (Soviet Union model), instead of being an ideal socialism for mankind, or far less being of Marxism, the theoretical basis of this ideal. Habermas focuses his analysis on the conventional ideas of socialism, namely, the conventional socialism of Marxism and democratic

---

[1] István Mészáros, *Beyond Capital: Toward a Theory of Transition,* Vol. 1, p15, Beijing: China Renmin University Press, 2003.

[2] Fredric Jameson, *Actually Existing Marxism*; Yu Keping, *Marxism in the Age of Globalization,* pp 69-85, Beijing: Central Compilation and Translation Press, 1998.

socialist ideas of social democratic parties in West Europe. On the basis of his analysis, he explains the realistic significance of Marxism. According to him, all the criticism on the early capitalism and on socialism schools raised by Marx and his direct inherits were deeply rooted in the production conditions and the narrow territories of the early industrialization and were inevitably imbedded with many shortcomings and deficiencies, which also appeared to varying degree in the theories of Marx, Engels and Kautsky. After Stalin's interpretation, this type of Marxism was transformed into a totally inhumane ideology.[1] The conventional socialism, that is, the Soviet model of socialism, has become outdated. But an outmoded idea, model of socialism, can not sufficiently prove that Marxism is out of date. After his analysis on dramatic changes, Jameson explains what Marxism and socialism are, the relationship between Marxism and the concept of "revolution", what communism is and the significance of capitalism in its late period. He sufficiently argues for the realistic significance and the eternal vitality of Marxism.[2] Jameson believes that Marxism is a science of capitalism, or more exactly, a science of the inner contradictions of capitalism. But capitalism is more than just a production system or a way of production, but a way of production with the high elasticity and adaptability. Capitalism relies on two basic strategies to achieve the above-mentioned goals: the expansion of the system, and new type of commodity production. Capitalism has strengthened its adaptability capacities by relying on these two strategies to a certain extent, but both of the two strategies cannot eliminate the capitalist crisis. Modern capitalism remains in crisis. According to Jameson, to prove that capitalism remains in crisis is equal to proving Marxism is not out of date. David Mc Lellan is another renowned researcher of Marxism. He notes that the series of revolutions in 1989 and the following years were no more than a regression to history after the roundabout route followed by Bolshevists. The revolution

---

[1] Jürgen Habermas, "What Does Socialism Mean Today? The Rectifying Revolution and the Need for New Thinking on the Left", *New Left Review*, Number 183, Sept/Oct 1990: 3-21.

[2] Fredric Jameson, *Actually Existing Marxism*; Yu Keping, *Marxism in the Age of Globalization*, pp 69-85, Beijing: Central Compilation and Translation Press, 1998.

have resumed to the orbit of history as suggested by Marx.[1] He makes it clear that Marxist historical materialism, the Marxist ways of probing into the society and the origins of political concepts have a great advantage. The development of Marxism remains with bright prospects.[2] Western Marxists believe in Marxism and have continued to defend Marxism still firmly after the dramatic changes and when the world socialist movement is at a low tide and Marxism faces severe challenges.

Third, Western Marxism trend offers a new understanding of socialism. After the dramatic changes, the world socialism is at a low tide. If socialism fails, what will be the historical fate of socialism? Many Western Marxists have studied these issues, and re-established their concepts on socialism on the basis of their strong belief in socialism. Habermas uses his theory of "communicative action" to re-establish socialist ideas. Habermas notes socialism should be a kind of independent public sphere as a result of communicative actions. Modern society satisfies its need of completing the function of controlling through three resources of money, power and solidarity. However, "a radical reformism no longer features with the key needs that it can possibly maintain, but due to its purpose being focused on the social process, it requires to re-distribute powers." This expectation is "socialist"[3]. The new concept of socialism raised by Habermas equals socialism with a non-restrictive ideal community based on communicative actions. According to this concept, socialism is not only a goal, but also a realistic movement that leads to the goal. I.Mészáros thinks that dealing with the structural crisis of capital must be beyond capital. The genuine target of socialist revolution is beyond capital. To be beyond capital, capital must be demolished from the process of social production.[4] I. Mészáros has been positive to Marx's ideas and socialist theories. After the dramatic changes,

---

[1] David McLellan, *Marxism after Marx*, 3rd Edition, p375, Beijing: China Renmin University Press, 2004.

[2] David McLellan, *Marxism after Marx*, 3rd Edition, pp377-380, Beijing: China Renmin University Press, 2004.

[3] Jürgen Habermas, "What Does Socialism Mean Today? The Rectifying Revolution and the Need for New Thinking on the Left", *New Left Review*, Number 183, Sept/Oct 1990: 3-21.

[4] István Mészáros, *Beyond Capital: Toward a Theory of Transition,* Vol. 2, p955, Beijing: China Renmin University Press, 2003.

he proposes that the goal of socialist transformation is beyond capital, which is highly valued. Through studies on the nature and the future of socialism, Jameson explains that Marxism, the theoretical base of socialism, remains vital. He stresses socialism has surely always meant to provide a cradle-to-grave protection for human beings: the ultimate safety net, which provides the beginning of an existential freedom for everyone by providing a secure a free human time over and above practical or material necessities thus opens the process where a true individuality begins to shape, by making it possible for people to live without the crippling anxieties of self-preservation. In this sense, socialism means guaranteed material life, free education, free health care and retirement subsidy, freedom of association, thorough and complete rights of grassroots democracy, rights of working, rights of enjoying non-colonized culture and recreation. Jameson asserts that "socialism is to get rid of unnecessary and avoidable economic and material restrains; it is a free collective practice."[1] In such a way, Jameson not only explains what socialism is from the prospective of Marxist Theory and enhances the understanding of socialism, but also points out the prospects of the practical socialist development. Western Marxists have conducted careful reflections on dramatic changes in the Soviet Union and Eastern Europe, analyzed the realistic significance of Marxism, and re-explored and enriched socialism.

---

[1] Fredric Jameson, *Actually Existing Marxism*; Yu Keping, *Marxism in the Age of Globalization*, pp 69-85, Beijing: Central Compilation and Translation Press, 1998.

Chapter 4

A Review of Socialist Movements and Thoughts in the Age of Globalization

After the dramatic changes in the Soviet Union and Eastern Europe, the relative strengths of socialism and capitalism has greatly changed, world socialist movement has descended to a low tide, and developed capitalist countries have enjoyed relative stability and prosperity. However, the new changes of capitalism still create preconditions for the realization of socialism, and socialist movement is an important driving force for the transformation and progress of capitalism. For a long time to come, socialism and capitalism will co-exist with both conflict and collaboration. In the process of globalization, the conflicts between the two systems will occur, but the ways of conflicts as well as the means of solving the conflicts will change. The confrontational relation between the two systems has shifted to a cooperative relation, which could be developed for a rather long time.

4.1 The New Changes of Capitalism Create Conditions for the Realization of Socialism

In the process of globalization, new socialist elements within capitalism increase and accumulate, and tendency toward socialism will create necessary conditions for a new society. The new developments in contemporary capitalism enable the human society to move toward socialism, and create conditions for realizing socialism.

4.1.1 Rapid progress of productive forces in capitalist countries

In the 1940s, the third technological revolution marked by the utilization of nuclear energy and the invention of electronic computer appeared. After the 1970s, micro-electronic technology has gained rapid development and been extensively used in production. As a result, technological revolution witnessed another surge. This technological revolution was a result of revolutionary development of natural sciences in the first half of the 20th century; information technology is more and more applied to production process; the use of advanced machinery and artificial brains has pushed production to a new height. The innovation and development of science and technology is not self-isolated, but it exerts enormous impact on social spheres. It greatly enhances economic growth, upgrades industrial structure and promotes the development of social productive forces, and at the same time brings about profound changes to developed capitalist countries.

The contemporary revolution of science and technology displays some key features: the integrated development of both science and technology, the spontaneous development of leading technologies, as well as the interactive development of science, technology with the societal development. Firstly, on the basis of closer infiltration and merger of science with technology, the contemporary technological revolution presents a tendency of integrated development. On the one hand, science relies increasingly on the support of technology, and the speed of scientific research achievements transformed into technologies has increased all the time high. On the other hand, modern high technologies are all based on profound modern theories of science, with high content of science or knowledge. The integrated development of science and technology has caused a close relation between science and technology, and the boundary between them is getting fuzzier.[1] The extensive use of the term "science and technology" as twins reflects this close relation and the tendency of integration. For example, in the domains such as information science and technology, bio-science and technology, new energy science and technology, advanced materials science and technology, space science and technology, and (oceanology) marine science and technology, the distinction between science and technology is hard to distinguish. Secondly, the contemporary revolution of science and technology is featured with the cluster development of leading technologies. Different from the previous technological revolutions with single leading technology, such as steam engine technology, electric power technology, and electronic technology, leading technologies are all interwoven in the current revolution. The high technologies bundle is composed of information technology, bio-technology, advanced materials technology, new energy technology, new manufacturing (processing) technology, laser technology, marine technology, and space technology. There are also internally related structures in them: advanced materials technology, new energy technology and information technology respectively correspond to matter, energy and information, the three pillars of human civilization. Space technology, marine technology and bio-technology represent the three directions human beings develop—the aerospace, marine and the complex earth system; new manufacturing (processing) technology and laser technology are technological tools that can be applied in various technologies and practices. However, the technologies in the cluster leading the science and technological revolution have varying nature and status, and

---

[1] Yin Dengxiang, "Basic Features of the Development of the Contemporary Revolution of Science and Technology", *Research of Party Building*, 2003 (5).

information technology plays a very special role. In the context of growing demand for labor efficiency, speed and quality, and with the appearance of large scale integrated circuits and microcomputers, the development of social production mode from mechanical, electrical and automated technologies to information technology, and increased application and penetration of information technology to all spheres of social production and social life, the society has been remolded profoundly.[1] Thirdly, the interactive development of science, technology and society is another key feature of the revolution in science and technology. The three motifs of science, technology and society form binary relations of science and technology, science and society, and technology and society, and ternary relations of science, technology and society. Each of the three—science, technology and society—enjoys a parent system, and each system contains its own sub-systems. There are various relationships between the sub-systems and the parent systems. The closer and more diversified the relations, the shorter are the cycles of transformation among science, technology and society. In the relations of the three, science is the basis, technology is the core, and society is the direction.[2]

Being driven by the contemporary technological revolution, new high technologies are in the ascendant, such as information, microelectronics, advanced materials, new energies, bio-engineering, aerospace, laser, and marine engineering. The industrial structure undergoes major adjustments. In developed countries, the application of information technology in economic and social life enables the tertiary industry to surge and become the leading economic sector in industrial structure, which includes information, education, research and development, consultancy and other various services. Information technology industry, with computer and web technology as the core, develops rapidly and greatly enhances the optimization of economic structure and the productive forces of developed capitalist economies, and provides material and technological basis for economic globalization.

---

[1] Yin Dengxiang, "Basic Features of the Development of the Contemporary Revolution of Science and Technology", *Research of Party Building*, 2003 (5).

[2] *Ibid.*

Capitalism enters into an age of "new economy", which extensively promotes knowledge-intensive production and services and is largely based on information industry. The United States of America has led this revolution and become the engine of the global economy.

Since the 1990s, the development of science and technology and the progress of economic globalization had greatly promoted economic prosperity of the U.S. economy. The U.S. economy had recovered since March 1991, and then kept a stable growth for a long period until March 2001 before going into recession. This was the longest expansion period in the history of economic cycles. This round of economic growth had displayed features different from the traditional economic cycles, with two highs and two lows, that is, high economic growth rate and high growth rate of productive forces, low unemployment and low inflation rate. Moreover, the 2001's recession in this cycle was not that sharp. Since the early 1990s, in the process of economic globalization, the United States has taken advantage of the opportunity provided by accelerating economic globalization and taken the lead in adjusting her domestic economic structure. As a result, she held a stronger position in the international economic competition. Her most remarkable achievement had been the improvement and surge of high-tech industries, information industry in particular. With her leading position in the high-tech sectors and sound strategies for economic development, the United States has seized an opportunity in the global division of labor in the world industrial complex and was the first developed nation to complete the adjustment of domestic economic structure, and had focused developing her high-tech industries. On the one hand, she imports labor-intensive products with heavy pollution and low added value from developing countries, including light industry products such as food, textiles, watches and other instruments, as well as steel, nonferrous metals, cement, plastics, petro-chemicals, ships and general machineries. These industries with low level of technology are shifted to developing countries. Between the United States and developing countries, a new type of division of labor in industries has been established, which enables the United States to focus her attention on developing high-tech industries. On the other hand, she exchanges knowledge- and technology-intensive products with other developed countries, which increasingly expands the horizontal division of labor among developed countries and further improves the division of labor, which enables her to concentrate on research and development of products with higher technological content. As a result, industries in the United States are promoted to a higher level of technology intensiveness and are advantageously positioned in international competition. In the 1990s, the outstanding feature of industrial adjustment in the United States was the rapid rise of IT industry. Currently, the number of CPU chips in the United States accounts for 90% of the world market, application software 50%. Replacing traditional industries such as steel, automobile and architecture, information industry becomes the largest pillar industry in the United States and adds the most to growth of her economy. During 1995 and 1998, 1/3 of economic growth in the United States came from the booming digital economy. In the average GDP growth rate 4.1% of this period, the information industry contributed 30%. The contribution of computer and telecommunication industries exceeded 24% on average.[1] Meanwhile, new and high technology has also promoted the technological level of traditional industries and increased productivity therein, and improved the management of businesses and the efficiency of management. Moreover, new technologies increase the relative profitability of traditional industries to a great extent. The use of computers in business management has greatly reduced the cost of production and operation. Since the 1990s, economy in developed capitalist countries has been operated in a stable way, technological innovation has boomed and productivity was greatly enhanced.

Then what major influence will this new age, with all-round technological revolution and accelerated development, impose on human social existence? Gao Fang, a Chinese scholar, believes that the new technological revolution led by developed countries indeed presents a golden

---

[1] Liu Shucheng, Zhang Ping, *Probing into the "New Economy"*, p 307, Beijing: Social Sciences Literature Press, 2001.

age for the major development of productive forces of the human society. But this major development of technology and productive forces do not show yet the rise of morning sun or the resurrection of capitalism, but rather the last glow of the setting sun.[1] In essence, modern technological revolution is a revolution of productive forces, management and knowledge, offering as well the most important material conditions for the emancipation of mankind.[2] According to the basic theories of Marxism, two pairs of contradictions, one between productive forces and relations of production and the other between economic base and superstructure, are the basic contradictions of the human society, and the interactive movement of them promote the development of the human society. The means of production of capitalism grew gradually in the womb of the feudal society. After the development phases such as household manufacturing, cottage industry and machine-based industry, with the increasing socialization of the means of production, of the labor process, and of the products, an antagonistic contradiction between the requirement of socialized production and the private ownership of production means appeared which reflects the contradiction between productive forces and relations of production in the capitalist society. The capitalist system cannot overcome this intrinsic contradiction and cannot remove the economic crises of capitalism. Marx and Engels drew the conclusion: "The demise of bourgeoisie and the victory of the proletariat are equally inevitable."[3] At the same time, the high degree of development of productive forces creates a more reliable and more sufficient material condition for discarding private ownership and eliminating class antagonisms and class differences; the high degree of development of productive forces lay a sound and full material foundation for realizing the socialist distribution principle, "from each according to his abilities, to each according to his needs"; furthermore, the high degree of development of science and technology as well as productive

---

[1] Gao Fang, Li Jingzhi, Pu Guoliang, *Theories and Practices of Scientific Socialism*, 4th Edition, p 296.

[2] Liu Dachun, "On the Essence of Modern Technological Revolution", *Journal of Adult Higher Education*, 2005 (5).

[3] *Selected Works of Marx and Engels*, 2nd Edition, Vol. 1, p 284.

forces is prerequisite for improving the capacities of people and the free and all-round development of people; the progress of productive forces and the society enables everyone to receive better education and social training and as a result, the ideological consciousness and new thoughts will flourish greatly. The good will be promoted, the bad discarded, and collectivism, a new humanism and fraternity will prosper while the evil nature of human beings such as ignoring the public interests to benefit one's own interests, or benefiting oneself at the expense of others, jealousy or vindictive mindset will be greatly lessened. The ideological conditions for the future "association of free individuals" will be prepared.[1] Thus, in a certain sense, the development and progress of productive forces in capitalist countries create conditions for socialism.

4.1.2 The growth of socialist elements inside capitalism

There are indeed many socialist elements inside the contemporary capitalism, which prepare for the transition to socialism. Marx had pointed that "the material conditions necessary for the emancipation of the proletariat was generated intuitively from the process of bourgeoisie production."[2] In the process, when adjusting the forms and systems of the production relations in capitalism, various new elements that facilitate the dismantling of the old ways of production have been generated, such as state-owned economy, cooperative economy, shareholders' economy, economic plans and social welfare practices. These new elements emerging in the economic system and contrasting capitalism prepare and inspire for the ultimate victory of socialism.

First, the ownership of capital in capitalist countries is socialized. Contemporary capitalism has adjusted the forms and systems of the relations of production. With private ownership core remaining unchanged, the forms of property ownership are adjusted, and the single and pure private

---

[1] Gao Fang, Li Jingzhi, Pu Guoliang, *Theories and Practices of Scientific Socialism*, 4th Edition, pp 297-298.

[2] *The Complete Works of Marx and Engels*, 1st Chinese Edition, Vol. 34, p 358, Beijing: People's Press, 1972.

ownership economy is transcended. State-owned economy, cooperative economy, shareholders' economy were also constantly developed, the features of mixed economy gradually appear, thus the ownership of capital is increasingly socialized. After the Second World War, state-owned economy was established in many capitalist countries. Lifelines of national economy became state-owned in West European countries, including postal services, telecommunication, electricity, gas, railway, aviation, and coal mining. But, after the 1980s, the proportion of state ownership in these countries began to descend. In 1979, after Margaret Thatcher took office, she vigorously promoted privatization and shareholders' economy. Over 15 years, state-owned companies were reduced to only three, London Buses, Post Office and UK Nuclear Power Generators, and shareholders in the United Kingdom increased from 3 million to 12 million, accounting for 22% of the population.[1] But state-owned economy remains to play decisive function in the lifeline industries of the national economy. In the developed capitalist countries, and shareholding is highly diversified.

Statistics show that about half of families in the United States hold stocks, and the number of shareholders amounts to 65 million, with the majority of belonging to working class. In these countries, stock ownership by employees also appears. Currently in the United States, employees holding stocks reach 47.04 million, accounting for 40% of the work force. There are 10,000 stockholding plans in the United States and about 10% of its work force participates in the plans. In 1995, the number of shareholders in Germany, Japan, France, Britain, the United States and Canada accounted for 5.4%, 9%, 10.1%, 17.5%, 21.1% and 25% of the population of each respective country. Shareholding is only a change of form of private ownership of capitalism, but to a certain extent it adapts to the need of socialization of production and favorable to the progress of productive forces.

In the relations of production of capitalism, new forms of realization and capital organization forms also occur, including public limited companies, multinational corporations, monopolized capital organizations as well

---

[1] Wu Jiang, *On the Communication of Socialism and Capitalism*, pp 59-60, Beijing: Chinese Social Sciences Academy Press, 2003.

as state monopoly capitalism. These are economic elements "passively discarding capitalism" and are the transitional forms of socialism leading to socialism. Shareholding may be a change, only in the form of capitalist private ownership, but to certain extent it adapts to the need of socialization of production and remarkably facilitates the rapid progress of productive forces. Marx and Engels had revealed from several perspectives that the progress of capitalism prepares for the advent of socialism, and shareholders' economy (stock companies) was one of the perspectives. Marx said, "An enormous expansion of the scale of production and of enterprises, that was impossible for individual capitals. At the same time, enterprises that were formerly government enterprises become public...." "Transformation of the actually functioning capitalist into a mere manager, administrator of other people's capital.... In stock companies the function (author's note: managerial function) is divorced from capital ownership, therefore labor is also entirely divorced from ownership of means of production and surplus-labor. This result of the ultimate development of capitalist production is a necessary transitional phase towards the re-conversion of capital into the property of producers, although no longer as the private property of the individual producers, but rather as the property of associated producers, as outright social property."[1] Marx also compared the cooperative factories of the laborers with stock companies. He noted, "The cooperative factories of the laborers themselves represent within the old form the first sprouts of the new, although they naturally reproduce, and must reproduce, everywhere in their actual organisation all the shortcomings of the prevailing (capitalist, underlined by author) system. But the antithesis between capital and labor is overcome within them.... The capitalist stock companies, as much as the cooperative factories, should be considered as transitional forms from the capitalist mode of production to the associated mode, with the only distinction that the antagonism is resolved negatively in the one and positively in the other."[2] Over a hundred years since Marx wrote those above, stock companies have experienced new adjustments, and new forms

---

[1] *Capital*, Vol. 3, p 494, Beijing: People's Press, 1975.

[2] *Capital*, Vol. 3, pp 497-498.

of industrial enterprises have appeared, all containing some "transitional forms" to socialism. As new forms of capital organization, these indeed do not touch the capitalist system itself, but provides social-economic conditions for socialism transforming private capital to social capital. Such adjustments show that the distance between developed capitalist nations and socialism is getting shorter.

Secondly, the new changes of industrial structure, employment structure and class structure shape a high quality workforce. In the second half of the 20th century, there appeared many new changes in terms of class structure and class relations in the West, promoted by the new technological revolution, the changes in industrial structure and employment structure, and improvements in standard of productive forces and living conditions. In developed capitalist countries, the working class refers to all wage earning workers except for managers, executives, professionals and self-employers. It covers blue-collar non-skilled or semi-skilled workers, as well as skilled white-collar workers. Sometimes white-collar office workers are regarded as the lower level of the middle class and are examined in the working class. With the huge changes in industrial structure and employment structure, the conditions of the working class have changed greatly.

Firstly, proportion of industrial workers has decreased and the number of workers in service industry has increased. Take the United Kingdom for example. Between 1971 and 1996, the percentage of employers in manufacturing industry decreased from 30.6% to 18.2%, and that in mining, energy and water supply decreased from 9.5% to 1.1%. Manchester, once the industrial center of the United Kingdom, underwent similar changes. The percentage of sales of the manufacturing industry in the total sales volume decreased from 70% in the early 1960s to 20%. In that period service industry developed rapidly. Between 1971 and 1996, the percentage of employers in the service industry in total workforce increased from 52.6% to 75.8%, and finance, insurance, education, healthcare and other public service organizations witnessed the most rapid growth.[1]

---

[1] Li Peilin, "Changes of Social Structure over Two Decades in the UK", from www.china.org.cn/chinese/ch.wzh/2.doc.

Secondly, the proportion of blue-collar workers has decreased and the number of white-collar workers has increased. Blue-collar workers refer to workers engaged in physical labor, while white-collar workers, non-physical labor. In the production sectors of developed countries, technologies and mechanical equipment are constantly upgrading, the level of automation improving, production monitored by computers spreading, and the technical requirements for workers keep increasing. Meanwhile, with the improvement of education, certain level of education and professional training has become compulsory for employment. Between 1968 and 1997, the percentage of blue-collar workers decreased from 66.5% to 34.5%. With the changes of technical structure in industries, both government departments and academia in the UK increasingly tend to categorize jobs by using terms of skilled, semi-skilled and non-skilled workers. If semi-skilled and non-skilled workers can be classified as blue-collar workers, then statistics in 1996, display that blue-collar workers accounted for about 20% of those total employed, including only 5% non-skilled workers. The semi-skilled and non-skilled female workers exceeded their male counterparts by nearly 5 percentage points.[1]

Thirdly, workers working in low-wage sectors face deteriorating working and living conditions. In the mid-1970s, it was regulated that those who worked for six months or above would be entitled labor protection in case of unemployment. By the mid-1990s, the regulation was reversed and only those who had worked for two years or above could be protected. Between 1975 and 1995, employees who were not entitled to labor protection in cases of unemployment increased from 9% to 30% total workforce. There is no minimum wage standard in the UK. The average wage of low-paid workers in Europe is lower than other developed countries in the world, and the number of low-paid workers is greater. Between 1976 and 1996, the income gap between the bottom 10% and top 10% wage earners in the UK widened from 2.5 to 3.5 times. In order to reduce the number of employees and save on necessary welfare spending, the employers always impose or force the workers to work overtime. Between 1984 and 1996, the number of

---

[1] Li Peilin, "Changes of Social Structure over Two Decades in the UK", from www.china.org.cn/chinese/ch.wzh/2.doc.

full-time workers working for 48 hours or above per week increased from 2.75 million to nearly 4 million, accounting for 1/4 of the total number of full-time workers, and most of them are manual labor workers. Industrial restructuring and rapid technological upgrading has caused higher percentage of unemployed due to deficit of skills. Among the unemployed in 1996 in the UK, those unemployed for one year or more accounted for 38%, unemployed for two or more years 24%, and unemployed for three or more years 16%.[1]

In terms of class relations, developed capitalist countries have adopted measures such as "people's capitalism", "mixed economy" and "welfare state" to ease class conflicts and adjust class interests. Class interests and class awareness tend to become similar. The changes of class structure and class relations in contemporary capitalist countries inevitably challenge the class consciousness and want of revolution in working class, the traditional revolutionary institutions. And in terms of consciousness on class relations, similarly the idea advocating "the inevitable fall of bourgeois and the inevitable victory of proletariat" seems vanishing. With the advancement of new technological revolution, the development of education as well as social progress, technological and cultural standard of the working class further improves. The progress of capitalist democratic politics promotes democratic awareness of the workers and educates new generations of the revolutionary class. After the Second World War, in developed countries, the status of workers was improved, and new regulations enabling the employees' participation in operation management was established. A system of "joint decision" councils was implemented in West European countries, which requires companies must have a number of workers to be on the board of counselors and take part in operation and workforce management. In Germany, the counselors committees of companies with over 1,000 employees must have 1/2 workers as representatives, who discuss and solve some major issues together with employers in the committee. For companies with more than 500 and less than 1,000 employees, the

---

[1] Li Peilin, "Changes of Social Structure over Two Decades in the UK", from www.china.org.cn/chinese/ch.wzh/2.doc.

committee must have 1/3 workers as representatives. At the same time, employees' committees are established in companies to protect the rights and interests of the workers. Companies are restricted to fire their workers at will. When a company needs to fire workers, it must negotiate with the workers' trade union and pay compensation. In France, according to labor laws, employers who refuse to consider the requests or the opinions of the representatives of employees are regarded disputing the law. In Sweden, the employers are obliged to provide workers appropriate information regarding production targets and personnel affairs, and major issues should be consulted with workers' representatives. Since the 1970s, it has been regulated in Sweden that any large company should allocate certain proportion of its profit transferred to workers' investment fund so that the workers can have greater influence on the company through that fund. This so-called "fund socialism" has received recognition and support from many people.[1] In 1980, the US government, Trade Unions and employers signed a tripartite collaboration agreement of "overall understanding". In line with this agreement, some companies started to co-opt workers' representatives into the board of directors, and quite number of companies started practicing people-oriented management, democratic management, or management with the participation of employees. Participation of employees in management is an element that disputes the private ownership of capitalists and the hired labor employment system, besides a positive element that the new society will rely on.[2] Co-opting workers to participate in the management of companies as implemented by many capitalist countries reveals that capitalism has to allow socialist elements to a certain extent under the pressure of working class struggle. The above analyses prove that the adjustments occurring inside capitalism after the Second World War represent accumulation of the historical process, socialism replacing capitalism.

---

[1] Luo Wendong, "On the 'New Social Elements' Inside the Contemporary Capitalism", *Journal of Theoretical Frontier*, 2004 (14).

[2] Tao Chengde, Ye Guanglin, "New Changes of the Contemporary Capitalism and the Growth of Socialist Elements", *Journal of Theoretical Horizon*, 2002 (3).

Fourthly, macro-adjustments and social welfare policies are implemented. After the Second World War, during a quite long period, the operational pattern of the market economy of developed capitalist countries was a combination of state's macro-economic adjustment with market self-operation. Currently, in these countries one can no longer observe an unrestrained anarchic social production. On the basis of the previous experiences, these countries pay attention to the role of economic plans, strengthen state interference, and step up macro-adjustment. The planned adjustment and macro-control of the national economy covers the whole process of social reproduction. And the turbulences, blindness and destructiveness of market economy are eased to a certain extent, and economic growth enhanced. During 1948 and 1992, France executed 10 national economic development plans, including both departmental and national level macro plans. These plans covered the speed of departmental development and quantitative quotas, overall strategies and directions, and the coordination and balance of departmental and regional economies. These planned adjustments enabled the French economy to enjoy an orderly growth. Meanwhile, Japan, Germany, Holland, Britain also carried out economic plans. By resorting to macro-adjustment, capitalist states have reformed their previous roles as "night-watchers" and passive observers of "the invisible hand", the market. Instead of "visible hand", state interference became a supplementary necessity to strengthen the adjustment of national economy. Though the decision-making power still depends on private companies, the adaptation of decisions is dependent on the negotiation between private companies and public departments. Governmental departments and banks play important indirect roles in the decision-making process. The state not only controls the economic lifelines and a great number of state-owned enterprises, but also directly adjusts the economy through economic, administrative, legislative and financial means to maintain the balanced development of national economy. To some extent, the anarchy of production and economic operation without regulations are bygone, and sharp fluctuations of the economy as in the early periods of capitalism have become lessened.[1]

To ease the intrinsic inner contradictions of the capitalist society, Western capitalist countries have made some adjustments and reforms in some aspects of the relations of production, those not antagonizing the fundamental system. They've learned many practices from socialist countries and carried out reforms beneficial for the improvement of living standard of the workers. Some measures are taken, including implementing labor law and minimum wage law, providing public welfare and public health system, levying heritage tax for the wealthy strata, progressive income tax, which are relatively complete and sound. At the same time, in terms of labor management, capitalists now gradually regard the workers as "economic individuals" and "social individuals" departing from the old conception of "living machines" or "talking machines". In management, different from purely relying on enforcement, regulations or disciplines, incentive measures are gradually taken and feelings and non-physical elements are taken into account, and as a result, the general conditions of the working class is improved. In terms of distribution, under the prerequisite of "distributing in line with capital accumulation" featured with surplus exploitation, capitalist countries have stepped up the income adjustments through primary and secondary distribution by means of taxation. Social welfare security system tends to cover more people. Distribution of incomes tends to be fairer. In some countries in West and North Europe, income distribution shows signs of bridging inequalities. In the early 20th century, the US government expenditures only accounted for 5% to 8% of GDP, which grew to 35% by the end of 20th century. Currently, Western states, only through taxation, annually centralize more than 13% of national income; EU countries centralize nearly 50% of national income. 60% of tax revenues are used for social welfare expenditures, such as poverty relief, free medical care, unemployment subsidies, for pensioners and education support. Welfare state system has promoted economic growth and has partly achieved the goal of

[1] Zhao Bin, "New Changes of the Contemporary Capitalism and Their Influence on World Socialism", *Journal of Contemporary World and Socialism*, 2004 (1).

social equality and justice. But it could not offer a remedy that can solve all social miseries of capitalism. The balance of economic growth and social justice cannot always be effectively maintained, and compromises between the employer and employee, between the state regulation and market cannot be attained. The "from cradle-to-grave" social security system in income distribution plays its role in improving the living conditions of the working class, guaranteeing the basic living of people of low income and narrowing the gap between the rich and the poor, and represents a socialist element in terms of fair distribution of income.

The unprecedented and compound developments realized in productive forces, relations of production, economic basis and superstructure elements of contemporary capitalist society generate major propelling effects on the maturation of socialism in the capitalist womb. The great leaps in science and technology in productive forces of capitalist societies, and the "new social elements" such as shareholders' and cooperative economy, social security, participation of employees in management, and improvement of welfare system, all prepare an expanding solid material and technological foundation as well as sufficient social and historical conditions for mankind to embark on the road of socialism and communism.

4.1.3 Class confrontation and disparity between the rich and the poor expand globally.

At present, class confrontation and disparity between the rich and the poor within developed countries in the West are eased to some extent due to macro-economic adjustments and implementation of welfare policies. But this does not mean confrontation or disparity has perished. Class society structure of advanced capitalism expresses itself through increasing tendency of paradoxical dualities: between the diversification of tiered social index and the polarization of social classes—including immigrants—between improvements in social openness and the relative rigidity in social mobility, the popularization of middle-class lifestyle and the expanding disparity between the rich and the poor. Though organized class struggles are decreasing, contradictions between classes do not vanish and capitalist society breeds complex and dangerous contradictions.[1] Studies illustrate that since the 1990s, class confrontation and disparity between the rich and the poor have aggravated. In the 1990s, "new economic miracle" had appeared in the United States remarkably propelling growth and economic competitiveness. But ordinary workers could not benefit from the "new economy". In 1979, the richest 20% earned 3.5 times more than the poorest 20%, and by the end of 1990s, this gap had expanded to 9 times. During 1992 and 1998, the gap had widened 9% and later during 1998 and 2001 the gap was widened by 70%. The top 20% high income earners seized 50% income of the country, and in 2000 the top 5% had earned 22.1% of the country's total income, which further increased to 22.4% in 2001. The problem of homelessness in the United States is nearly as severe as at the end of the Second World War. Over the recent 10 years, information and information service industries in the United Kingdom grew in an overwhelming speed with the fastest growing number of employees. In the past decade the GDP growth of the United Kingdom has remained relatively low and stable, but income gap and disparity between the rich and the poor was widening. According to the statistics of inland revenues in the UK, in 1994 the total value of net assets in the UK was 1.3 trillion pounds, in which net value of real estate assets accounted for 60% and net value of mobile properties for 40%. During 1980 and 1994, the adult population with individual assets had increased from 4.135 million to 4.5 million. Among the total individual wealth including commercial wealth, the 5% richest accounted for 38% of the total wealth, up from 36%; the population with 100,000 pounds of wealth or above rose from 1% to 8%; while 50% of those in the lower segment of wealth owners saw a decrease of their wealth from 9% to 7%. And thus Gini coefficient—a measure of inequality of income distribution or inequality of wealth—rose from 0.65 to 0.66. If career pension insurance assets and state pension assets—which have no trading value—are added in the calculation,

---

[1] Li Jingzhi, *Evolution and Conflicts of the Contemporary Capitalism*, pp 131-132, Beijing: China Renmin University Press, 2001.

the disparity of income will be smaller than the disparity of income with trading value. But evaluating on the whole, the disparity of income over the past decade has widened. During 1980 and 1994, in the distribution of individual wealth (wealth with trading value as well as career pension insurance equity and state pension equity), the share of the top 5% rose from 24% to 25%; while the share of the 50% of those in the lower segment wealth owners decreased from 21% to 17%; Gini coefficient rose from 0.46 to 0.49. The main reason for the widening gap of income distribution was that: a part of those in the middle level of wealth owners had become wealthier, while another part had lost.[1] Since the 1990s, generally the disparity between rich and the poor in developing capitalist countries has also aggravated, along with the deteriorating tendency in the whole world capitalism.

At the same time, class confrontations and disparity between the rich and the poor have expanded globally within the countries. The inequality in acquiring benefits from the process of globalization has widened the gap between the south and the north, illustrating the Matthew effect and denoting the phenomenon that "the rich get richer and the poor get poorer". Facts indicate that with the progress of the economic globalization, the disparity of development between the south and the north is enlarging. While wealth in the north is bulging, the poverty in developing countries of the south is aggravating. Since the 1950s, calculated according to GNP, the material wealth globally produced has increased only six times. But the gap of social wealth between a small number of rich countries, with 20% of the world population, and many poor nations, has expanded from 30: 1 in 1960 to 74: 1 in 1997. At present, 1/5 of the world population with higher income live in the United States, Japan, Germany, France, the United Kingdom and Nordic countries, which control 86% of the world exports and 68% of foreign investment. The average income of the top 20% richest countries in the world is 37 times of that of the top 20% poorest countries. The wealth owned by 200 large companies of Group 7 club countries, the richest countries,

---

[1] Li Peilin, "Changes of Social Structure over Two Decades in the UK", from www.china.org.cn/ chinese/ch.wzh/2.doc.

accounts for 33% of the world production value in 1997, and the wealth owned by 500 large companies of these rich countries' club accounted for 45% of the world production value. In developing countries, 800 million people are unemployed or half unemployed, and this number exceeds the total number of workers in the industrialized countries. According to the report of Food and Agriculture Organization (FAO) of the United Nations on Nov. 25, 2003, the target of halving—by 2015—the number of people facing seems impossible to be achieved. In the 1990s, only 19 countries, including China, had reduced the number of people faced by hunger. There were another 17 countries having reduced the number of people in hunger in the early 1990s, but generally the number of people with malnutrition has grown sharply in the mid and late 1990s. There are about 921 million individuals in the world who suffer from malnutrition, and the figure grows by 5 million each year.[1] The global disparity between the rich and the poor is becoming an important issue attracting general concern by the whole world, and it calls for an urgent solution to guarantee a healthy development of global economy.

4.1.4 Basic contradictions of capitalism deepen.

The conclusion asserted by Marx and Engels that "the fall of bourgeoisie and the victory of the proletariat are equally inevitable" was neither based on any indignation towards capitalism, nor on a blind desire for socialism, but on their scientific analyses on the basic contradictions of capitalism. The inevitable fall of bourgeoisie and the inevitable victory of the proletariat is a natural and historical process independent of the will of people, and caused by existence and movements of the basic contradictions of capitalism. Till recent times, the basic contradictions of capitalism have still existed and deepened with new forms of expression. As globalization proceeds, domestically, the deepening of the contradictions is displayed in the structural imbalances of the economy, and internationally, in the global expansion of those contradictions.

---

[1] Xu Chongwen, *New Changes of the Contemporary Capitalism*, p 641, Chongqing: Chongqing Press, 2004.

Firstly, when we examine the structural imbalance of the economy within capitalist countries. The basic contradictions do not appear as serious social crises, but they have not disappeared and keep producing troubles in the capitalist society and accumulate self-negating elements on the ownership form of the means of production of capitalism. Meanwhile, the variety of problems faced by capitalism is not only an accumulated, either in forms or quantities, of the basic contradictions, but a further development towards structural contradiction or crisis because of the state monopoly capitalism, and a deepening confrontation of basic contradictions. The state macro-adjustment of capitalist economy overcomes market deficiencies, but at the same time brings new contradiction and obstacle for the development of social productive forces through financial deficit, growth of state debts as well as stagnation; science and technology promotes the development of social productive forces, but at the same time the application of science and technology in capitalist society confronts with laborers and brings about structural unemployment; science and technology creates the possibility of continuous expansion of production, but realizing the possibility is increasingly restrained by the consumption capability of the residents; the prospering economic life as driven by profit rate is accompanied not only by the imbalanced socio-economic relations, but also the imbalance between human and nature. Capitalist industrial development and consumerism lifestyle in developed countries result directly in the exploitative development and serious waste of natural resources. Severe ecological problems are caused worldwide. There remain many institutional problems in the contemporary capitalist economy, and the most outstanding ones are the crisis of welfare system and the serious risk imbedded in the world monetary and financial system which is not sound. All these crises and contradictions are attributed to the fact that it becomes increasingly difficult for the relations of production on the basis of private ownership to drive the overwhelming development of science and technology and the expanding social productive forces. As a whole, the biggest dilemma and fundamental contradiction faced by the developed capitalist economies remain to be the contradiction between the highly socialized production and the private ownership of the means of production. It is possible for capitalism to partially improve the relations of production by adjusting the economic system and policies, but it is not possible for it to surpass the narrow boundary of the ownership of capitalist means of production. Capitalism is just creating various physical conditions and social forms unconsciously for the fundamental self-negation.[1]

Secondly, the insurmountable contradiction in the global expansion of capital. To a large degree, economic globalization is a result and representation of the development of the contemporary capitalism. Economic globalization expands the achievements of capitalism to the global scope, and inevitably expands the intrinsic contradictions of capitalism globally, and various contradictions and chronic illnesses of capitalism recur in the global scope. Globalization keeps expanding the ways of production and simultaneously expands its basic contradictions, and as a result, it causes a worldwide crisis of the whole system of capitalism. Globalization causes the basic contradictions of capitalism to expand from within one country to the globe and many other territories. The basic contradiction is the contradiction between the socialized production and the private ownership of the means of production. In the global economy, this basic contradiction is interpreted as many concrete contradictions, such as the contradiction between the planned and adjustable national economy and the global economy without plan and lacking adjustment, the contradiction between strict organization and scientific management and the blind expansion and chaos of the world market, the contradiction between the unlimited expansion potential of the world production capacity and the limited capacity of the world market, contradictions between countries, and contradictions between multinational corporations. Since the 1990s, turmoil and crises in the financial sector happen now and then and bring about huge influence on the global economy and politics. For example, the turmoil and crisis of the European monetary system in 1992, 1993, 1995, financial crisis in Mexico in 1994, the sweeping financial storm that started in Southeast Asia in 1997, and

[1] Li Jingzhi, Lin Su, *Contemporary World Economy and Politics*, pp 100-102.

financial crisis in the autumn of 1998 in Russia and in the spring of 1999 in Brazil. The contradictions in the global economy also result in various structural imbalance, such as the frequent huge trade deficit in the United States, the large scale structural unemployment in Europe, and the long-term economic stagnation in some developing countries. All these seriously restrain and destruct the development of global productive power, and negatively influence the development of some countries and regions, as well as the stable, continuous and healthy development of global economy. At the same time, globalization has resulted in more serious basic contradiction of capitalism and more serious split globally. In the triumphant progress of globalization, the critical voice and the movement of anti-globalization surge; the contradiction between the high degree of organization and plan in multinational corporations and the world market without order intensifies; globalization also intensifies the contradiction between the employers and employees within developed countries in the West, and intensifies social division and confrontation between the rich and the poor; the contention among the capitalist powers, including the United States, European Union, and Japan, has shifted from contending for "territories" to contending for global economy and the power in the global market; with the advancement of capital globalization, the division and confrontation between developed and developing countries also intensify.[1] The intensification of these contradictions result in the dislocations between the aggregate supply and demand of world economy, between sectors and territories of world economy, and in turn incite turmoil and crises, in particular, the clashes between "developed capitalist countries" and "developing capitalist countries", and between "the central area" and the "periphery" of world economy. Obvious that along with the unlimited squeezing of surplus value by capital brought about by the progress of globalization, the contradiction between the private ownership of capitalism and socialized production has been intensified in the global scope, which will gradually sublate capitalism and eventually replace

---

[1] Wang Yonggui, "The Trends of Economic Globalization and the Historical Destiny of Capitalism", *Journal of Contemporary World and Socialism*, 2003 (3).

it with socialism and communism.

However, the intensification of the basic contradiction of capitalism does not mean that capitalism will demise in a short course. As Marx emphasized, "No social order ever disappears before all the productive forces for which there is room have been developed; and new higher relations of production never appear before the material conditions of their existence have matured in the womb of the old society."[1] The internal adjustment of capitalism eases the contradictions to a certain extent, and globalization wins certain space and time for the development of the contemporary capitalism. But the relations of production of capitalism cannot fetter the progress of social productive forces long, and will ultimately be replaced by a new higher social order, communism.

4.2 Socialist Movement Is an Immense Driving Force for the Changes of Capitalism

Since the birth of socialist movement, the two forces of socialism and capitalism have been competing and influencing each other and have become two most important forces molding the development of the human society. Socialist movement is influenced by capitalism and capitalism is also influenced by socialism in a broad and extensive way.

4.2.1 Socialist movement directly promotes the changes of capitalism.

As well known, the past century was a time when capitalism experienced great changes. Capitalism, especially after the Second World War, encountered enormous changes as compared with a century ago. At the same time, the last century witnessed the major development of socialist movement. Socialist movement here refers to its broadest sense, which includes left-wing political movement and new left-wing social movement, with the working class as the

---

[1] *Selected Works of Marx and Engels*, 2nd Edition, Vol. 2, p 33, Beijing: People's Press, 1995.

social basis of communist parties and social democratic parties in capitalist countries, as well as theoretical and practical explorations of socialist countries. The new changes of capitalism are caused by the development of productive forces in its fundamental sense, and adjustments and reforms do not transcend the scope allowed by the system of capitalism. The adjustments and reforms are largely the result of pressures on it by "the internal socialist movement" and "the external communism", instead of its own will or at its own initiative.[1] Socialist movement is the necessary product of the development of capitalism at certain stage and is meant to overcome and solve the contradictions of capitalism, and find a new prospect for social development. Socialist thinking and movements direct the target of attack on the system of capitalism. During various periods in history, socialist movement has exerted profound influence on the changes of capitalism.

The development of socialist movement in the late 19th century forced capitalism to give in and adopt some reformist policies to ease the relations between employers and employees as well as social contradictions. With the progress of industrial revolution, the social polarization in capitalist society was intensified, so did the struggles between workers and capitalists. In the 1830s and 1840s, organized and massive political strikes or armed uprisings had appeared. The most famous uprisings were: textile workers' (canuts) uprising in Lyon, France in 1831 and 1834, the workers' chartist movement in the United Kingdom during 1836 and 1848, and the uprising of Silesian textile workers in Germany. The target of the proletarian in these three uprisings was not restricted to revolutionary democracy or solely for the aim of improving their living conditions. They directed the spearhead of the fighting to the whole class of bourgeoisie and the system of capitalism. Workers' movement in this period was presented with distinctive and extensive political nature. In 1848 with its birth, Marxism became the important guideline for socialist movement. From Communist League to the First International and the Second International, the focus of socialist

---

[1] Tao Wenzhao, "Internal and External Resistance: The Interpretation of the New Changes of Capitalism by Socialist Movement", *Journal of Teaching and Research*, 1999 (4).

movement was positioned in Europe and North America. During this time, socialist movement and capitalism were in direct confrontation and their struggle had a high degree of violence, for example, the French February Revolution and June Uprising in 1848 European revolution, and Paris Commune in 1870-1871. The capitalist governments had excluded socialist movements from the democratic system of capitalism, announced socialist organizations as illegal, deprived basic democratic rights of the working class, such as the right for general election, and carried out bloody suppressions on strikes through extreme measures. After decades of resistance from socialist movement, capitalism gradually became adaptive in the late 19th century. For the need to consolidate the capitalist system, the capitalist class adopted reformist measures and started to handle its relations with socialist movement through rule of law. Importantly, capitalist class accepted the legality of the socialist movement in its system. Workers' parties were gradually legalized and entered into the power organs of capitalist political system such as the parliament. Socialist movement turned from confrontations outside the system to appeals within the system. Some requests of the movement were accepted or realized, such as limiting working hours, and establishing trade unions. But taken as a whole, socialist movement in the 19th century had a weak and small influence on capitalism, and capitalist system was forced to accept some requests of socialist political movement—reluctantly— after many twists and turns.[1]

Between the two world wars, capitalism started to absorb the advanced experiences and management of socialism to rescue itself from crises. The direct confrontation between modern socialism and capitalism started after the victory of the October Revolution of Russia in 1917. The international imperialist forces resented the Russian Revolution and the Republic of the Soviet Union and tried in veil to smother the socialist country in its infancy. The capitalist world had to tolerate the existence and growth of a large socialist state locating on two continents; Europe and Asia, a new state with

---

[1] Tao Wenzhao,"Internal and External Resistance: The Interpretation of the New Changes of Capitalism by Socialist Movement", *Journal of Teaching and Research*, 1999 (4).

utterly different political system. Later on, despite political and ideological differences, some capitalist countries, unwilling to give up that large Soviet market and a major trade partner, had started trade and political exchanges with the Soviet Union. In the late 1920s, the capitalist world had suffered from grave economic and political crisis, while in contrast the Soviet Union had made brilliant economic achievements. Socialist industrialization of the Soviet Union strode forward, and its national economy had prospered. The superiority of socialist system was distinctively displayed for the world working class and other politically progressive personages. In such a context, some wise people in the capitalist countries realized that in order to continue ruling, capitalism needed to view positively the effective measures adopted by socialist countries in developing their economy and to absorb the positive elements of socialism. In the process of adjusting policies to tide over the economic crisis, though Germany, Italy and Japan took the road of fascism, the United Kingdom, France and the United States chose the reform road. In the United Kingdom, in 1929 the Labor Party led by MacDonald took its second term of office and decided for state interference in the economy. It implemented some policies with socialist features in the aspects of labor relations and labor management, social welfare and employment. In 1931, MacDonald, as the leader of the Labor Party and Prime Minister, appointed left-wing and radical Hewlett Johnson as the Dean of Canterbury who was very friendly to Soviet Union. Since then, socialist thinking started to have an important position in social and political life of the United Kingdom. The Labor Party inaugurated the history of taking office by left-wing parties and the influence of left wing force went deep into the political system and was extended to the life of the whole society. In France, in June 1936, the new Popular Front government under Blum, a member of Socialist Party, was formed. The radical Socialist Party took part in the cabinet. The Communist Party was not in office, but had supported Blum government's policies. In the United States, in 1932, Roosevelt started "New Deal Policy", which was attacked as "socialist" measures by the rightists. Roosevelt's New Deal changed the laissez-faire mode economic policies, and had strengthened state interference in the economy. The New Deal generated profound influences on future policies in capitalist countries. Without exception, modern capitalist market economies are market economy under the state macro-adjustment, which constitute the important element of modern market economy. Roosevelt's New Deal Policy showed that capitalism had started to treat certain policies of socialist movement seriously and in a systematic manner, and absorb them in a possible scope.

After the Second World War, socialist movement influenced developed capitalist countries and promoted changes in the relations among capitalist countries. After the Second World War the establishment of a socialist bloc led by the Soviet Union had formed a world pattern based on the opposition of socialism and capitalism. For the first time, the capitalist world had to face a global opponent and felt the realistic threat of collapse. During the Cold War, both domestic affairs and foreign affairs in capitalist countries were designed by "anti-communism" elements. In some context, the issue of "communism" was put on the top of the agenda. As a result, if the element of "communism" is not taken into account, it would be very difficult to understand many major policies implemented in Western capitalist countries during the Cold War. For example, in 1958 the Soviet Union's successful launch of space satellite had greatly shocked the United States and urged her to pass the National Defense Education Act. As a respond the United States had also started researches on the Internet technology. Within capitalist countries in the West, left-wing parties either had assumed governments or become the main opposition. Social Democratic Parties and Communist Parties were the main parties in some European countries and had become important left-wing forces in the political framework. A new era was opened; either left or right-wing parties were winning the power and the monopoly of liberal and/or conservative parties' governments were bygone. The new political landscape after the Second World War in some countries illustrated that the left-wing elements had infiltrated political, economic and social life in a comprehensive way, and were institutionally consolidated. New Left social movement was also the product of this period and had emerged as a new element in the left wing.[1] After the Second World War, a strong communist bloc outside the capitalist countries and a strong left-wing movement inside these countries had initiated changes in the relations among these countries. No war occurred between major capitalist countries after the Second World War. Such a kind of new relationships between capitalist countries, on the one hand, was due to the easing and containment of contradictions through the internationalization of economies, and on the other hand was due to the existence of a powerful socialist bloc. In the face of powerful socialist countries, capitalist countries had to contain their internal contradictions and disputes. To confront socialism, capitalist countries in the West, headed by the United States, formed an alliance in terms of international strategies and manifested a strong tendency of cooperation. Pressure from socialism had driven the traditional imperialist countries which used to be rivals to join hands. The United Kingdom, France and Germany which had warred throughout the history had then embarked on the policy of lasting alliance. If there was no pressure from socialism, it would be hard to imagine that they could join hands so fast. Another example, Germany and Japan had initiated the Second World War and were defeated; normally they should be severely punished. But from the perspective of confrontation between capitalism and socialism, the United States included Germany into the Marshall Aid Plans, which injected a new blood to Europe, and also aided Japan after the Korean War. This had provided conditions for the rapid rise of these two defeated countries. As an American scholar, Leste C. Thurow noted, "In face of world socialism, response of a single capitalist country is apparently not enough. There must be some global measures to contain global communism."[2] After the Second World War, capitalism continued to learn from socialist countries successful methods of planned management and macro-adjustment of the economy, and reduced to a large degree the blindly, speculative and

[1] Tao Wenzhao, "Internal and External Resistance: The Interpretation of the New Changes of Capitalism by Socialist Movement", *Journal of Teaching and Research*, 1999 (4).

[2] Leste C. Thurow, *The Future of Capitalism: How Today's Economic Forces Shape Tomorrow's World*, p 114, Beijing: China Social Sciences Press, 1998.

destructive features of the market economy; capitalist countries introduced welfare policies and social security mechanisms from socialism, and adjusted income distribution, thus have eased class contradictions to a large extent.

Additionally, socialist movement has promoted many political changes in capitalist politics. Over the past century, capitalist countries in the West have made great achievement in modernizing political democracy, and some goals strived by socialists have been reached, which are shown in the following aspects: Firstly, socialist movement was allowed into the democratic political system in the West. In the 19th century, most capitalist countries had adopted high-handed oppressive policies toward socialist movement, cruelly suppressed workers' movements, cleansed workers' organizations or socialist groups, and had not admitted legal status of workers' parties. Currently, social democratic parties and communist parties are mostly legal parties, and socialist forces are recognized both factually and legally. Left-wing parties play important roles in political life and rule the governments. Secondly, promoted by socialist movement, general election system has been gradually implemented in the Western countries; various conditions restricting the right of election have been abolished; the working class and other lower classes have gained equal political rights by law; and women and minority groups, once discriminated, have also won election rights. Thirdly, new forms of democracy, such as participatory democracy, appear. The workers are able to participate in industrial relations management sphere within a certain scope, and trade unions have important say in labor affairs. All these were the goals that socialists strived for in the 19th century and have eventually come true.

At the same time, socialist thoughts and their development have greatly enhanced the plurality of ideologies in capitalist society. Without socialism, there could be no plurality in ideological sphere. Currently, socialism has remarkable influence on the capitalist ideology. The popularization of school education advocated by socialist movement has contributed to the implementation of compulsory education. Especially, the popularization of higher education, open schools and distance education systems promoted and implemented by left-wing forces, have provided opportunities for the middle and lower classes to receive higher education. Community colleges and loans granted by the state to those receiving higher education to a certain extent guarantee the middle and lower classes to receive education; these cultural reforms favorable to lower-level people should be recognized. But it is to be stressed that these new changes of capitalism are compromises made by capitalists to socialist movement within the scope allowed by the capitalist rule, and not change the nature of capitalist system.[1]

4.2.2 Capitalism absorbs the elements of socialism.

Socialism was born opposing capitalism, but socialism and capitalism cannot be fully exclusive. Socialism develops on the basis of capitalist development and absorbs outstanding achievements of capitalism. Examining the history of relations between capitalism and socialism over the past century, we find that capitalism has also absorbed many elements of socialism that are favorable to the development of capitalism. We can even say that many elements shown in the new changes of the contemporary capitalism have grown from socialist elements absorbed.

After since socialist movement had emerged, socialism and capitalism appeared to be confrontational over rather a long time, and were incompatible in many cases. But it was in such kind of confrontation that capitalism had absorbed socialist elements and initiated reforms. As a result, capitalism has gained greater vitality. Socialist movement inside capitalist countries had played very important role especially in the reforms of domestic affairs. This was more markedly shown in European countries with a long history of workers' movement. Parties in capitalist countries that are based on the working class are communist and social democratic parties. They are left-wing political parties, commonly regarded as socialist parties. Since the second half of the 19th century, the unremitting struggles by these parties both inside and outside the capitalist system have changed greatly

---

[1] Tao Wenzhao, "Internal and External Resistance: The Interpretation of the New Changes of Capitalism by Socialist Movement", *Journal of Teaching and Research*, 1999 (4).

the traditional form of capitalism. The main features of the changes in contemporary capitalism, including nationalization, applying a certain degree of planning in economic and social issues, welfare state system, etc., are closely linked to the efforts of the left-wing parties. These policies were initially proposed by left-wing parties and promoted by them. It is worth noting that after the British Labor Party took office as the first left-wing party in 1920, after the Second World War, other left-wing parties had also won power in several other countries and became major parties in Europe. While the left-wing parties were in office, they vigorously implemented their ideas and policies, which could hardly be reversed by the right-wing parties resuming office, but were kept effective, as they were in line with the trend of social development and reflected the demands of the majority. The so-called new changes in capitalism, in terms of their origin, are the outcome of some policies of the left-wing parties, which became policies of the state through parliamentary struggle, or ruling practices by the left-wing parties. Left-wing movement, in particular socialist movement, has left strong reformist marks on capitalist system, in various aspects. Take economic policies as an example. The basic demands of socialism include planned economy, public ownership, and distribution "to each according to his work". There exist variations of these economic ideas in modern capitalist countries. Laissez faire attitude and myopia of liberal capitalism have resulted in violent cyclical turbulences and crises. After the Second World War, developed countries in the West had generally promoted Keynesianism; they had not only intervened in the economy and regulated markets, but had also established a relatively sound social welfare and security system. Supported by international workers' movement and the development of socialist countries, Western democratic countries had generated an ideological consensus, which especially promoted democratic socialism theories and policies to an advantageous position. The consensus suggests that the state should play more important and active roles in market economy; besides correcting market malfunction, the function of the state should focus on realizing socialism, social equality, providing necessary social welfare; and the state should recognize the functions of labor organizations. Fundamentally, these adjustments and reforms of capitalism were not voluntary. A century after the first economic crisis in 1825, more destructive economic crises had occurred. The great crises in the 1920s and 1930s, in particular, had shaken the fundament of capitalist system. Currently, the governments in capitalist countries no longer assume the role of "night watcher", but rather that of a "social housekeeper". Today governments have a strong ability of macro-adjustment. This kind of planning was indeed demanded by economic development and plays an important role in stabilizing modern economic and social development. Today many have realized that planned economy isn't equal to socialism, and market economy isn't equal to capitalism, too. However, observing from the perspective of historical development, planned economy has been a basic principle consistently advocated by socialism. The plans in capitalism no doubt have borrowed some successful practices from socialist countries, which were the direct result of efforts and governments of the left-wing.

After the Second World War and over a rather long period of time, the economic growth rate in socialist countries had far exceeded that of capitalist countries and socialist economy was thriving. The challenges and defects of the capitalist system and the value orientation of socialism have offered the people in capitalist countries, another choice of value and new hopes. The appearance of socialist system and the tremendous achievements had brought huge impact on capitalist system and had forced capitalist rulers to make painstaking choice: either to eliminate socialism, or to accept certain values of socialism. While capitalism had failed to smother socialism, was forced to adapt and include some socialist elements. Considering Marxist theories criticizing capitalism and comparing capitalist practices with socialism, capitalist countries have discovered the intrinsic defects and diseases of capitalism and the advantages of socialism. As a result, capitalist rulers on the one hand "reform" and solve many problems in the system to adapt to the demands of the era, and on the other hand absorb what's favorable from socialist system to improve capitalism. Thus, it is reasonable to suggest that capitalist system is stamped with marks of socialism, and socialist elements appear and grow in capitalist society. To certain degree, the people in capitalist countries enjoy merits created by socialism, which displayed in the following aspects: Inspired by socialist public ownership, capitalist countries have the state-owned economic sector; inspired by planned economy of socialism, capitalist countries started to have planned adjustment of the economy; inspired by socialist practice of workers being the masters of their own affairs, capitalist countries started to allow employees' participation in managing production and joint decision system; inspired by the improved living standards of the people in socialist countries, capitalist countries started to implement social welfare system. Measures that would be practiced by the proletariat after winning political power—as proposed in the *Communist Manifesto*—such as levying high progressive taxes, eliminating urban and rural differences, popularizing free education for children, have already realized by contemporary capitalism. In particular, high progressive income tax, high progressive heritage tax and unemployment security system, etc., were included in the legal system and can be operated and implemented. Over the past decades, in terms of the intrinsic contradiction of socialized production and the private ownership of means of production of the capitalist system, capitalist countries have accepted the remedies of Marx without changing the fundamental system of capitalism. Absolute private capital was transformed to social capital through stock holding and securities trading; private ownership was transformed to partial state ownership through levying heritage tax. Production mode has been highly socialized; moreover, many famous family-owned monopolistic consortiums, like Rockefeller's in the United States and Siemens family in Germany, have withered or disappeared. These measures do not endanger the rule of capitalism, but ease the contradiction between socialized production and private ownership of the means of production. After the Second World War, in the capitalist world, especially in West Europe, there were rounds of struggles and debates between state ownership and privatization. Basically, left-wing parties had implemented nationalization of some important industries in various methods; while right-wing parties had privatized the state-owned enterprises. But on the whole the degree of nationalization had increased substantially since the Second World War. In France, state-ownership was as high as 30%. Several key industries were nationalized. For example, in the United Kingdom, seven major industries were state-owned including coal, ship building, electricity, gas, railway, post service and telecommunication. Banks, the lifeline of modern economy, were nationalized, such as the Bank of France. Though state economy in capitalism is different from public ownership of socialism, it is a form of negation of the traditional private ownership of capitalism.[1]

A fair income is a goal of socialism. Under the leadership of trade unions, the working class had waged a long-term and intense struggle to protect their interests in terms of wage, working hours, employment and social security. For instance, in 1872, American workers waged a general strike for 8-hour work day, and in 1962 they had demanded for five working days per week and a seven hour work day. The policies of income distribution in Western countries are based on the contribution of capital, which lay on the private ownership base. But as permitted by this base, a possible adjustment could be made and income distribution was more socialized. The government intervenes in income distribution at different levels and with varying methods, adjusts income disparity and narrows the difference of income. Though the polarization of income distribution in the West remains to be serious and the gap between the top and the low income earners is growing, the efforts made shall not be ignored. Measures such as minimum wage regulation, progressive income tax levied on high income earners, social security coverage for the jobless, and general social welfare practices have narrowed income gap to certain extent. The gap could well be greater if there were no measures like these. Socialist movement has won concessions for the working class by a pressure on the capitalist class, under the condition that the fundamental interests of private owners have not been essentially endangered. Lester Thurow noted, "In the past 150 years, socialist system and welfare state system provided a new source of thought. Some elements

---

[1] Tao Wenzhao, "Internal and External Resistance: The Interpretation of the New Changes of Capitalism by Socialist Movement", *Journal of Teaching and Research*, 1999 (4).

from these two systems penetrated into the structure of capitalist system."[1]

The new changes of contemporary capitalism in fact have proven the historical inevitability of socialism replacing capitalism. History reveals that the new changes are not simply attributed to the voluntary self-adjustment of capitalism, and they are also the outcomes of the struggle of the working class and assimilation of socialist elements into capitalism. The driving force or inner secret of the changes of capitalism will not be fully explained if the in-depth criticism of Marxist theories on capitalism and the impact of the world socialist movement on capitalism are not taken into account.[2]

4.2.3 Socialist movement remains to be the important driving force for capitalist changes.

Currently, the world socialist movement is at the low tide, but it has not disappeared and socialist thoughts still have much influence. Not all socialist countries could be transformed by "peaceful evolution" strategy, and socialism, as the opposition and criticizer of capitalism, still plays an important role in shaping several changes in capitalism.

First of all, the world socialist movement exists and exerts influence on capitalism. After the dramatic upheaval in the Soviet Union and Eastern Europe, regional international meetings by communist parties and left-wing parties are being organized regularly, which has become an important form of international liaison, exchanges of experiences and mutual support among communist and left-wing parties. The influential ones include Athens Conference of Communist and Workers Parities, and Sao Paulo Forum. Athens Conference, an international meeting of regional communist parties and left-wing parties started in the 1990s, takes place once or several times a year. In January and June, 2002, two meetings were held in Athens. One was held by 13 communist parties in the Middle East, and another by 62 communist parties and workers parties from Asia, Europe, America and

---

[1] Lester Thurow, *The Future of Capitalism*, p17.

[2] Luo Wendong, "Theoretical Analysis on the Relations of Contemporary Capitalism and Socialism", *Journal of Theoretical Front of Universities and Colleges*, 2004 (12).

Oceania. They discussed the impact of 9.11 terrorist attack on global politics and prospects of the communist movement. They agreed that in the new scenario, communist parties and workers parties should take new measures to oppose the expansion and war policies of imperialism. Athens Conference represents a new trend of allied struggle by the communist parties and the workers parties. Sao Paulo Forum is an international conference of left-wing movement with the longest history, hosting the greatest number of parties and organizations and has the largest influence. In 1990, suggested and hosted by the Workers' Party of Brazil, the first meeting was held with 48 left-wing parties and organizations from 13 countries (including the Communist Party of Cuba). Starting from the third meeting in 1992, the Forum invited other communist parties and left-wing parties and organizations from all the five continents. At the 10th meeting in 2001 in Havana, capital of Cuba, the Forum was defined as "a left-wing forum, against imperialism, against neo-liberalism, against all kinds of colonialism and neo-colonialism; and a platform of solidarity, mutual assistance and debating for an alternative". The 11th meeting in 2002 that took place in Antigua, Guatemala reinstated the resolution of opposing imperialism and the demand of establishing a new international order. Its target of struggle in the near future was agreed, as striving for peace and democracy, and promoting an alternative integration process in Latin American continent. Sao Paulo Forum has become an important annual gathering of the left-wing parties in Latin America and the whole world. Other types of exchanges have also become frequent, such as participation in festivals of party's newspaper festivals and party congresses. In 2003, representatives of 110 parties and organizations in different countries were invited to take part in the L'Humanité Festival held by the French Communist Party. Delegations and representatives of 39 parties and organizations from more than 30 countries, including Vietnam, North Korea, Laos, Cuba, participated in the Avante! Festival of the Portuguese Communist Party. Frequent and various types of exchanges and cooperation contribute to sharing experiences, promoting unity and expanding influence. Apart from the communist and left wing parties, another kind of political forces:

anti-globalization movement, anti-war movement which embrace recently booming new peace movement, ecological movement and environmental protection movement have enriched the world socialist movement.

As a criticizer of capitalism, socialism continues to influence the changes of capitalism. Communist parties of some developed countries study the present and future historical status of capitalism and socialism in a criticizing spirit. They hold that Marxism will remain to lead important socialist movements in developed countries and continue to exist with the criticism on capitalism. Socialist ideal will remain to inspire people in developed capitalist countries. Various socialist forces continue to regard transforming and criticizing capitalism as their mission, reveal the deficiencies of the capitalist system and oppose exploitation and suppression in the capitalist society. At present and in a long time to come, some serious problems brought about by globalization may intensify the basic contradictions of capitalism. And new contradictions and problems, unprecedented in the Cold War period have appeared in some countries. They pose new challenges to the ruling class, and at the same time bring several new opportunities for socialist movement and form a new driving force to oppose and criticize capitalism.[1]

Secondly, some schools of socialist thinking in capitalist countries remain to be influential. After the dramatic changes of the Soviet Union and Eastern Europe, the world socialism entered a phase of reflection and exploration. Various schools have carefully summarized the historical lessons from those dramatic changes, reviewed the realistic issues in capitalism and the future of socialism and capitalism. Among these schools, (social) democratic socialism, market socialist theory, Western Marxism theory, Trotskyite socialism, ecological socialism and new-left socialism have gained remarkable development, which expands the influence of socialism and consolidates people's hopes in socialism. After the dramatic changes of the Soviet Union and Eastern Europe, left-wing scholars deeply concerned with the prospects and fate of socialism have held many academic meetings.

---

[1] Chai Shangjin, "The Current Status and Prospects of the Communist Parties in Other Countries", *Journal of the Contemporary World*, 2005 (2).

In the beginning of the 21st century, international seminars of socialist scholars continue to be held, and the influential ones include seminars hosted by the academic society of French Communist Party, the World Marx Congress (Espace Marx), organized by professor Jacques Bidet, International Seminar of Socialist Scholars organized by Professor Aleksandr Buzgalin from Moscow State University, International Seminar of Marxist Scholars organized by Professor Beckerman from Stuttgart University, Socialist Scholars Conference organized by left-wing scholars in New York and Socialist Conference organized by left-wing scholars in London. They take place either once a year, or every two or three years. Their participants vary from a few dozens to several thousands, coming from different social classes of different countries, representing different left-wing parties. The themes of these seminars or meetings are major issues related to Marxism, socialism and the development of the human society. While socialist movement is at the low tide, the significance of these seminars and meetings far exceeds the meetings themselves in sharing socialist theories and thoughts, strengthening the exchanges and collaboration of Marxists in the world, boosting the morale of socialists, and expanding the influence of socialism.

Thirdly, the achievements of socialist countries remain to be an important pressure for the changes of capitalism. As the opponent and the innovation and the replacement of capitalism, existing socialism produces a major pressure on capitalism and forces it to change constantly. After the dramatic changes of the Soviet Union and Eastern Europe, the previous 9 socialist countries split apart forming 27 countries that are no longer socialist, and socialist countries in the world was reduced from 16 to 5.Thus socialism has encountered a major setback. But over the recent decade, the reforms of socialist countries have made noted achievements. These socialist countries have insisted on combining the basic tenets of Marxist theories with their national conditions, and exploring and building socialism with their own characteristics. As a result, the reputation and influence of socialism has been re-enhanced. The Chinese economy has achieved continuous high growth rate, upgrading industrial structure, and presents a pattern of joint growth of different types of ownership with public ownership as leading and the main body. Meanwhile, market economic system is developing and improving and a system of socialist market economy has been initially established. While China achieves remarkable economic growth, its political system also makes major progress. The basic political system, including the National People's Congress, multi-party cooperation with political consultation under the leadership of the Communist Party of China, and the autonomy of ethnic regions, keeps improving. The social strata in China evolve toward a modernized structure, the initial shape of which has been formed. Cultural development scores major achievements, the ethical quality of the people greatly improves, and Marxism in the process of innovation shows strong dynamism and energy and is further consolidated as the guiding ideology in the superstructure. The all-round national strength of China is notably enhanced and its influence in international affairs notably increases. Vietnam also makes great progress in economic development during its renovation (doimoi) and opening up. Since the 1990s, the economic growth in Vietnam has displayed a higher speed. The growth rate of GDP was 6% in 1991, 8.6% in 1992, 8.1% in 1993, 8.8% in 1994, 9.5% in 1995, 9.34% in 1996, and 9% in 1997. After 1997, as impacted by the financial crisis in Southeast Asia, GDP growth in Vietnam was slowed for some time, which was 6% in 1998 and 4.8% in 1999. But the growth rate rose again in 2000 to 6.7%, 6.8% in 2001, 7.04% in 2002, and 7.2% in 2003.[1] Vietnam also reforms its political system in a very steady and positive way. Life long tenure for leaders has been abolished, democratization of political life promoted, rule of law improved, and anti-corruption practices being developed. Laos also makes remarkable achievements in reform and opening up. In rural areas, it implements household contracting responsibility system, and in urban areas it conducts reforms. Political system is gradually reformed in a steadfast way. Other socialist countries all have performed reforms at varying degree and scored progress. The achievements of these countries show that socialist course in the world is progressing, and the great practice initiated in the 20th

---

[1]　Gao Fang, Li Jingzhi, Pu Guoliang, *Theories and Practices of Scientific Socialism*, 4th Edition, p 194.

century continues. Socialism remains to be a major pressure for capitalism to change.

4.3 The Confrontation and Cooperation Between Socialism and Capitalism in the Age of Globalization

Economic globalization exerts huge influence on the relations of capitalism and socialism. In the age of economic globalization, the two systems will co-exist in peace for a long term, with both conflict and collaboration between them. But as economic globalization proceeds, the forms and contents of the conflict or collaboration will undergo many changes.

4.3.1 The conflict between the two systems will constantly occur.

As long as the two systems co-exist, the confrontation and conflict between them will be inevitable. It is not plausible to deny that the two systems will conflict with each other in the condition of economic globalization or exaggerate the idea that the influence of economic globalization will push more similarities in two systems.

First of all, from the perspective of ideology, the confrontation of the two systems is inevitable. The purpose of foreign policies of any country is to protect its national interest, and as an important element, ideology includes and serves the national interest and effects the selection of goal of foreign policies by shaping the ideas of decision-makers. To reach the goal of foreign policies at the lowest cost with long-lasting effects, ideology can be the best way by deploying its attractiveness.[1] It is fair to say that at most time the core motive of international exchanges of nations is not ideology, but ideology has important influence on international relations. As a result, at the level of international relations, countries with different ideology may well be

[1] Xing Yue, "The Role of Ideology in Foreign Policies", *The Pacific Journal*, 2004 (9).

confrontational or even hostile.

Secondly, from the perspective of values, the values of socialism and capitalism have fundamental differences. Capitalism is a social system or social form based on private capital and ruled by the capitalist class.[1] Socialism is a social system or social order based on socialized production and the power sets with the working people.[2] The ultimate goal of capitalism is to exploit the surplus value to the largest possible extent. "All means of improving social productive forces are realized against sacrifices offered individual laborers. All means of developing production turn to means of ruling and exploiting the producers. Laborers develop in an unbalanced way and become partial."[3] The purpose of the development of socialist productive forces is to achieve the free and all-round development of the people. The contrasts of the value of socialism and capitalism can be confirmed from the ideas of Bertrand Russell. He had asserted that "socialism essentially means common ownership of land and capital under a democratic form of government. It implies production for use and not for profit and its fruits distributed if not equally to all, at any rate according to inequalities justified only in the public interest."[4]

Viewed from historical practice, the confrontation of socialism and capitalism had existed from the start of socialist movement, which becomes even more direct and severe after the establishment of socialist system. After the October Revolution in 1917, capitalist countries joined their military forces to intervene the new-born Soviet political power and intended to smother it in its cradle age. After the Second World War, capitalist countries had embargoed, contained or enclosed the newly emerging socialist countries. While military force had failed to demolish socialism, capitalism promoted the strategy of "transforming by peaceful evolution". After the

---

[1] Gao Fang, *Probe into the World Affairs*, p 184, Beijing: China Books Press, 2002.

[2] Gao Fang, *Probe into the World Affairs*, p 188, Beijing: China Books Press, 2002.

[3] *The Complete Works of Marx and Engels*, 1st Chinese Edition, Vol. 23, p708, Beijing: People's Press, 1972.

[4] Quoted from Jean Maret, Alain Houlou, *Livre - Histoire Des Socialiste,* p8, Beijing: Commercial Press, 1999.

dramatic changes in the Soviet Union and Eastern Europe, capitalist countries continued to regard socialism as rival and threat. In reality, it is highly dangerous to compromise the conflict between the two systems or to deny the confrontation between them. Gorbachev had proposed "New Thinking of International Politics" and asserted that there were two types of contradiction worth noting: one was the contradiction between two fronts, socialism and capitalism, and the other was the contradiction between war and peace, and between life and death of mankind. According to him under the impact of nuclear threat and globalization, the contradiction between life and death of mankind had become the principal contradiction of modern international relations, and the confrontation between socialism and capitalism had retreated to a secondary position. Gorbachev had sought a proposition based on the principles of humanism advocating that the interest of all humankind is supreme. This idea was the core of his "New Thinking of International Politics". But his naive dream of globalism fell into the trap of "peaceful evolution" of the West, and had thus ruined the future of the Soviet socialism.

But in the age of globalization, the forms of contradictions between the two systems and methods of solving them are changing. It is wiser to expect massive military or face-to-face confrontations to take place, instead there will be arising abundant rivalries that are not directly confrontational. Jr. Joseph Nay, an American scholar, points out, "Today, countries no doubt use military force. But in the past half century, the role of military prowess has changed. Many countries, big powers in particular, come to realize that pursuing their goals with warring means pays a higher cost than in the past."[1] Why has this change occurred? He suggests that there are four reasons: Firstly, the latest military tool, nuclear weapon, is hard to deploy. Secondly, the cost of using conventional military force to rule people with nationalist emotions is much higher than that in the past. Thirdly, choosing military force will bring great political risk for the domestic rule. Fourthly, economic interdependence, telecommunication, international systems and

---

[1] Jr. Joseph Nye, *Understanding International Conflicts: An Introduction to Theory and History*, p14, Shanghai: Shanghai People's Press, 2002.

multinational entities sometimes play greater roles than military force. Military force as one of the tools is not out of date, but the cost and effect of using this tool have changed, and as a result today's international politics is more complex than that in the past.[1] The possibility of massive confrontation exists, though much reduced.

In the context of globalization, contradiction of the two systems is basically competition that is indirectly confrontational, including economic competition, cultural competition and competition in ideological spheres. Since the mid-1990s, as a larger socialist country, China has established strategic partnerships of various nature with capitalist powers, which shows that those big powers are intending to reach a strategic understanding to solve their differences without using military force. "A world war without smoke of gunpowder", famous in United States refers to economic, political, ideological, cultural and religious influence and infiltration using indirect measures that exclude wars or military actions, which strive to coach socialist countries to act in line with Western norms, or evolve toward the direction desired by the West. Against this backdrop, "harmony with differences" becomes the new way of co-existence of the two systems. All the successful experiences of capitalism should and can be drawn upon by socialist system. As an open social system, socialism can exist in peace with capitalism. But during this process of contesting and competitive co-existence of the two systems, socialist movement is at the low tide, which lays a disadvantage, but capitalism is able to expand as globalization proceeds. In today's world pattern, the power of socialism is positioned on the weaker end. Developing socialist countries are facing the negative impacts of developed capitalist countries in terms of economy, politics, culture, military affairs and even state (national) sovereignty.

In the context of globalization, the result of competition of countries with different systems would probably reach a "win-win" or "multiple win". In the Cold War period, socialism and capitalism aimed to defeat each

---

[1] *Ibid*, p 15-16.

other in competition. Both in theory and in practice, the popular pattern for international relations was "zero sum", that is, the gain of one party would be the loss of the other. In economic globalization, the links between socialist and capitalist countries is getting closer, exchanges are more frequent, and interdependence intensifying. As a result, the competition of countries with different systems starts to shift from the pattern of "zero sum" to "win-win" or "multiple win".

In the age of globalization, the methods of solving international contradictions become much moderate, including negotiation, compromise, mediation and arbitration or striving for establishing collectively abided international system. Generally speaking, there are three ways of solving international contradictions. The first is two parties ease their confrontation and reach a compromise by means of discussion, negotiation or mediation. The second is one party surpasses the other. One party has greater power and has the decisive win, and the other party accepts failure or defeat. The third is both parties will perish, as no party is willing to compromise. At present, international conflicts have the following features: one is that international conflicts show a tendency of being globalized. The second, they cover extensive and larger spheres such as politics, economy, military, cultural and environmental affairs. The third, conflicts are interdependent and interact with one another. For example, economic conflicts push political conflicts. The fourth, the frequency of international conflicts notably grows. The destructiveness and risks of international conflicts increase. Against such a background, conflicts between a bigger country and a small one may result in both parties' loss, if proper measures are not designed, let alone this may prove true in dealing with conflicts between two big countries. The abuse of military force by the United States after the Cold War is a typical example. The Kosovo War showed that the illegal humanist interventional military actions were unable to solve human crises issues. War in Afghanistan and Iraq showed that anti-terrorist wars which tackle violence with violence had not achieved the anticipated goals, and military measures are unable to solve various threats to security. In March 2003, the United States declared war on Iraq and for some time U.S had showed off her hard power. But the war to Iraq had not only displayed the limitations of her material resources and personnel, but also lessened the charisma of American culture, the charm of its ideology, as well as its capability of using international mechanisms. The soft power of the United States was remarkably damaged and lessened.[1]   In this situation, solutions that are more rational, more effective and in line with the interests of all parties are important, and less acute methods work better.

Opposite systems as they are, socialism and capitalism should adopt moderate measures to solve conflicts between them, examining the common interests of both sides and of the whole international community in the age of globalization with interdependence. They can even form a joint global governance mechanism and follow the generally abided international systems.

4.3.2 Confrontation of the two systems changes to more collaboration.

As economic globalization accelerates, the essential differences of socialism and capitalism will not disappear and the fundamental opposition between them will continue to remain. Basically they will be both confrontational and cooperative. As the two systems are opposite, their conflicts and confrontation are inevitable; as they co-exist within the common international society, cooperation between the two will be necessary. As economic globalization proceeds, the previous predominance of confrontation will be replaced by a predominance of cooperation.

Globalization intensifies interdependence of nations and the world is more closely linked as a whole. To seek cooperation is in line with the goals: peace and development, which constitute the most important trends of today's age, and also in line with the requirements of world development as well as the common interests of both socialist and capitalist countries.[2] It also

---

[1]   Xiong Guangqing, "Iraq War Weakens the Soft Power of the United States", *Journal of Academic Exploration*, 2005 (2).

[2]   Zhang Senlin, Liu Taiping, "The Features of the Relations of Socialism and Capitalism in Economic Globalization", *Journal of the Party School of Changchun City Committee*, 2003 (2).

accords with the common interests of the international community. Robert Keohane and Joseph Nye note: "We live in an age of interdependence. This observation tends to indicate that the nature of world politics is changing."[1] Assessing that globalization have changed the nature of world politics may exaggerate its impact on world politics, but its influence is indeed enormous. For example, globalization is changing the role and functions of the state. For the national states of the past, the tasks of politics used to be preparing and winning wars (armed force), maintaining domestic order (police), and establishing systems of unity and mutual assistance (compulsory education, medical care and insurance, unemployment subsidy, guarantee pensions). In the context of globalization, the role of the states is changing and the states shoulder responsibilities at two tiers: to be responsible for its own people, and to be responsible for the international community. The state can no longer act arbitrarily as she wishes under the pretext of sovereignty, but is under the control of its people, non-governmental organizations, appraisal bodies, and international organizations. The control overlaps and takes various forms. The bad image of a state will deter investors and cause international financial institutions' hesitation. Under the new historical conditions of accelerating economic globalization, the interdependence of countries and regions is intensifying and international cooperation becomes essential in the life of international society.

Economic globalization integrates many countries with different and particular economic and political systems into the international community, and the relations between them display new features. With the dramatic upheaval in the Soviet Union and Eastern Europe, the dissolution of the Soviet Union and the gradual establishment of socialist market economy in China, market economic system is able to expand globally, and a unified and single world market comes into full being. Both socialist and capitalist economies are integrated into the world economic system. The need for market, resources, and technologies of other countries is growing, and the increasing and intensifying economic links will result in transcending

---

[1] Robert Keohane, Joseph Nye, *Power and Interdependence*, 3rd Edition, p1.

ideological conflicts, adopting more open policies, and seek for broader participation and cooperation. On the one hand, while sticking to the basic principles of socialism and giving full play to superiorities of socialism, socialist countries have taken initiative to integrate themselves into the world market system, and vigorously developed economic exchanges and cooperation with capitalist countries. On the other hand, developed capitalist countries, from the prospect of their own interests, in particular to responding needs of economic development, also enhance the collaboration with socialist countries and actively develop the commodity and investment market of socialist countries, in order to gain greater interests. As a result, economic globalization can promote world economic growth and provide opportunities for all countries to develop. Both socialist and capitalist countries can take more active actions to take part in international competition and cooperation, and may enjoy a deeper and longer cooperative relationship.[1]

Under economic globalization, most countries will be part the same world system, exchanges of countries will grow, and cooperative areas will grow broader and stronger between socialist and capitalist countries in economy, politics, culture, science and technology, foreign affairs and military affairs. However, common global problems will also increase, for example, environmental pollution, terrorism, smuggling, drug-trafficking and other organized criminal activities. These cannot be solved only by a single country, but need coordinated efforts from all members of the international community, both socialist and capitalist countries. After the dramatic upheaval in the Soviet Union and Eastern Europe, developed capitalist countries have sought negotiation and cooperation with socialist countries in many spheres, and socialist countries have participated in international cooperation and conducted dialogues and exchanges with capitalist countries. As economic globalization proceeds, there will be more and deeper cooperation between socialist and capitalist countries.

The themes of the 21st century may be co-existence, peaceful competition, two-side learning and joint development of socialism and capitalism. As a new social system, socialism needs to carry on and make use

---

[1] Ying Xiaoli, "The Relations of Socialist and Capitalist Countries in Economic Globalization", *Journal of Academic Forum*, 2002 (2).

of social productive forces and cultural achievements created by capitalism and make new innovations summing up her new practices, in order to build socialism in a smoother way. After the establishment of socialist system, the achievements of socialist modernization are largely based on learning and absorbing what has been achieved by capitalism. In the age of economic globalization, socialism and capitalism will co-exist for further generations, and it is inevitable for the two systems to learn and absorb each other's achievements and favorable elements in the process of both conflict and cooperation. With increasing exchanges between them, interdependence will intensify. The achievements of socialist countries after the dramatic upheaval of the Soviet Union and Eastern Europe prove that socialist course in the world is making progress, and socialism remains to be an important pressure for capitalist changes. Capitalism will continue to be inspired by socialist movement, and to learn and absorb some of socialist elements. As far as socialism is concerned, as the successor to capitalism, its negation of capitalism is a dialectical negation at a higher level than capitalism. Socialism needs to draw the achievements created for the progress of mankind by capitalism to the end of surpassing and replacing capitalism. Contemporary capitalism has made remarkable progress in technological, economic, political and cultural territories and possesses many advanced experiences that can be learned by socialist countries. The need by socialism to learn from capitalism to promote its growth is also the need by capitalism to pay greater attention to social justice and orient to socialism. In summary, as economic globalization proceeds, the two systems will learn from each other in a more intensified way.

Chapter 5

The Re-Positioning of the Contemporary Socialism in China

To identify the position of Chinese socialism is the important basis for China to set out national development strategy and international strategy. How to make clear the position of Chinese socialism from the perspectives of history and the world socialist development is an issue explored by the Communist Party of China for a long time, with setbacks and relapses during the course. The re-positioning of socialism with Chinese characteristics is the basic foothold for the modernization of Chinese socialism, and policies since China's reform and opening up are had all followed this direction. In the age of globalization, socialist China is the criticizer and competitor of the contemporary capitalism, and it also learns from the strengths of the contemporary capitalism. The development of China to a large extent relies on how to adopt what is useful and discard what is not of the contemporary capitalism.

5.1   TheComplications and Relapses of Identifying Socialism with Chinese Characteristics

After the Opium War in 1840, China was gradually changed into a semi-colonial, semi-feudal society. When the nation's existence was in peril, the advanced elements and leading spirits in China made painstaking endeavors to try to find the truth from the West. Many explorations failed, starting from "Learning from the West to subdue the West" and Westernization Movement, to the Reform Movement in 1898. The bourgeois democratic revolution led by Sun Yat-sen finally ended the feudal rule running for over 2,000 years and founded the Republic of China. Though the Revolution of 1911 overthrew the Qing Dynasty, it did not fundamentally change the backwardness of the semi-colonial, semi-feudal society of China. As Mao Zedong pointed out, "Hong Xiuquan, Kang Youwei, Yan Fu and Sun Yat-sen were the leading spirits seeking the truth from the West before the birth of the Communist Party of China."[1]   But their efforts failed. "The situation of China was worsening, and people could hardly make a living."[2] Some democratic personages, in all their depression and hesitation and through reflection, started to realize that to save the country, "the evilness of producing autocratic monarchs must be uprooted", old ideas and ethic concepts eradicated. If the people were not to be emancipated from the trammels of old ideas, "the new system of China"[3] would not be created. The failure of the old democratic revolution directly resulted in the surge and rapid development of the New Culture Movement around the time of the May 4th Movement in 1919. In the Chinese academia, an upsurge seeking the truth from the West on a broader scope was set off. Various schools of ideas were introduced to China, for those thirsty for new knowledge. "Any book will be read, as long as it is about new ideas from the West."[4] Social reformism, capitalist enlightenment period ideas, pragmatism and socialist ideas were passionately introduced, and there were many

---

[1] *Selected Works of Mao Zedong*, 2nd Edition, Vol. 4, p 1469, Beijing: People's Press, 1991.

[2] *Ibid*, p 1470.

[3] *Works of Li Dazhao*, Vol. 1, p 175, Beijing: People's Press, 1984.

[4] *Selected Works of Mao Zedong*, 2nd Edition, Vol. 4, p 1469, Beijing: People's Press, 1991.

schools of socialism such as anarchism, Narodnism, New Village movement, Guild Socialism, Marxism, etc. As Qu Qiubai noted in 1920, "Discussions on socialism always inspired our endless interest. But we were more like the youth in Russian in the 1840s. We were like looking at the morning mist through a screen window. The influence was vague, the schools of socialism and the significance of socialism were divided and not very clear."[1] But amid continuous research, comparison and argument of various schools of ideas, some advanced intellectuals started to have initial understanding of scientific socialism, and the victory of October Revolution eventually brought about a leap of this understanding. Marxist works were translated into Chinese, and groups that studied or advocated Marxism mushroomed. In conclusion of the history of this period, Mao Zedong pointed out, "The Chinese learned a lot from the West, but it was not workable and the ideal could not be realized."[2] "Russian revolution in 1917 awakened the Chinese, who learned something new, namely, Marxism and Leninism."[3] As a result, the advanced elements in China started to "use the proletarian perspective of the universe as tools to observe the fate of the nation, and to reconsider their problems. To take the road Russian took was the conclusion."[4] The first Marxists and advanced elements with primary communist ideas, including Li Dazhao, Chen Duxiu, Mao Zedong, Cai Hesen, started their research and publicity of Marxism and used its scientific principles to analyze issues and observe the society. In articles including "My Perspective of Marxism", Li Dazhao systematically explained the basic theory of historical materialism, and proposed to use the Marxist materialism to equip the mind of the Chinese to the end of reforming China. Li pointed out that "Now it is the age for the common people in our world. We should know about our forces and unite rapidly, to meet our needs in life, and to create a new history of the common people in the world."[5] According to Chen Duxiu, the workers "will have to form a class, and will

[1] *Works of Qu Qiubai*, Vol. 1, p 23, Beijing: People's Press, 1986.

[2] *Selected Works of Mao Zedong*, p 1470.

[3] *Ibid*, p 1514.

[4] *Ibid*, p 1471.

[5] *Works of Li Dazhao*, Vol. 2, p 365, Beijing: People's Press, 1984.

have to occupy the position of the class of forces through revolutionary means, and to destroy the old ways of production by using that forces."[1] Mao Zedong not only raised that "materialistic conception of history is the ground of the philosophy of our party"[2], but also raised that to reform China, various ideas should be studied deeply and the conditions of the country should be understood. He believed that "if we want to do something in today's world, we will have to do it in the territory of China. And the conditions of the territory of China need to be surveyed and studied on the spot."[3] Though the early Marxists did not yet have a mature command and application of scientific socialism, scientific socialism turned from simple introduction, evaluation and dissemination to voluntary application. At the same time, the early Marxists fought with various non-Marxism and anti-Marxism schools by applying the basic theory of Marxism. In one of their debates, "Problems and Ideas", they criticized reformism and believed that only if social problems could be tackled at the source, "there would be hope to solve each and every concrete issue", and solving economic issues would be fundamental. "Before the transformation of economic organizations, none of the problems would be solved at all."[4] In the debate on socialism and anarchism, they criticized the reformist ideas of capitalism, believing that to save China, socialism must be implemented. And to implement socialism, a revolution should be carried out to take over political forces. On the other hand, they criticized the adverse comments on Marxism by the anarchists and noted that the outcome of class struggle must be class dictatorship. No command of political forces would not protect revolution and prevent counter-revolution. The class overthrown would rise again and revolution would achieve nothing.[5] The arguments and debates widened the influence of Marxism, helped the dissemination of scientific socialism, and moreover,

[1] *Selected Articles of Chen Duxiu*, 2nd Vol., p 8, Beijing: SDX Joint Publishing Company, 1984.

[2] *Works of Mao Zedong*, Vol. 1, p 4, Beijing: People's Press, 1984.

[3] *Materials of New Democracy Society*, p 63, Beijing: People's Press, 1980.

[4] *Works of Li Dazhao*, Vol. 2, p 37, Beijing: People's Press, 1984.

[5] *Works of Cai Hesen*, p 51, Beijing: People's Press, 1980.

urged the early Marxists to further study scientific socialism and to use it in a more correct way to observe and analyze social phenomena and solve social problems.

The wide spread of scientific socialism in China and its combination with workers' movement gave birth to the Communist Party of China. "The Communist Party was born in China, and it is an epoch-making event."[1] "When the Communist Party of China was born, Chinese revolution had taken on an entirely new look."[2] The establishment of the Communist Party of China marked that scientific socialism entered a grand new stage in China. But in the course of development, the historical positioning of Chinese socialism by the Chinese people has experienced twists and turns.

During the mid-1930s and early 1950s, in the course of practices of the new democratic revolution and construction, the Communist Party of China applied the basic theories of Marxism to Chinese reality, and created and proved a unique theory of new democracy. The background of this theory was an understanding of the conditions of the nation, the opening remark was an analysis on new democratic revolution, the main part of it was an analysis on the new democratic society, and the concluding part of it was an analysis on the transition of new democracy. As the trunk of the theory of new democracy, the theory of new democratic society was the direct outcome of the theories and practices from new democratic revolution, the logical starting point of the transition from new democracy to socialism, that is, socialist revolution, and a special strategy of social development based on the backward conditions of China. The theory of new democratic society regarded new democratic society as the direct end-result of new democratic revolution, as a transitional phase between terminating the semi-colonial, semi-feudal society and establishing socialist society, and as a special form of social development. New democratic social system included political, economic and cultural system. The political system of new democracy: to implement the people's democratic governance under the leadership of the

---

[1] *Selected Works of Mao Zedong*, 2nd Edition, Vol. 4, p 1514.
[2] *Selected Works of Mao Zedong*, 2nd Edition, Vol. 4, p 1357.

proletarian and its party, on the basis of the alliance of workers and peasants, and with the unity of all democratic classes and all ethnic groups in the country; to be against imperialism, feudalism and bureaucratic capitalism; to fight for the independence, democracy, peace, unity and prosperity of China. The economic system of new democracy: to be led by state-run economy; each of the various economic elements that fit with the development level of productive forces, including cooperative economy, individually-owned economy, private capitalism economy, state capital economy, having its own share of work to do and cooperating with each other, with each in its proper place, to the end of promoting the development of social economy as a whole. The state would not eliminate capitalism, but encourage the operational initiative of all private businesses benefiting the national economy. Externally, the state carried out and controlled foreign trade to confront the exploitation of foreign capitals; internally, the state carried out controlled capital to check the monopoly tendency of capital to avoid any damage to the national economy. The cultural system of new democracy: to implement cultural education which was national, scientific and for the mass; to eliminate ideas that were feudal, comprador, fascist and colonially enslaving; to upgrade the level of culture and cultural qualities of the whole nation.

"The combination of new democratic politics, new democratic economy and new democratic culture makes the republic of new democracy." "This is the new China we are going to create."[1] According to new democracy social theory, the future China would surely enter the stage of socialism. "This is a definite prospect, and there is no doubt about it." [2] "But socialism can only be reached through democracy. This is the natural law of Marxism"[3], as well as the inevitable path of history. The reason was that the economy and culture of China was extremely backward. The aim of new democratic society was to change China into a country with political freedom, prosperous economy,

---

[1] *Selected Works of Mao Zedong*, 2nd Edition, Vol. 2, p 709.

[2] *Selected Works of Zhou Enlai*, 1st Vol., p 368, Beijing: People's Press, 1980.

[3] *Selected Works of Mao Zedong*, 2nd Edition, Vol. 3, p 1060.

advanced culture, to fight for industrialization and modernized agriculture. This was a process in preparation for material basis for transiting to socialism. Therefore the central task of the new democratic society was "to motivate all forces to resume and develop production"[1]. All other works "surrounding the central task of production and construction had served this central task."[2] After new democratic construction and reform, when all conditions got ready, the new age of socialism could be reached in an unflinching and proper way. When it was immature politically or economically, and change was not benefiting the majority of people in the country but harmful, change should not be considered. "To establish socialist society on colonial, semi-colonial and semi-feudal ruins would be idle dream"[3] if new democracy was not to be fully fledged. By the time the People's Republic of China was founded, theory of new democratic society had been widely accepted by Chinese people of all classes, and its basic spirit was shown in the Common Guideline, the provisionary constitution of New China. It guided the rapid recovery and development of the national economy and laid the basic material foundation for the upcoming socialist transformation.

Theory of new democratic society was a strategy of social development proposed by the Communist Party of China based on the backward conditions of China. That was the working class took the political forces of the country; the leadership of state-run economy was a prerequisite; each of the various economic elements had its own share of work and cooperated with each other; each was in its proper place, to the end of promoting the development of social economy as a whole. This was a fundamental constructive strategy with its ultimate goal of "developing production and economy", changing an agriculture country into an industrialized one in a stable way, and preparing the material basis for the transition from new democracy to socialism. The new democratic society was a necessary transitional phase in history between semi-colonial and semi-feudal society and socialist society. But it was not just

---

[1] *Selected Works of Mao Zedong*, 2nd Edition, Vol. 4, p 1429.

[2] *Ibid*, p 1482.

[3] *Selected Works of Mao Zedong*, 2nd Edition, Vol. 3, p 1060.

a phenomenal substitute between the new and the old, rather it was a complete social process needing to consolidate its foundation. "The foundation of the new democratic society were factories (social production, public ownership and private ownership) and cooperatives (including labor-exchange teams). It was not scattered individual economies…machines, not handicrafts."[1] This stage of society had its own independent economic form, the form of state and political forces, and cultural form. So the new democratic society can be regarded as a special form of social development. Its establishment and consolidation showed that China had broken away from the capitalist track, and its development and prosperity would ensure its final merger into socialism. The new democracy wasn't equal to socialism, but it would develop toward socialism. "Every new factory, every new mine pit, and every new machine marked a step to that goal."[2] The theory of new democratic society basically completed the theoretical exploration of the relation between the special stage of social development of backward countries and Marxist transitional phase; this exploration was started by Lenin, though unfinished. With a specific denotation, Marxist transitional phase refers to the historical phase of capitalism changing to socialism. Its prerequisite condition was that due to the sufficient development of capitalism, means of production and the political forces of the state were commanded by capitalists, and when the proletarian took over the political forces, they could directly conduct the revolutionary transformation of socialism. In his late years, Lenin endowed a new connotation of construction to the concept of "transitional phase". But Lenin did not clarify the essential difference between the concept he redefined and the original meaning of Marxist "transitional phase" he once used. Meanwhile, some non-standardized wordings, such as "retreat" and "outflanking", had usually made people understand the implications of this idea from the tactic perspective, thus the position of social development strategy in the new transitional phase could

---

[1] *Selected Letters of Mao Zedong*, p 238-239, Beijing: People's Press, 1983.

[2] Harry Pollitt, "Solute to the People's Republic of China", quoted from Qu Shu, *The Preliminary Study on New Democracy*, p 54, Hong Kong: The South Bookstore, 1949.

not be solidly established. As a result, the genes of renewed "attack" in the future were laid. But the new democratic society theory in China made clear its nature of constructive phase of economic growth and social development, and its central task was to motivate all forces to develop production and fight for industrialization and agricultural modernization. When enough material bases had been accumulated in the new democratic society, it would become possible to assume the peaceful transition to socialist society. The transitional phase for China in the future (from new democracy to socialism) would be a peaceful transition in a progressive and stable way. Liu Shaoqi exemplified the specialness of the transitional phase in China when he made a speech at the forum of business leaders in Tianjin. "At present, in the new democratic society, you capitalists can fully bring into play your initiative. How would you do when it transits to socialism? Last time I talked with Mr. Song Feiqing (director of East Asia Company). I said, 'Now you only have one factory. You can run two, three or eight factories in the future. When it comes to socialist society, when the state demands it, you can hand over the factories to the state, or the state buys them from you. If the state has no money at the moment, it can issue bonds. Then the state would have you manage these factories. You are still a director, but one of the state-owned factories. If you are capable, you may be given eight more factories to manage. When you run 16 factories, your salary will be increased, but you need to run them well. Would you take up the responsibility?'"[1] Mao Zedong also noted that, after the reforms of new democracy, when economic and cultural development of the country prospered in the future, all conditions were ready. "The new period of socialism would be entered in an eased and proper manner."[2] At that time, for capitalists who contributed to the course of the country and the people, "there is no reason the people or the government of the people will desert them, and there is no reason they will give them no chance of living

---

[1] *Reference Materials of the History of the Communist Party of China* (Seven), p 8, Beijing: People's Press, 1980.

[2] *Works of Mao Zedong*, Vol. 6, p 80, Beijing: People's Press, 1999.

or chance of working for the people."[1] In brief, "when class is demolished, individual will be relieved"; "when conditions are ripe, success will come."[2] These were the most concrete statements of Chinese communists on the transition from new democracy to socialism. In such a way, not only the independent social and historical status of new democratic society was enacted, the transition from new democracy to socialism was also clearly defined. Therefore, experiencing a special phase of new democratic society in backward countries was not an expedient measure, nor a "retreat", but an inner logic of social development. Theoretically, the disputes of retreat or attack, strategy or tactic on new economic policies, and the early termination of these polices as happened in the Soviet Union could be easily avoided. Hou Wailu, a historian, made a statement: "New democratic countries indeed drew upon lessons of the Soviet new economic policies (NEP), and enabled the development of the backward to rely on the advanced or overcome the backwardness through fighting against the advanced. However, in new democratic countries, overcoming the backwardness was the guideline for the progress of democracy, much different from the Soviet way of overcoming the backwardness. In new democratic countries in a certain sense there was a big step of retreat for the purpose of moving forward. The former (new democracy) contained capitalist elements, and the latter temporarily resumed socialist elements; the former smashed the old world before the prelude of socialism, and the latter prepared for socialist construction after the establishment of socialism; the former was one of the phases of normal economic growth, and the latter was known as transitional economy."[3]

Mao Zedong had pointed out for several times that new democracy and socialism were the two chapters of an article. If the first chapter was not well written, the second one would not also be well written. The new democratic society was the transition between the two chapters. The theory

---

[1] *Works of Mao Zedong*, Vol. 6, p 81, Beijing: People's Press, 1999.
[2] *Selected Works of Zhou Enlai*, 2nd Vol., p 106, Beijing: People's Press, 1984.
[3] Qin Kehong, *New Democracy and New Democratic Countries*, p 12, Tianjin: Knowledge Press, 1949.

of new democratic society had proposed such a pattern of development: in the context that productive forces was extremely backward and development uneven, various relations of production fit in the level of productive forces and respective superstructures should be allowed to give play to their functions, in order to promote the progress of the society as a whole. Viewed from historical facts, in the brief practice of building the new democratic society, various economic, political and cultural elements and the systems of the society had achieved remarkable integration of functions, under the conditions of low productive forces, backward economy and culture, and low degree of democracy. Thus miracles were created in recovering from war and resuming development of production. In analyzing the success and failure of Mao Zedong's economic and political theory, some analysts from other countries acknowledged that Mao Zedong created an effective economic and political theory through his long-term practices in fighting wars. The golden period of his theory was during the anti-Japanese war period and the early 1950s. The main experience of this theory was to create a mixed economy with the mutual influence of state-run, cooperative or private economy and of both market and planning, and to encourage the growth of individually-owned and cooperative economy.[1]

Regretfully, this pattern was easily discarded without extensive practices. In September 1952, Mao Zedong had noted a new viewpoint at the meeting of the Secretariat of the Central Committee of the Communist Party of China that "socialism can be basically completed in 10 to 15 years. No need an extra transition period to socialism of 10 years."[2] It was an essential change of Mao Zedong's notion on the steps and ways of changing of new democracy to socialism. However, at least Mao Zedong had thus perceived new democratic society and transitional phase as two different concepts. Previously it was new democracy, then there was socialist transformation

[1] Mark Seldon, "Political and Economic Theory of Mao Zedong on the Transition to Socialism", *China Report Quarterly*, 1988 (2).

[2] Party Literature Research Centre of the CPC Central Committee, *Biography of Mao Zedong (1949-1976)*, Vol. 1, p 236, Beijing: Party Literature Press, 2003.

(transition). Originally Mao Zedong had identified 1953 as the starting time for the transitional phase.[1] But, in June 1953, at the Politburo meeting of the Central Committee of CPC, Mao had seriously criticized "establishing new democratic order", noting, "After the democratic revolution succeeded, some people stay where they are and do not understand that the nature of revolution has changed. They continue to carry on new democracy; they do not undertake socialist transformation. They are prone to make right-deviationist mistake." He made it clear that in the transitional phase, "the Principal Line is the beacon lighting all works."[2] The direct outcome of Mao's this critic was a negation of the theoretical and practical exploration of building new democratic society. Thus a new connotation was endowed to new democratic society, that was, a mixture of it with the transitional phase concept. At that meeting, Mao had also said, "Since the founding of the People's Republic of China until the basic completion of socialist transformation, it was a transitional phase. The Principal Line and task of the Party in the transitional phase is to basically complete industrialization in the country, and conduct socialist transformation of agriculture, handicraft industry and capitalist businesses."[3] This statement became the master copy of the Principal Line in the transitional phase for the Communist Party of China and was officially promulgated soon after. Endeavor to Motivate All Forces and to Build Our Country into a Great Socialist Country—Outline of Our Party's Principal Line in the Transitional Phase for Study and Publicity, compiled by the Ministry of Publicity and approved by the Central Committee of CPC to publish to the whole Party, explained the Principal Line of the Party in the transitional phase. The final version was penned by Mao Zedong: "It is a transitional period from the founding of the People's Republic of China to the basic completion of socialist transformation. The Principal Line and the principal task for the Party in this transitional phase is to gradually realize

---

[1] Party Literature Research Centre of the CPC Central Committee, *Biography of Mao Zedong (1949-1976)*, Vol. 1, p 254, Note 1, Beijing: Party Literature Press, 2003.

[2] *Mao Zedong's Articles Since the Founding of P.R. China*, Vol. 4, p 251.

[3] *Biography of Mao Zedong (1949-1976)*, Vol. 1, pp 253-254.

industrialization in the country, and the state will gradually conduct socialist transformation of agriculture, handicraft industry and capitalist businesses over a long time to come. The Principal Line is the beacon lighting all works, and any work will make either left- or right-deviationist mistakes without this beacon."[1] After Mao Zedong fully raised the Principal Line in the transitional phase, he then pointed out that "many policies of this Principal Line had already been raised in the resolution of the Second Plenary Session in March 1949, and they are now handled according with those principles, too." As a result, those who continued the theory of building new democratic society were accused as "arguing something else which was not in line with the principles of the Second Plenary Session, or even openly disobeying the principles of the Second Plenary Session."[2] In this way, Mao had made major changes to the initial original theory of new democratic society in two aspects. First aspect, a complete and a separate social form as a new democratic society concept was cancelled, and was replaced by the transitional phase term in a very general sense. Second aspect, the focus of Party work was shifted from construction to both construction and transformation tasks, and this new understanding with double-focus was eventually characterized by a shift from "the object" to "the subject", hence position of radical revolutionary action was raised and construction was descended to secondary position. Thirdly, to transform the relations of production was taken as the axis of social development. Though the peaceful nature of social transformation was stressed, class struggle was over-emphasized and the confrontations of conflicts were improperly exaggerated. On the one hand, national bourgeoisie was excluded from the scope of the people; it was believed that "after the landlord class and bureaucratic-capitalist class were overthrown, the principal contradiction within China was the contradiction between the working class and national bourgeoisie."[3] On the other hand, the transitional phase was outlined as a stage of

---

[1] *Works of Mao Zedong*, Vol. 6, p 316.

[2] *Mao Zedong's Articles Since the Founding of P.R. China*, Vol. 4, pp 301-302.

[3] *Works of Mao Zedong*, Vol. 6, p 231.

completing the transition from a society of complex and plural economic structure to "a society with single-unitary socialist economic structure."[1] Fourthly, the proposition that "there must be cooperatives before deploying machineries" was raised.[2] In a lopsided way, the backward labor-exchange and mutual assistance movement under the conditions of natural economy, and the collective laboring retaining the residual features of old village commune in the countryside were regarded as direct socialist elements. The ideas "simple cooperation generating new productive forces" by classic Marxist authors when analyzing cottage industry was simply copied, and it was regarded that collective work would improve labor productive forces and was of the real nature of socialism. This strategic evolution had two results. First aspect: the task of construction in new democratic society was transplanted to the transitional phase and was regarded as equally important as socialist transformation. Second aspect: the definition of early stages in the transitional phase showed a theoretical absence. For the realization of the first aspect, transformation should match with construction and changes of the relations of production should be achieved at the same time spontaneously with industrialization of the country. But practices showed that, the change of focus had resulted in the lagging behind of construction as compared with transformation work. To make up for the latter, only two propositions were possible. One proposition could be the transition from the semi-colonial and semi-feudal society to socialism, but this was already denied by the initial theory of new democratic society, and was once strongly criticized by Mao Zedong and some other people. As a result, a new proposition was chosen as "transitional phase from capitalism to socialism"[3]. But this proposition not only denied the special character of Chinese society and dogmatically used some conclusions of classic authors, but also paved the way for the later mistaken theories of "major transition" and a series of theoretical mistakes. When the Principal Line was originally identified in 1953, it was predicted that three five-year-plans or more time would be needed to transit to

---

[1] *Selected Works of Liu Shaoqi*, Vol. 2, p 142, Beijing: People's Press, 1985.

[2] *Works of Mao Zedong*, Vol. 6, p 432.

[3] *Biography of Mao Zedong (1949-1976)*, Vol. 1, p 397, p 400.

socialism. But by the end of 1956, socialist transformation of agriculture, handicraft industry and capitalist businesses were completed. As announced officially, socialist society had been entered. In the painstaking exploration of the communists in China, socialism was the direction of new democratic society, and the correct understanding of socialism was a direct result of the creative thinking new to the full transformational process of new democratic theory and practice. But due to the unexpected rapid victory of the War of Liberation (1946-1949), the task of constructing the country had become impeding. However the new democratic societal construction had not been fully fledged, and thought on socialism was quite unclear. As a result, Mao Zedong and his comrades were unable to have deserved rational creation that was independent on the higher level of political philosophy, but to inherit the basic theoretical propositions (principle) and the Soviet pattern, and take them as the logical premise of theory and the direction of practice, with no need to prove or test, after the fundamental changes of political relations in the Chinese society. Mao had pointed for several times that the Principal Line of the transitional phase "was based on Lenin's theory on the transitional phase."[1]. In December 1953, the publicity paper outline compiled by the Ministry of Publicity and approved by the Central Committee of CPC was the most systematic material explaining the Principal Line. There were as many as 21 quotations of Lenin and Stalin, among which, 11 of Lenin and 10 of Stalin. These quoted statements of Lenin were from some articles of Lenin during 1918 and 1919. So-called Lenin's theory on the transitional phase was some statements during the period of war communism policies, while war communism was soon replaced by new economic policies. The pattern of Stalin's socialism had advocated the full nationalization of industries, and the replacement of any form of market regulation mechanism by planned economy; heavy industries were stressed while agriculture and light industries were ignored; the expansion of construction and accumulation was stressed while the simultaneous improvement of people's living conditions ignored; and also enforced implementation of collective farming being in line

---

[1] *Works of Mao Zedong*, Vol. 6, p 389.

with the nationalization of industries, due to the incompatibility of socialist industrialization and individual agriculture was advocated. In the propaganda at that time and in the mind of most people, "today's Soviet is our tomorrow", and "the path taken by the Soviet Union is the role model we should follow." This mentality to some extent had restricted the theoretical recreation and rethinking of communists in China.

During the whole process of transformation, the national industrialization was regarded as the main body, and socialist transformation as the two wings of a bird, but "the essence of the Principal Line of the Party in the transitional phase is to enable socialist ownership of the means of production to become the only economic basis of our country and our society."[1] That was to say, "the Principal Line can be interpreted as solving the issue of ownership structures."[2] As the understanding on this issue deviated from the determining position of the level of productive forces and only emphasized the changes of the relations of production, changing the relations of production was also simplified as solving the issue of ownership in line with Stalin's view of ownership as the basis of the relations of production. As a result, "the most basic thing of socialism was the completion of socialist transformation, and the demolishing of private capitalist ownership of the means of production. Nationalization meant that agriculture and handicraft industry became collectively owned."[3] This abstract pattern of socialism structure without considering the level of productive forces and the level of economic development inevitably stressed "big, public and pure" things in a lopsided way. According to this pattern, to realize socialism in China was to thoroughly eliminate capitalist elements in urban and rural areas as well as all kinds of private ownership of means of production, which aimed to sweep bourgeoisie and capitalism completely in China.

In the process of socialist transformation, Mao Zedong tended to identify the transitional phase as "from capitalism to socialism."[4] But this

---

[1] *Works of Mao Zedong*, Vol. 6, p 316.

[2] *Ibid*, p 301.

[3] *Selected Works of Zhou Enlai*, Vol. 2, p 105.

[4] *Biography of Mao Zedong (1949-1976)*, Vol. 1, p 397, p 400.

phase actually referred to the period from the founding of the People's Republic of China to the basic completion of socialist transformation. Driven by complex factors, socialist transformation witnessed surges of climax before being terminated within only three years (1953-1956). And in 1956, it was announced that China had entered socialist society. In such a way, industrialization in the country once again became a "leftover issue inherited from history". In the 8th National People's Congress of the Communist Party of China held in 1956, it was pointed out that "because socialist revolution has been basically completed, the main task of the state changes from liberalizing productive forces to protecting and developing productive forces." "The principal contradiction in the country is already the one between the requirement of the people of establishing an advanced industrial country and the reality of a backward agricultural country, and the one between the people's need for the rapid development of economy and culture and their insufficiency to meet the people's need. The essence of this contradiction, under the conditions when socialist system has already been established in China, is the contradiction between the advanced socialist system and the backward social productive forces. The principal task of the Party and the people of China should focus on the efforts in solving this contradiction in order to transform China from a backward agricultural country into an advanced industrialized one."[1] In the early 1957, Mao Zedong had made a general description of the historical process covering 150 years: the 20th century and the first half of the 21st century. In the 20th century, the first half was for revolution, the second for construction. The time period he had described was a transitional time from revolution to construction. The central task for the 100 years from now on till the mid-21st century should be the construction of China.[2] But at the same time Mao believed that since the new social system was newly established, there should be a period for consolidation. "The fight to consolidate socialist system, and the fight between capitalism and socialism, would undergo a rather long historical

---

[1] *Selected Important Literature Since the Founding of P.R. China*, Vol. 9, p 350, p 351, Beijing: Party Literature Press, 1994.

[2] *Biography of Mao Zedong (1949-1976)*, Vol. 1, p 648.

period."[1] Though class struggle on a massive scale had basically ended, class struggle was not yet finished; in the ideological area, class struggle will continue for a long time. That who would be the winner in ideological domain remained to be a question.[2] In the Anti-Rightist Struggle launched later, Mao made this idea clearer: "Socialist revolution in the economic front in 1956 alone is not enough, which is also not consolidated as well. The Hungarian Crisis is a proof. There must be a thorough socialist revolution in the political and ideological front."[3] "There is no doubt that the principal contradiction of Chinese society is the contradiction between the proletariat and bourgeoisie and the contradiction between socialist road and capitalist road."[4] "The resolutions of the 8th National Congress stated that the principal contradiction at present is that between the advanced socialist system and the backward social productive forces. As this contradiction will remain in the future, this statement sounds correct even in the long term. But it is not proper at present."[5] With these new ideas the resolutions of the 8th National Congress was altered. The second meeting of the 8th National Congress held in May 1958 confirmed and legalized Mao's statement in procedure, in the form of work report delivered by Liu Shaoqi on behalf of the Central Committee. It was delivered as, "During the whole process of transitional phase, that is to say, before socialist society is established, the fight between the proletarian and bourgeoisie, and the fight between socialist road and capitalist road, remain to be the principal contradiction inside our country."[6] In this way, the correct judgment of the first meeting of the 8th National Congress on the principal contradiction of the Chinese society was officially changed, which was a major shift in the guiding idea of the Communist

[1] *Works of Mao Zedong*, Vol. 7, p 268, Beijing: Party Literature Press, 1999.

[2] *Biography of Mao Zedong (1949-1976)*, Vol., p 646.

[3] *Mao Zedong's Articles Since the Founding of P.R. China*, Vol. 6, p 548, Beijing: Party Literature Press, 1992.

[4] *Biography of Mao Zedong (1949-1976)*, Vol. 1, p 720.

[5] *Ibid*, p 719.

[6] *Selected Important Literature Since the Founding of P.R. China*, Vol. 11, p 288, Beijing: Party Literature Press, 1995.

Party of China. The meaning of the transitional phase was once again greatly changed, with the lower limit as that "before socialist society is established". At the 10th Plenary Session of the 8th Central Committee of the CPC in 1962, the meaning of the transitional phase concept was revised again and changed to "the whole historical period of capitalism transforming to communism." The communiqué of this session stated, "During the whole historical period of proletarian revolution and rule (which will take decades or longer time), class struggle between the proletarian and bourgeoisie exists, and the struggle between socialist and capitalist road exists." "The class struggle is complicated with twists and turns, and sometimes can be very acute. The class struggle will inevitably be reflected inside the Party. The pressure from imperialism outside the country and the influence of the bourgeoisie inside the country are the social root for revisionism inside the Party."[1] The statement on class struggle in the transitional phase in the communiqué basically formed a complete statement later known as the Principal Line of the Party in the whole historical period of socialism. A series of major events happened afterwards, including the debate between China and the Soviet Union, the socialist educational movement, as well as the Cultural Revolution, which were all extensions and development of this thought. Until the end of the Cultural Revolution, the historical positioning of Chinese socialism by Mao Zedong was not able to come back to the correct orbit. The understanding of socialism by the Chinese communists had hesitated between the abstract statements of classic authors and the reflections on their own experiences in the revolution period.

5.2 The Historical Re-Positioning of Socialism with Chinese Characteristics

In October 1978, the Cultural Revolution lasting for 10 years was ended.

---

[1] *Selected Important Literature Since the Founding of P.R. China*, Vol. 15, pp 653-654, Beijing: Party Literature Press, 1997.

In 1978, a discussion that "practice is the only benchmark to test the truth" had swept across the country. The long-confined thinking broke down the barriers of doctrines and swiftly awoke the energy and vitality of the whole nation. The discussion was both an ideological issue related to the attitude toward scientific socialism, and a political issue related to the future and the fate of the Party and the country. This discussion had created an enormous driving force for the complete and accurate understanding and application of Mao Zedong Thought, the liberation of thinking mode, for the practical and realistic evaluation of the work done, and for the rectification of all aspects of work in the country. It had also laid the ideological foundation for re-identifying the correct ideological line of Marxism at the 3rd Plenary Session of the 11th Central Committee of CPC, and created ideological conditions for the formation of theory of building socialism with Chinese characteristics. The 3rd Plenary Session of the 11th Central Committee of CPC held in December 1978 had marked a great historical turn in the Party's work. The Party re-defined the ideological line, political line and organizational line of Marxism and drew an end to the situation of hesitation between October 1976 and December 1978. The Party had started in a careful and comprehensive way to correct mistakes made during the Cultural Revolution and also the leftist mistakes before that period, and solved in a step-by-step manner many inherited problems since the founding of New China and other realistic issues, and direct the theoretical exploration of building socialism with Chinese characteristics back to the correct orbit. At the 12th National Congress of the Party in September 1982, Deng Xiaoping had pointed out: "Our modernization construction must start from the realities of China."[1] "Direct copy of experiences and patterns of other countries will never succeed. We had many lessons in the past. Our basic conclusion based on the long-term historical experiences is to combine the general truth of Marxism with China's actual conditions, to take our own road, and to build socialism with Chinese characteristics."[2] This was the first time Deng Xiaoping had

---

[1] *Works of Deng Xiaoping*, 1st Edition, Vol. 3, p 2.
[2] *Ibid*, pp 2-3.

explicitly raised the key preposition and basic theory of "building socialism with Chinese characteristics."

The 13th National Congress of the Party in October 1987 had summarized the experiences and lessons of building socialism with Chinese characteristics since reform and opening up was initiated, and further clarified the basic principles of economic development and reform of systems. It held high the great banner of socialism with Chinese characteristics, comprehensively elaborated the theory of the primary stage of socialism and promulgated the basic line of the Party. The theme of the report of the congress was "to march on the road of socialism with Chinese characteristic". The congress had announced that, "at the primary stage of socialism, the basic line of our party is to build socialism with Chinese characteristics that is, to lead and unite the people of all ethnic groups, to take economic development as the central task, to adhere to the Four Cardinal Principles and persevere in reform and opening up, to be self-reliant and to make arduous efforts in building China into a prosperous, democratic, and spiritually advanced socialist modernized country. The Four Cardinal Principles, to adhere to the socialist road, to adhere to democratic dictatorship of the people, to adhere to the leadership of the Communist Party of China, to adhere to Marxism, Leninism and Mao Zedong Thought are the very foundation for building our country. To adhere to the general line of reform and opening up is a new development of the line of the Party since the 3rd Plenary Session of the 11th Central Committee of the Communist Party of China, which endowed new updated contents for the Four Cardinal Principles. The two basic points: adhering to the Four Cardinal Principles and to reform and opening up are both interconnected and interdependent, and are unified in the practices of building socialism with Chinese characteristics.[1] This was the first time that the Party had raised the concept of "building socialism with Chinese characteristics" as the guiding idea and basic theory of the Party in an explicit way, and closely linked and unified the primary stage of socialism with the basic line of "one central

---

[1] *Selected Important Literature Since the 13th National Congress*, Vol. 1, p 15, Beijing: People's Press, 1991.

task and two basic points". It was also the first time that the 13th Congress outlined 12 key points of the theory of building socialism with Chinese characteristics and made it clear that this theory had given some initial answers to basic questions such as the stage, task, driving force, condition, layout and international environment of building Chinese socialism, and planned for the way of marching forward. The 13th National Congress also proposed the strategic goal of socialist modernization construction in China that could be taken in three steps: The first step was to have GNP doubled that of 1980 and have people adequately fed and clad. The second step was to have GNP doubled again by the end of the 20th century with people having a fairly comfortable living. The third step was to have GNP per capita reach the level of moderately developed countries by the middle of the 21st century, with people living a relatively affluent life and modernization tasks would be basically achieved.

Another important contribution of the 13th National Congress was its systematic elaboration of the theory of the primary stage of socialism. According to the theory, the primary stage of socialism in China does not refer to the initial stage that any country will have to go through for entering socialism, but refers to a specific stage China has to experience in building socialism in the context of backward productive forces and underdeveloped commodity economy. The period from the 1950s when China had basically completed socialist transformation with scarcity of means of production, to the basic realization of socialist modernization belongs to the primary stage of socialism, which will last for at least a hundred years. This stage differs from the transitional phase when socialist economic foundation has not been laid; it also differs from the phase when socialist modernization is realized. China previously was a large semi-colonial and semi-feudal society. Over the past hundred years since the mid-19th century, after the struggle of various political forces, after the many failures of old democratic revolution and the final victory of new democratic revolution, it was proven that capitalist road is not workable in China, and the only way is to overthrow the reactionary rule of imperialism, feudalism and bureaucratic capitalism under the leadership of the Communist Party, and to take socialist road. However, as

Chinese socialism was born in the semi-colonial and semi-feudal society, its productive forces lags far behind that of developed capitalist countries, which determines that China will have to undergo a rather long primary stage to realize industrialization, socialization and modernization of production that many other countries have realized under the conditions of capitalism. On the whole, the primary stage of socialism in China is a stage for China to gradually get rid of backwardness, a stage for an agricultural country based on the manual labor of the over-helming agricultural population to gradually change to a modernized industrial country with non-agricultural population becoming the majority, a stage to change the high proportion of natural and semi-natural economy into highly advanced commodity economy, a stage for the establishment and development through reform and exploration of socialist economic, political and cultural system that is full of vitality, a stage for the great revitalization of the Chinese nation through the endeavors and hard working of the Chinese people.

It is fair to say that the theory of the primary stage of socialism is a new kind of essential regression to the initial theory of new democratic society. The task of construction at the primary stage of socialism is what left over from the new democratic society and uncompleted in the transitional phase. The enormous change of the Chinese society brought about by socialist system must be mentioned, but the basic implications of the essential content of social construction have not been changed. Therefore, it can be said that this primary stage of socialism, not in the sense of time order, is a remedy for the gap of new democratic society. The connotation of theoretical regression is that for socialist theory, the theory of new democratic society is the only successful exploration of social construction that the communists of China can draw upon as their own. In terms of the thematic connotation of construction and the extension of construction, the connectivity of the two to certain extent surpasses the reference of revolutionary experiences. But the regression of the theory of the primary stage of socialism to the theory of new democratic society is not a historical retrogression, but rather a major progress of the theory of social construction of the Communist Party of

China. It is shown in the following aspects. First of all, as compared with that of the period of new democracy, the indexes and criteria of modernization given in the theory of the primary stage of socialism is more profound in understanding and bears more scientific expressions. Take industrialization as an example. Industrialization is the goal of new democratic society, the transitional phase as well as the primary stage of socialism. But for a long time, the understanding of industrialization is not comprehensive and had lagged behind understanding of the contemporary times. The standard of industrialization was inherited from that of the Soviet Union, namely, industrial product accounts for 70% of the gross product of both agriculture and industries. As a matter of fact, the result of industrialization of all advanced industrialized countries is that industrial and non-agricultural population account for the majority of the population, the proportion of agricultural population greatly decreases, and agricultural productive forces greatly improves. Meanwhile, contemporary industrialization is a dynamic domain, a process with ever improving and renewing technological level. The goal of industrialization must take the level reached by world modernization as its benchmark. But Chinese communists used to have a fuzzy understanding of the importance of world technological revolution waves, and had kept a static standard for the development of industrialization. Another example, the level of development of commodity economy and market economy is an important measure for a country's modernization. But there was no clear statement of commodity and market economy in the initial theory of new democratic society, and later all these was regarded as the synonym of capitalism and was denied. Practices show that if there is no sufficient development of commodity and market economy, it is not possible at all to break the enclosure status of natural and semi-natural economy. The theory of the primary stage of socialism has drawn upon experiences of construction practices and is able to become a new theoretical abstraction against the broad backdrop of world modernization, assessing the positive results of economic and political progress both at home and abroad. In the primary stage of socialism, the historical topic to be solved or answered by developing productive forces is to realize industrialization, socialization and modernization of production. On the one hand, it requires to promote the traditional type industrial revolution already completed by developing countries. On the other hand, it needs to target the goal of the development of world technological revolution. To this end, the reform of the parts not adaptable to the development of productive forces in the relations of production and superstructure should be realized, in order to establish a socialist economic, political and cultural system that is vigorous. Meanwhile, modernization of people is one of the key parts in the index of modernization. As a result, though "a prosperous, democratic, morally advanced socialist modernized country"[1] and "an independent, free, democratic, unified and prosperous new country"[2] do not have essential difference in the abstract sense, in terms of the richness and depth of their connotation, the former is endowed with content keeping up with the times that the latter one lacks it. Secondly, "What is socialism and how to build socialism is still being explored."[3] "We did not have a very clear understanding of this issue."[4] In the theories of new democratic society and the transitional phase, the understanding of socialism showed an idealistic coloring and a subjective bias, and this theoretical defect was more notably shown in a more extreme way. After the historical reflections and practices of reform, the understanding becomes much clearer and more mature. The theory of the primary stage of socialism has transcended the idealistic tendency of "the single unitary economic basis", and advocates that it is socialism as long as public ownership, then with a population of 600 million, it insists on the principle of distribution "to each according to work" as the main form of distribution. At the current stage, productive forces in China has some features: some modern industries co-exist with a large number of industries lagging behind modern standards in several decades or even a hundred years; some regions have advanced level of economies while there remain many regions that are less developed or poor; there are a few advanced technologies, but generally

---

[1] *Selected Important Literature Since the 13th National Congress*, Vol. 1, p 15.

[2] *Selected Works of Mao Zedong*, 2nd Edition, Vol. 3, p 1030.

[3] *Selected Works of Deng Xiaoping*, 1st Edition, Vol. 3, p 227.

[4] *Ibid*, p 63.

the level of technology is low, and illiteracy and semi-illiteracy still have a high proportion in the population. To adapt to this great variety of productive forces, the single rigid mode needs to be broken and the flexibility and variety of social structures need to be "resumed", in light of the successful experiences of new democratic society building. The resumption, in the ultimate analysis, is a result of the uneven development of productive forces. At the primary stage of socialism, the level of productive forces is still low, but the overall national conditions and its strength compared to the new democratic society are enormously far advanced. In the new democratic society, state-run economy took the lead but its predominance was far from established and private capitalism had not only existed, but was allowed to fully develop within certain limit. But at the primary stage of socialism, private and individually-owned economies are allowed to exist and develop, but private economy under socialist condition is not equal to the pure private economy in its nature. It is the product adaptive to the level of productive forces under the condition of socialism, and the intrinsic and inevitable element of the primary stage of socialism, instead of just what was inherited from the old society. Fundamentally the diagnosis that China is at the primary stage of socialism embodies two-tiered and two-aspect meanings: One is that the Chinese society is already a socialist one, and socialism must be adhered to. The other is that Chinese socialism is yet at the primary stage. Under the historical conditions of modern China, it is dogmatic not to recognize that China can embark on the road of socialism without experiencing the stage of full development of capitalism; it is utopian in terms of revolution and development to believe that the primary stage of socialism can be passed over without the enormous growth of productive forces.

To understand the historical stage of Chinese society in a correct way is the primary problem of building socialism with Chinese characteristics and the main basis on which to decide and implement correct policies. To build socialism in China, in a backward oriental country, is a new topic in the history of development of Marxism. What China faced was different from the ideas founders of Marxism who had predicted building socialism on the basis of highly developed capitalism, and it had also differed from the situation of other countries. An indiscriminate copy of theory or the experience of other countries would not work. The road of building socialism with Chinese characteristics should be opened in practice, from the perspective of China's actual conditions and by combining the basic theories of Marxism with China's conditions. On this particular issue, the Communist Party of China has made creative explorations and great achievement, and has experienced setbacks and paid huge costs. Since the late 1950s, as influenced by leftist thinking, Chinese communists had experienced the impatience for success and the blindness regarding the purity of social structure. It was believed that productive forces would be dramatically improved only by relying on revolutionary mass movements or solely out of good will, and it was believed that the form of socialist ownership should only be large and public. For a rather long time, CPC had put the task of developing productive forces to the inferior position, and insisted "taking class struggle as the key link" after the basic completion of socialist transformation. Many things restricting the development of productive forces and without considering the real essential nature of socialism, or many things which were only results and had accorded to some specific conditions in the history were taken as eternal correct things and were obeyed as the principles of socialism. Many things favorable to the development of productive forces and commodity economy, socialization and modernization of production under the condition of socialism were regarded as "capitalist restoration" and were opposed. The overly single and unitary ownership structure and the rigid economic system thus resulted, and the political system, linked to this economic system, with overly centralized power, had seriously restricted the development of productive forces. The new understanding on socialism was a crystallization of experiences of long-term exploration of socialism with Chinese characteristics, as well as a positive result of reform and opening up. As far as the historical positioning of socialism with Chinese characteristics is concerned, theory of new democratic society serves as the initial origin of theory of socialism with Chinese characteristics, which has been re-established on the basis of the theory of the primary stage of socialism and it was the continuation, development as well as improvement of the positive results of the initial theory of new democratic society.

If we say that "the theory of primary stage" had focused on identifying the historical position of socialism in China, then "the theory of Chinese characteristics" completes at two levels the theoretical positioning of Chinese socialism. One is that, the disconnection in principle of the practice and the abstraction embodied in "Chinese characteristics" is what between universality and particularity, and between individuality and commonness is in the philosophical sense. The other is that, the disconnection of unique significance embodied in "Chinese characteristics" and the theories and practices of other countries is what between particularity and particularity, and between individuality and individuality. With its profound culture, China is not a country whose destiny can possibly be controlled by an outside force, either materially or spiritually. But over a rather long period of time in modern history, the efforts of the Chinese people of getting rid of the control of external force had been greatly restricted. The reason for it was that the country was not interdependent, and there were continuous wars and various political forces that needed to rely on the strength of the others for survival and development. These political forces also needed to rely on different ideas to equip themselves. It was true for both anti-revolutionary and revolutionary forces. As a result, there appeared a conflict of control and anti-control, but this contradiction had a different form of expression in different periods or for different groups of people. For Chinese communists, their fight for independence was aimed against the Soviet Union, both in the period of revolution and construction, and theoretically it was aimed at Stalinism. That was the reason behind the rectification campaign started in Yan'an (1942 to 1945), and raising the Mao Zedong Thought banner. The essence of Mao Zedong Thought on the one hand is Marxism and Leninism, and on the other is a Chinese-style combination of Marxism and Leninism with Chinese realities. After Stalin passed away, Mao had asserted that a better road could be designed examining the Soviet Union as a mirror. But after many detours, China could not indeed step out of the shadow of Stalin.

Later there appeared the disputes with Khrushchev and essentially these were disputes and differences on the essential issue that what socialism is and how to build socialism. For Khrushchev, the Soviet road could fit all countries, and they should follow suit. Even if national realities were to be taken into consideration, some common principles still needed to be followed. For Mao Zedong, the Soviet way was not the best and China could find a better and faster way, as proven by the victory of Chinese revolution. Khrushchev criticized China for being dogmatic, and China criticized him as revisionist. Both sides believed the other was wrong and not adhering to Marxism and Leninism, and requested the other to rectify for not building socialism. The outcome was that the relationship between the two parties and the two countries was broken up. The theory of Chinese characteristics to a large extent took this lesson and avoided disputes with others. As Deng Xiaoping put it, "Whether the domestic policies of a party of a country are right or wrong is to be judged by the party and the people of that country. Only the people of the country can best understand its actual conditions."[1] "When a party comments on the rights and wrongs of parties of other countries, it usually bases on some existing formulas or fixed schemes. In fact, that is not workable."[2] "Even if the formulas are Marxist, when combined with the actual conditions of different countries, it is hard to avoid mistakes."[3] The disputes between the Soviet Union and China were firstly about the rights and wrongs between concrete practices and abstract principles, secondly about the rights and wrongs between concrete practices and concrete practices. As to the first aspect, Mao Zedong had done well during the period of revolution, but during the period of construction, he had sunk into the disputes with Khrushchev on abstract principles. Behind the disputes on principles were the disputes on practices: whether the principles had been adhered to or not by each side. Unconsciously Mao Zedong had become the defender of Stalinism in the disputes. In terms of the second aspect, it was the

---

[1] *Selected Works of Deng Xiaoping*, 2nd Edition, Vol. 2, p 318, Beijing: People's Press, 1994.
[2] *Selected Works of Deng Xiaoping*, 2nd Edition, Vol. 2, p 318, Beijing: People's Press, 1994.
[3] *Ibid.*

inevitable extension of the first aspect. The theory of Chinese characteristics of Deng Xiaoping follows the exploration which was uncompleted by Mao and progresses into a new stage. Historically, the significance of this new stage and new exploration is as great as Mao's exploration of the road of revolution unique for China. Deng's theory thoroughly separates the practices of building socialism in the contemporary China from the abstract theoretical principles. According to Deng, "We cannot require that Marx should provide ready-made answers to questions that appeared a hundred years or a few hundred years after his death. Similarly, Lenin could not complete the task of providing answers to questions that appeared 50 or 100 years after his death."[1] What he praised is to answer newly appeared questions under new situation through one's own practices, that is, "to say what was not articulated by our ancestors", but to speak "new words"[2]. Deng's theory also differentiates China from the Soviet Union and all other countries. He had believed that only its own people could understand better a country's conditions and could judge the rights and wrongs of the country, and people from other countries should not make indiscreet remarks. He acknowledged that China had made that kind of mistakes in the past. It is because of the basic positioning of Chinese characteristics, the historical positioning of primary stage had become possible. The primary stage itself is a concept with strong Chinese characteristics, and the theory of Chinese characteristics has the same philosophical basis as the theory of primary stage, that is, seeking truth from facts, and the theory of white and black cats. The best theory will not be counted as a good one if it cannot lead the people to a prosperous life. Whether the theory is good or not, the people have the final say. The rights or wrongs of other countries are to be judged by their own people. "Things in China should be tackled in line with China's conditions and rely on the strength of the Chinese people. To be independent and self-reliant was our foothold in the past, and it is now and will be the same in the future. The Chinese people cherish the friendship and cooperation with other countries

---

[1] *Selected Works of Deng Xiaoping*, 1ˢᵗ Edition, Vol. 3, p 291.

[2] *Ibid*, p 91.

and peoples, and we cherish more the right of independency and self-reliance we have secured through long-term efforts. No country should expect that China would be its appendage, or China would swallow the bitter fruit of infringing upon China's interests."[1]

The re-positioning of socialism with Chinese characteristics is the basic foothold of socialist modernization construction of China, and the starting point for various policies since reform and opening up. Over the past two decades, China has scored some achievements that attract the attention of the world, which shows that the policies and guidelines of the Party are correct, the direction and strategy of development are correct, and the re-positioning of socialism by the Party in the new historical period is accurate and realistic.

5.3 The Relation Between Socialist China and the Contemporary Capitalism

5.3.1 Socialist China is the criticizer of the contemporary capitalism.

The identified role of socialism has decided that it has a confrontational and negating relation with capitalism. Socialism is the response to the institutional deficiencies of capitalism, the opposite of capitalism and the inheritor of capitalist civilization. In essence, it falls into the domain of post-capitalism as an ideology, movement and social system that tries to apply measures of social adjustment and control in order to overcome the institutional deficiencies of capitalism, to the end of realizing social justice and achieving social progress and emancipating mankind. Heated struggle had existed between socialism and capitalism ever since socialism was born. The ultimate mission of socialism is to defeat, demolish and replace capitalist system. And capitalism does not ever forget to overthrow the new system that may bring it to an end. It intends to smother socialism in the cradle, imposes economic sanctions or military embargo, or urges socialism to "peacefully

---

[1] *Selected Works of Deng Xiaoping*, 1ˢᵗ Edition, Vol. 3, p 3.

evolve" into capitalism. The struggle between the two systems had never ceased ever since the first socialist country was born. Bolshevik forces in Russia encountered allied attack of 14 imperialist countries immediately after it was established. The revolutionary forces in Hungary and Germany was nipped in bud. Later the Soviet Union was embargoed, while Cuba and Vietnam were attacked militarily. By the late 1980s and early 1990s, socialist forces of the Soviet Union and Eastern European countries were "evolved peacefully". Though this peaceful evolution was much related to mistakes made by the ruling communist parties in polices, international capitalist forces had contributed to that process. China has chosen socialist system. As a socialist country, China inevitably criticizes and denies capitalist system, in terms of the following aspects: Firstly, "only socialism can save China, and only socialism can develop China."[1] This has been the basic fact in the modern history of China. China was a semi-colonial and semi-feudal society. In more than a hundred years since the mid-19th century, various political forces fought each other. The choice of capitalist road in China was proven as failure after many rounds of failure of old type democratic revolution and the final victory of new democratic revolution. "The civilization of Western bourgeoisie, democracy of bourgeoisie and the solution of a bourgeoisie republic went bankrupt in the mind of Chinese people."[2] The only way out was to overthrow the counter-revolutionary rule of imperialism, feudalism and bureaucratic capitalism under the leadership of the Communist Party and take the road of socialism. "Capitalist democracy gives way to people's democracy, and the capitalist republic gives way to people's republic. As a result, it will become possible that through the people's republic, socialism and communism can be realized, and classes demolished, the great harmony of the world achieved."[3] Secondly, in the modern history, the colonial expansion of capitalism had brought about disasters to the Chinese people. Emotionally the Chinese people had an instinctive dislike, hatred and repulsiveness toward capitalism. The backward China had its door forcedly

---

[1] *Selected Works of Deng Xiaoping*, 1ˢᵗ Edition, Vol. 3, p 331.
[2] *Selected Works of Mao Zedong*, 2ⁿᵈ Edition, Vol. 4, p 1471.
[3] *Selected Works of Mao Zedong*, 2ⁿᵈ Edition, Vol. 4, p 1471.

opened by the weapons of Western imperial forces and Chinese people in turn started to learn from the West. But "the imperialist aggression broke the dream of the Chinese to learn from the West", because "though the Chinese learned much from the West, what they learned did not work. Chinese people could not have their ideal realized." "The teachers used to commit aggression against the students."[1] These are facts in the history. Eventually, the Chinese discarded the road of capitalism and chose the direction of socialism. In 1949, the Chinese people had stood up, which is an undisputable fact. In comparing what had happened in history, the Chinese people have a distinct judgment as to which is better between socialism and capitalism. Thirdly, capitalism will inevitably demise and socialism will win the victory in terms of the laws of social development. For China, socialism was built in a backward and large oriental country. Over a few decades of practices, China paid heavy cost and was brought to understand a basic Marxist idea, that is, "no social order ever perishes before all the productive forces for which there is room in it have developed; and new, higher relations of production never appear before the material conditions of their existence have matured in the womb of the old society itself"[2], But, "socialism will inevitably replace capitalism after a long process of development, which is a general trend of social development,"[3] and the basic rule for the historical development of mankind. Chinese people believe that only socialism can save China and develop China, and has set forth the idea that to stick to Four Cardinal Principles with "adhering to the road of socialism" as the first one.

The socialist role of China determines the position of international anti-socialist forces that they never forget to deploy any possible means to promote peaceful evolution of China, and China never forgets the threat of capitalism aiming her survival. To change the social system of socialist countries and to resume the rule of the world by capitalism is the consistent strategy of capitalist countries in the West. To this end, they have used

[1] *Selected Works of Mao Zedong*, 2nd Edition, Vol. 4, p 1470.
[2] *Selected Works of Marx and Engels*, 2nd Edition, Vol. 2, p 33, Beijing: People's Press, 1994.
[3] *Selected Works of Deng Xiaoping*, 1st Edition, Vol. 3, pp 382-383.

military intervention, economic embargo, as well as "peaceful evolution". After the People's Republic of China was founded in 1949, international anti-socialist forces started to regard New China as one of the major threats to "a free world". On the eve of the founding of the People's Republic of China, Dean Acheson, the then Secretary of State of the United States, lamented, "The unfortunate but inescapable fact is that the ominous result of the civil war in China was beyond the control of the government of the United States.... Nothing that was left undone by this country has contributed to it. It was the product of Chinese internal forces, forces which this country tried to influence but could not."[1] To handle with the upcoming "threat", Acheson put forth very clearly a view, that was, to deploy non-military and peaceful means to influence the elements, nature, domestic and foreign policies of the Communist Party of China, to urge CPC to give up its aspiration of communism, in particular to distract China off the Soviet policies, and eventually to include China into the world capitalist bloc. This was the most original, most direct, most concentrated, most authoritative and most explicit statement of the United States' official policies of promoting "peaceful evolution" of New China.[2] On January 5, 1953, in his testimony at the Capitol Hill, Dulles had made it clear that, to deal with socialist countries, "more forceful and more active policy has to be adopted", "which must be and possibly be a peaceful way."[3] Dulles had proposed a long-term plan for putting the hope of "peaceful evolution" on the third or fourth generation of leaders of the Communist Party of China. Ever since, "peaceful evolution" became a basic tenet of United States government toward the Soviet Union, the Eastern European countries, as well as socialist China. According to Holmes, former Secretary of State of Foreign and Commonwealth Affairs, "in the long run, defeating the communist road lies in infiltration of our

---

[1] Quoted from *Selected Works of Mao Zedong*, 2nd Edition, Vol. 4, p 1486.

[2] Lin Limin, "Ancheson, Dulas and the Origin of American's Peaceful Evolution Policies on China", *Journal of Party History Research Documents*, 2001 (3).

[3] Quoted from Wu Renzhang, *The Dramatic Changes in the Soviet Union and Eastern Europe and Marxism*, p 200, Beijing: World Affairs Press, 1998.

ideas into communist countries."[1] The development of globalization, the dissolution of Cold War pattern and the efforts of China in merging with the world cannot alter the strategy of "peaceful evolution" of capitalist countries. On this point Deng Xiaoping was much concerned: "It may well be that one cold war is ended, and two others may start. One is aimed at the south, the Third World. The other is aimed at socialism. Western countries are fighting the Third World War without the smoke of gunpowder. By without the smoke of gunpowder, I mean the peaceful evolution of socialist countries."[2] He warned for several times that imperialism puts its hope of peaceful evolution on our later generations. "The policies of developed countries insulting the backward countries do not change. China must hold steady to its faith, otherwise we will be targeted."[3] On this issue, Jiang Zemin had also clearly noted, "China is now the biggest socialist country in the world, with growing strength. The Western hostile forces have stepped up their political strategy of 'Westernization' and 'split apart' in China through various means and ways. They intend to overthrow the leadership of the Communist Party of China and socialist system in China. Their political intention never changes." "The fight between China and hostile forces both at home and abroad in terms of infiltration and anti-infiltration, overthrow and anti-overthrow will last long and be complicated."[4]

5.3.2 Socialist China is the rival of the contemporary capitalism.

After repeated hot wars and the long confrontation of the Cold War, despite the dramatic changes of the Soviet Union and Eastern Europe, there remains an undisputable fact in the contemporary world: for a long time to come, socialism and capitalism will not be able to defeat and destroy each other and the two systems will co-exist for the foreseeable future. Socialist China must learn to deal with the capitalist world in developing normal economic and trade relations, as well as political, military and cultural

[1] Quoted from Wu Renzhang, p 202.
[2] *Selected Works of Deng Xiaoping*, 1ˢᵗ Edition, Vol. 3, p 344.
[3] *Ibid*, p 319.
[4] Jiang Zemin, *On the Three Represents*, p 61, Beijing: Party Literature Press, 2001.

exchanges and collaboration. It is a relationship of peaceful co-existence, collaboration and exchange, and peaceful competition.[1] The status of peaceful co-existence of the two systems was displayed soon after the birth of socialism. As the efforts of international imperialism using military force to overthrow the Soviet Union were frustrated, a very fragile and unstable status, though on the whole an equilibrium, was formed. Socialist republic could not survive under the enclosure of capitalism, and the enclosure could not also continue long. Imperialism was much stronger than Soviet Russia, but unable to abort it. Imperialism had to acknowledge it or partly acknowledge it and needed to have economic, political and cultural relations with it. Meanwhile, for Soviet Russia, "it was not possible for a socialist republic to survive if it did not have any relation with the world." "The survival of the country should be connected with the relation of capitalism."[2] Countries of two different systems have common economic interests, the basis for establishing normal relationship between countries and for peaceful co-existence. As Lenin put it, "There is a force surpassing the wishes, will and decision of any hostile government or class. This force is the economic relationship common to the whole world. It was this relationship that forced them to take the road of communicating and exchanging with us."[3] "If we do not have certain interrelations with capitalist countries, we will not possibly have any stable economic relations. The situation clearly shows that capitalist countries will not possibly have stable economic relations either."[4] Gradually, peaceful co-existence, cooperation and exchange had become a basic pattern of the relationship between the two systems. Both sides tried for several times to break this balance, but eventually had to acknowledge this balance as a win-win choice, the best choice so far available.

After the founding of the People's Republic of China, the Five Principles of Peaceful Co-existence were set forth. But over a long time, limited by the overall international situation and China's foreign strategies, China was

---

[1] Quoted from Wu Renzhang, *The Dramatic Changes in the Soviet Union and East Europe and Marxism*, p 202.

[2] *Complete Works of Lenin*, 2nd Chinese Edition, Vol. 41, p 167, Beijing: People's Press, 1986.

[3] *Complete Works of Lenin*, 2nd Chinese Edition, Vol. 42, p 332, Beijing: People's Press, 1987.

[4] *Ibid*, p 328.

in a serious Cold War confrontation with the capitalist world, in particular, with the developed countries in the West. Chinese leaders had believed that as long as imperialism existed, war could not be avoided. "Only by relying on the mass and waging a tit-for-tat struggle against policies of aggression and war of imperialism, can peace be effectively protected." As a result, at the same time of stressing and supporting the revolutionary struggle against imperialism and capitalism by the peoples in the world, China also based itself upon some strategic notions of waging wars early, waging big wars and nuclear war. Under the conditions of serious hostility, capitalist countries in the West had exercised military embargoes and economic sanctions on China, and in turn China had carried out revolutionary foreign policies and practiced a highly closed pattern of development, and held an extreme repelling and hostile attitudes toward capitalism. Unconsciously, China had stepped into a blind alley of self-enclosure from being embargoed. Deng Xiaoping noted when reflecting on this part of history, "The world now is an open one. China lagged behind since the industrial revolution in the West. After the founding of New China, we were embargoed, and to some extent we remained to be closed. This was one of the key reasons that China closed itself to international exchanges"[1] "Since the founding of New China, for a long time, we remained in a state of separation from the world. The separation was not due to China for some time, and it was because of international forces against China and against Chinese socialism that China was forced to be separated and isolated. Since the 1960s, we were in the position to strengthen exchanges and cooperation with the international community, but instead we had isolated ourselves."[2] Facts showed that though there were some achievements, "there was not much progress on the whole"[3] to construct the country with its door closed. It was during the late 1960s and the 1970s that the gap between China and the world was rapidly widened. That decade had witnessed booming development of the world. The economic and technological progress was not calculated on a yearly basis, not on a monthly

---

[1] *Selected Works of Deng Xiaoping*, 1st Edition, Vol. 3, p 64.

[2] *Selected Works of Deng Xiaoping*, 2nd Edition, Vol. 2, p 232.

[3] *Selected Works of Deng Xiaoping*, 1st Edition, Vol. 3, p 90.

basis, but on a daily basis. But China at that time was immersed in its own dream. Experiences have proven that "to construct the country with its door closed will not bring success. China's development is not isolated from the world.[1] After the 3rd Plenary Session of the 11th Central Committee of the Communist Party of China in 1978, the views on war, on international situation and on capitalism were gradually adjusted, and opening up to the outside world was taken as a basic strategy of social development. China opened up not only to socialist countries and to developing countries, but also to developed capitalist countries. In an open world, to have economic, cultural and even political cooperation with capitalist countries, the basic prerequisite is to accept the possibility of peaceful co-existence and mutual development of these two systems. On the basis of summarizing the experiences and lessons in dealing with the capitalist world, Deng had stressed that no matter what changes international situation might bring, the international community should advocate the five principles of peaceful co-existence, and take these principles as benchmark in handling international relations. Countries with different social systems and ideologies will co-exist in the world for a long time to come, which is an objective reality. In order to maintain the world peace and stability, relations between countries shall be developed in the spirit of the five principles of peaceful co-existence. "When China observes the relations between countries, it does not do so from the perspective of social system"[2], but "questions are viewed and answers are given with China's national interests as the supreme benchmark."[3]

However, socialism and capitalism are two different social systems and ideologies. The peaceful co-existence, cooperation and exchanges will not disguise the struggle between them as to which is better. In the context of peaceful co-existence, the struggle as to which is better turns from military contest at battlefields to competition of economic strength, cultural attractiveness and other national capabilities, which is a peaceful competition

[1] *Selected Works of Deng Xiaoping*, 1st Edition, Vol. 3, p 78.
[2] *Ibid.*
[3] *Ibid*, p 330.

that will last long. The history of the relations of the two systems teaches that, within a short run it is neither realistic nor possible that any one of the two will replace and defeat the other, whatsoever means and measures are taken. Due to the fact that socialist system was first established in backward countries determines that socialist countries will have to spend a rather long time to get rid of their backwardness, before people start to consider which is better as compared to capitalism. Out of this consideration, Deng pointed out, "To build socialism, productive forces must grow advanced. Poverty is not socialism. For us, in order to insist on socialism and to build socialism which is superior to capitalism, we must get rid of poverty. Though we are building socialism now, actually we are not yet qualified."[1] This understanding is the cornerstone to identify the theory of the primary stage of socialism. In the process of peaceful competition with contemporary capitalism, China should not try to tell capitalism that China's system is superior, but should develop productive forces in a sound way, develop socialist democracy and improve the living standard of its people. On the one hand, China should have confidence in the future of socialism and insist that only socialism is the way for China, not capitalism. On the other hand, China must follow the guideline of seeking for the truth and being practical and focus on construction and devote herself to development. As long as the socialist banner of China is held high, and as long as China stands firm and achieves its goal of development, socialism will show its superiority. Reform in China is an experiment both in China and for the world. As long as China stands firm, there will be at least 1/5 of the world population that adhere to socialist road, and socialism will stand firm in the world and have great influence internationally. "This not only opens a road for the Third World which has three quarters of the world population, and more importantly, it shows to mankind that socialism is the only way and is superior to capitalism."[2]

---

[1] *Selected Works of Deng Xiaoping*, 1ˢᵗ Edition, Vol. 3, p 225.

[2] *Ibid.*

5.3.3 Socialist China is the learner of contemporary capitalism.

In terms of historical logic, socialism is the negation of capitalism and the natural inheritor of all the excellent achievements of capitalism. The fact that socialist system was first born in backward countries decided that for a long time socialism should constantly learn from capitalism for its advanced technology and managerial expertise. Between it and capitalism is a relation between the forerunner and later comer of modernization. As one of the forefathers of Soviet Russian socialism, Lenin came to have a very clear understanding of this point soon after the Soviet Union was founded. He emphasized that all the things having true scientific value developed in Europe and America should be absorbed. He suggested that some knowledgeable and reliable people should be dispatched to Germany, United States, United Kingdom and Canada, to study advanced technologies and managerial issues. He believed that "it is good to absorb good and useful things of other countries: Soviet political forces + Prussian management order of railways + technology and trusts in the United Sates + national education of the United States + … + … = total sum = socialism."[1] "Whether socialism can be realized is decided by how well the Soviet forces and administration organization is combined with the latest and the advanced components of capitalism."[2] Lenin pointed out that, we could not imagine there is other kind of socialism apart from the socialism with all the experiences obtained with the huge capitalist culture as the basis. However, Stalin to some extent noticed this issue, but his understanding was limited by the theory of two parallel and confrontational world markets (he was also the initiator of this theory), thus Soviet Union became more conservative in learning from the advanced experiences of capitalism. Leaders after Stalin also refused to open up and reform, and continued to be closed and refused to introduce advanced technological achievements and managerial expertise, even when technological revolution boomed in the West and the Soviet productive forces

---

[1] *Complete Works of Lenin*, 2nd Chinese Edition, Vol. 34, p 520, Beijing: People's Press, 1985.
[2] *Ibid*, pp 170-171.

lagged behind. This was one of the important reasons of the Soviet failure in the competition with the West, in particular, with the United States.

Chinese socialism evolved from a semi-colonial and semi-feudal society with its level of productive forces lagging far behind that of capitalist countries. As afore-mentioned, that is the real basis for the theory of the primary stage of socialism. For the whole period of primary stage of socialism and even longer time to come, China will be in the status of catching up with developed countries. Learning and borrowing economic, technological and managerial experiences from developed capitalist countries thus becomes one of the important contents of China's reform and opening up. In the future when China will be developed, learning from others will remain as a norm of social development and progress.

Upon entering the socialist period, Mao Zedong had a very clear understanding, "Strengths of all nations and countries should be learned, and anything that is genuinely good, political, economic, scientific, technological, literature and arts, should be learned."[1] "Any corrupt systems and ideas of the bourgeoisie in other countries should be resisted and criticized. But this should not hinder us from learning the advanced technologies and scientific aspects in business management."[2] Facing up to the realities after China completed socialist transformation, Mao Zedong once had doubted that and said, "The new economic policies (NEP) of Russia had ended too early. The retreat only took two years before turning into attack. By far social material resources were not sufficient." He then proposed an idea that "capitalism could be built even after it was demolished."[3] It is fair to say that the above-mentioned understandings of Mao Zedong were profound and far-sighted; unfortunately they were not adhered to. Later on, leftist ideas got the upper hand. In terms of the relations with capitalism, China had implemented polices of "cutting the tails of capitalism", and had criticized "worshipping and having faith in things foreign", "slavish mentality for foreign things", and "ideas that betray China". As a result, many things under the condition of socialism that could be well favorable to the development of

---

[1] *Works of Mao Zedong*, Vol. 7, p 41.

[2] *Ibid* , p 43.

[3] *Ibid,* p 170.

productive forces, commodity economy, market-orientation, socialization and modernization of production were regarded as "capitalist restoration" and were opposed. But as practices have shown, a country cannot be developed with its doors closed and when it is complacent and conservative. It is unwise not to learn or borrow all the civilized achievements of mankind.

After the 3rd Plenary Session of the 11th Central Committee of the Communist Party of China, the re-positioning of the primary stage of socialism was gradually developed and the strategy of reform and opening up was identified. In this context, the relations between China and the contemporary capitalism had correspondingly changed. Opening up is to all the nations in the world, including developed capitalist countries. Opening up is not only in economic sphere, but also in various areas such as science, technology, education and culture. Opening up is to actively expand international exchanges and cooperation on the basis of equality and mutual benefit, to fully use two markets, two resources both at home and internationally, to improve resource allocation and economic benefits, to give play the comparative advantages of China's economy, to speed up economic growth in China, to actively participate in international economic cooperation and competition, to develop external-oriented economy, to connect and mutually complement China's economy with international economy, and to improve China's international competitiveness. The essential objective of opening up is to create higher productive forces on the basis of learning and absorbing all the achievements of mankind. Deng Xiaoping had asserted that: "To win advantage over capitalism, socialism must absorb and draw upon all the achievements created by mankind in a bold manner, and all the advanced operation and management methods reflecting the rules of modern and socialized production of all countries in the world, including developed capitalist countries."[1] In this way, "our system will improve on a daily basis. It will absorb all the progressive elements that we can absorb from all countries and become the best system in the world."[2]

---

[1] *Works of Deng Xiaoping*, 1st Edition, Vol. 3, p 373.
[2] *Works of Deng Xiaoping*, 2nd Edition, Vol. 2, p 337.

China's Foreign Strategy and Prospects on the Relations of Two Systems in the Age of Globalization

Globalization is both an objective process and a trend of development. Accepted or not, globalization has merciless impact on the process of world history and no doubt that of China. Globalization in the 21st century will be containing many layers and domains, and enjoy a broad scope and high speed. For China, a correct assessment of the opportunities and challenges is an important prerequisite to utilize advantages and avoid disadvantages, and formulate an appropriate national strategy. To face the opportunities and challenges of globalization, China should make appropriate strategic options, actively participate in and respond to globalization, thus take initiative for self development and open up a bright future in her socialist development.

6.1　Opportunities Brought to the Development of China by Globalization

In her modern history, regretfully China had missed many opportunities of development. However, today globalization provides an important opportunity for her economic growth, political progress and cultural prosperity. After introducing the grand policy of reform and opening up, the Communist Party of China has profoundly summarized the past experience of China's closed-door policies and has regarded opening up as one of the long-term basic national policies, and stressed that the policy of reform and opening up need not to be changed in the future for at least hundred years. China has developed ever closer links and continues integrating into the world economic system, which provides important conditions for China to utilize the opportunities brought by globalization.

6.1.1　Globalization brings opportunities for Chinese economic growth.

First of all, China should seize more opportunities to obtain those external elements she lacks. Economic globalization means massive cross-border movement of various productive elements such as commodities, services and many more. The proportion of these elements in different countries varies a lot. Some elements are rich and some are scarce. When a country lacks some key elements of production, it needs to get them from outside. The basic conditions of China can be assessed as follows: China has rich labor resources which account for 1/4 of the world; but China has scarce natural resources and agricultural land, and her oil and gas reserves per capita are far lower than world average; China is short of capital, and the volume of domestic investment only makes about 6% of the total volume of investment in the world. Only when labor combines with certain amount of capital, can it get employment opportunity and contribute to economic growth. Therefore, China needs not only to import resources, but should also utilize foreign capitals. As economic globalization proceeds and global movement of productive elements speeds up, China may seize more opportunities to use external productive elements such as capital, technology, managerial expertise, and talents. Some Western scholars have also noted that foreign investment, combining with labor-intensive industries, has enabled rapid growth of Chinese economy. China increasingly welcomes foreign investment, as it is generally accompanied by advanced technology, managerial expertise and skills, and other such facilities, which greatly enhance the increase of production and efficiency of her economic sectors.[1] After joining World Trade Organization, China has strictly abided by her commitments, continued to improve the environment for investment and provided more favorable investment conditions for transnational corporations. As a result, China has attracted more investments. Take Jiangsu Province as an example. In 2001, the average contract value per project by transnational corporations was 21 million US dollars, much higher than 13.8 million US dollars in 1994. The number of projects with total investment contract values above 100 million US dollars, and above 50 million has remarkably increased, and so have package cooperation and affiliated investment across sectors. For instance, Phillips, the Dutch giant, has invested in 10 projects in Jiangsu, mostly in electronic industry, and its aggregate investment volume had surpassed 200 million US dollars. This trend provides precious opportunities for China to attract more foreign capital, technologies and managerial expertise.

Secondly, globalization delivers a significant growth effect on China's economy. The most direct benefit of economic globalization for China is the reduction of custom tariffs and trade barriers, and thus growth of commodity exports. Economic globalization also promotes upgrading of industrial structure sustainable growth of economy, and facilitates obtaining scarce productive elements from other countries, in particular, foreign capital. According to Kondratieff's theory on 50 years' long economic cycles, the rising period of the fifth long wave cycle of world economic development

---

[1] Paul M. Augimeri, "The Effects of Globalization on China, a Developing, Newly Industrialized Economy", *Ecodate*, March 2001, Vol. 15, Issue 1.

has started in 1993 or 1994, which may last until about 2015. At the time when this book was edited, world economy was in the middle stage of the rising period of that fifth cycle. Just at this time, China substantially reformed her economic system, adopted market economy and basically completed integration with the world economy. China's timely participation in economic globalization has enabled China to join the ascending trend in the world economy and thus grow with this general trend.[1] The economies in the 21st century will witness two fundamental changes. One is the shift from industrial economy to a knowledge economy in developed countries, and secondly a shift from agricultural economy to industrial economy in developing countries. On the whole, the Chinese economy is in the early and middle stage of industrialization. At this stage, industrialization will be completed, and China's economy will enter the stage of information and knowledge economy. Today's take-off stage of Chinese economy is closely linked with the shift in the world from industrial economy to an information-based one. The structural adjustment—the shift of industrial focus and the development of information technologies—provide China an important opportunity to enter into the new age of economy. Thus China is able to transplant the extension of industrial chain, and at the same time catches up the wave of informationization and fully enjoys the benefits of the growth of world economy. Seizing this opportunity to guide industrialization process with the advantages of informationization forms China's recent basic strategy.

Thirdly, with the globalization trend China becomes "a central manufacturing house" of the world. Thus China utilizes many advantages of her: First, it has low-cost labor force, the most prominent one among its advantages. Second, the qualities of labor force keep improving. With the popularity of nine-year compulsory education in China, the basic workers are better educated. At the same time, the number of college graduates there is rapidly growing. In 2001 the number was 1.17 million, and 3.4 million in 2005 respectively. Thirdly, bottlenecks in infrastructure are basically

---

[1] Zhao Ziwen, "Globalization Process in the 21st Century and the Historical Opportunity for China", *Journal of International Business Research*, 2005 (1).

bygone. Today, industries such as energy, transportation, telecommunication, engineering, construction and equipment installation are able to provide sufficient support for manufacturing. Due to these achievements, capital from other countries continuously come into China; and on the other side the investment of large transnational corporations enables the improvement of the level of manufacturing in China in terms of technology, equipment, production and management. The combination of China's human resources advantage with the advantage of capital and technology of transnational corporations results in huge comparative advantage and brings the best possible efficiency of resource allocation between developed and developing countries. China has the biggest potential market, and the enormous potential brought by the rapid rise of Chinese economy is being tapped. The first half of the 21st century is a period for China to build a moderately prosperous society that will benefit more than one billion population, and the market potential can well be anticipated. As many comment, China has unique advantages of growing into a world centre of manufacturing. The first 20 years of the 21st century will possibly be the cluster period during which international capital moves to China.[1]

Fourthly, globalization enhances the improvement of market economic system and facilitates radical transformation of economic growth modal. Sustainable growth is a common strategy of both developed and developing countries in coordinating the relations of population, resources, environment and economy. It is the only way for the survival and development of mankind. In terms of economic growth and sustainable development of the environment and resources, economic growth should be shifted from extensive-oriented to intensive-oriented mode. Globalization provides opportunities for changing the mode of economic growth. Economic system and the mode growth are the carriers and forms of resource allocation and directly affect the efficiency and improve resource allocation. In the process of globalization, while resources choose the best location to be allocated,

---

[1] Zhao Ziwen, "Globalization Process in the 21st Century and the Historical Opportunity for China", *Journal of International Business Research*, 2005 (1).

they also choose the best carrier and form. The level of marketization in China is still low; market economy is not mature enough; market economic system is not well developed; the mode of intensive-oriented growth with high consumption, heavy pollution and low proficiency has not been radically changed. All these are extremely unfavorable for China to become the world centre of manufacturing and to the sustainable social and economic growth after that. The more China participates in globalization, the greater external pressure and internal motivation there are on the two radical changes in China. China will be forced to choose the newly industrialized road with less energy consumption, less pollution and high proficiency.[1]

6.1.2 Globalization promotes the political development in China.

Since the 1990s, globalization has speeded up and become the irreversible objective trend of world economy and international relations. When globalization removes national boundaries and requires a new interpretation of concepts such as sovereignty, independence, human rights and civil society, globalization enhances not only economic, trade and financial exchanges, but also political and cultural relations and exchanges.[2] Phenomena such as cultural infiltration, value changes and system transplantation accompany the process of economic globalization. Obviously economic globalization inevitably raises corresponding political requirement. For China, globalization is an unavoidable reality. Reform and opening up can be regarded as a positive response of China to this growing trend. The political appeal brought along by globalization will exert remarkable influence on the goal, value orientation and strategic choice of political development in China. Research shows that China's "opening up policies not only achieved extraordinary economic success and drove the growth of domestic economy, but also motivated the support for reform from key departments and regions. For this reason, in the following 15 years, despite

---

[1] Zhao Ziwen, "Globalization Process in the 21st Century and the Historical Opportunity for China", *Journal of International Business Research*, 2005 (1).

[2] Mikhail Titarenko, "China and Globalization", *Far Eastern Affairs*, 2003, Vol. 31, Issue 4.

resistances, China's reform was able to continue."[1] It is fair to say that globalization enhances the process of political development in China.

First of all, globalization promotes the process of democratization in China. Indirectly or directly, globalization urges countries to participate in international economic life to establish a set of more democratic and effective political system in order to ensure a stable and peaceful environment for economic development, and to ensure people to enjoy increased economic benefits as well as political benefits.[2] With deepening reform and opening up and economic integrating into the process of globalization, Chinese government formulates many measures corresponding to international trend to facilitate integration to international economic practices. Economic globalization brings about profound changes in domestic economic and social structure, and increases the differentiation of social stratums. As a result, social interests gradually become diversified and distinct. Economic globalization intensifies the complexity and difficulties in decision-making, and no decision can be made only through relying on the knowledge, experience and talent of just a small number of people. Similarly, it becomes difficult for a small number of people to make comprehensive forecast and summary of the outcome of decision. Decisions will be feasible and accurate only when decision-making becomes more scientific and democratic, and major errors in decision-making can be avoided.

Secondly, globalization promotes the process of rule of law in China. Economic globalization raises many political and legal issues on a global scope, such as international business and trade, market access, securities and futures, business taxation, information exchange, environmental protection, population and immigration, international crimes, etc. To have international cooperation in these aspects, China has to speed up its connection with

---

[1] Robert Keohane, Helen Milner, *Internationalization and Domestic Politics*, p 199, Beijing: Peking University Press, 2003.

[2] Yu Keping, *Globalization and Political Development*, p 25, Beijing: Social Sciences Literature Press, 2003.

the world in laws and regulations in various spheres. As a result, legal construction in China will be profoundly influenced. In the backdrop of globalization, legislature departments in China must further change their mentalities to learn more and draw upon experiences of other countries, and to improve the standard of legislation. At the same time, organizations and individuals in China must voluntarily improve their awareness of abiding by laws and regulations, as well as rules of the international community.

Thirdly, globalization promotes governmental reform in China. Economic globalization requires that China in the stage of institutional transformation break off the limit of the old system and integrate into the process of economic globalization. To share more the benefit brought about by economic globalization, China took the initiative to make the major strategic choice of joining in World Trade Organization. Transparency is one of the basic principles of WTO and the basic request for modern democratic politics. China's accession to WTO objectively raises a higher requirement for the political openness and transparency of the Chinese government.[1] Strengthening the restriction on governmental behaviors is another basic request of WTO from its member states, and also an important feature of modern democracy. China's accession to WTO also objectively raises a higher requirement for the Chinese government to improve its behaviors in legal and institutional spheres.[2] Generally speaking, similar to other developing countries, the lack of competitive technologies and high-tech products in China is largely due to the insufficient supply of soft technology and soft environment.[3] The process of integrating in globalization is necessarily a process of improving soft technology and soft environment in China, the key link of it is to continuously push forward the reform of

---

[1] Liu Dexi, *WTO and Sovereignty*, p 299, Beijing: People's Press, 2003.

[2] *Ibid*, p 303.

[3] Jin Zhouying, "Globalization, Technological Competitiveness and the 'Catch-Up' Challenge for Developing Countries: Some Lessons of Experience", *International Journal of Technology Management & Sustainable Development*, 2005, Vol. 4, Issue 1.

administrative system of the government.

6.1.3 The role of globalization in promoting cultural development in China

Culture is the crystallization of human civilization and penetrates every area of social life. Culture has an irreplaceable role in establishing a correct world view, view on life, view on history and values. Globalization provides a strong driving force to speed up the cultural merger of different countries, regions and nations, provides historical opportunity for exchanges and mergers of cultures, and promotes the development of Chinese culture.

First of all, globalization enriches cultural life in China and increases the dynamism of Chinese culture. The global movement of commodities and production factors (including labor force) is an economic phenomenon, but it embodies and brings along many cultural elements, reflecting values of consumption, lifestyles as well as cultural significance. The inflow of commodities and production elements to China enables the Chinese to have greater choices of consumption and to know the styles and cultures of different nations in the world. On the other hand, globalization speeds up the exchanges between cultures, and enables more contents to infuse between cultures. In the diversified world cultures, only through clashes, exchanges and mergers with other cultures, can Chinese culture display its unique charm, gain greater dynamic and get a better reception from rest of the world. Whether it is exchange or merger, it is no longer simple a "transplantation" or an "assimilation", but a creation of a more brilliant new Chinese culture keeping up with the contemporary age.[1] In this way, Chinese culture will not lose its uniqueness. Mao Zedong had once elaborated the relations of absorbing excellent foreign cultures and developing China's own national culture, taking music as an example. "Do not be afraid to play some foreign

---

[1] Li Chunyu, "On Economic Globalization and Cultural Diversity", *Journal of Business Economics*, 2004 (11).

music. In history, in the nine-piece music and ten-piece music in the Sui and Dang dynasties, most were music pieces from the West regions, and some were Korean and Indian music. Playing foreign music will not degrade our own music, and it will continue to develop. We can digest foreign music and absorb what is good in it, which is favorable to us."[1] "We accept the strengths of foreign countries, which will enable our things to grow remarkably."[2] American scholar Peter Berger notes, "The global culture is accepted but with significant local modifications." Globalization no doubt will create some conditions for the development of Chinese culture.

Secondly, globalization enhances the prosperity and development of cultural undertaking in China. To adapt economic globalization and merge in the world economic system, China had needed to reform its old system of planned economy and establish a new socialist market economy system. The historical changes will generate significant influence on Chinese culture. As globalization proceeds and reforms in economic and cultural systems deepen, cultural undertakings in China shows unprecedented prosperity. At the end of 2004, there were 2,599 performing art groups in China, 2,858 cultural venues, 2,710 public libraries, 1,509 museums, 282 radio stations, 314 TV stations, 60 educational stations. There were 114.70 million households as cable TV users. There were 30 cities with digital TV business with 1.22 million households as users. Radio coverage reached 94.1%, and TV coverage was 95.3%. In 2004, 212 feature movies, 44 science and education, documentary and cartoon movies were produced. 25.77 billion copies of newspaper at national and provincial levels were published, and 2.69 billion copies of various magazines, 6.44 billion volumes of books were published.[3]

---

[1] *Works of Mao Zedong*, Vol. 7, p 82.

[2] Samuel Huntington, Peter Burger, *Many Globalizations: Cultural Diversity in the Contemporary World*, p 9, Beijing: Xinhua Press, 2004.

[3] Source: National Statistics Bureau, "Statistic Communiqué of National Economy and Political Development of the People's Republic of China 2004", *People's Daily*, 2005-03-01.

What's more significant is that a modern culture which is more in line with socialist market economy and material civilization, which is diversified and encompassing, is being formed and developed.

Thirdly, globalization widens the space of thinking of cross-cultural exchanges and better helps people view and compare the diversified cultural behaviors from a global perspective, and in turn promotes cultural development. In the context of globalization, exchanges between nations and peoples become broader, and national cultures are more enriched and colorful, full of vitality and showing more distinctive cultural diversity. It is because of the new historical conditions of globalization that culture shows greater national features as well as diversity. The economic interdependence of nations is based on mutual understanding and trust, which can be reached with cultural exchanges as a most convenient channel. Take educational exchanges and cooperation as an example. Over the past two decades and more, China has sent 320,000 students to study to more than 100 countries and regions, and received more than 340,000 students to study in China from 160 countries and regions in the world. 1,800 teachers and scholars were dispatched to teach abroad; 40,000 foreign teachers and experts were invited to China to work; the number of Chinese experts and scholars taking part in international meetings abroad and the number of foreign scholars and experts coming to China for meetings equally exceeded 11,000. In 1996 alone, China had sent 10,000 students to study, to nearly 100 countries and regions, and received nearly 33,000 students to study, both short and long term, in 267 colleges in China from 160 countries and regions in the world. To help other countries in training technical, cultural and translation talents, China sent Chinese teachers to more than 30 countries opening Chinese language courses, and more than 5,000 Chinese teachers were sent on a long or short term basis. In that year, 3,760 foreign teachers and experts were invited to China to teach or work. The number of Chinese scholars dispatched by colleges or universities under the direct supervision of the Ministry of

Education to take part in international meetings abroad reached 2,099. The number of international seminars that Chinese scholars participated in had reached 1,316. The number of international seminars hosted by Chinese colleges or universities was 140, and more than 5,000 foreign scholars and experts were invited to China for meetings, and the number of delegations had nearly reached 130. The clashes, exchanges and merger of different cultures enable these cultures to absorb in the process of their development the advanced elements of other cultures; they enjoy a new dynamic. Against the backdrop of globalization, Chinese culture will gain greater dynamic and energy by drawing upon and absorbing elements favorable to its development in the process of external exchanges.

6.2 Challenges Posed to the Development

Globalization brings important opportunity for China's development, but at the same time it poses a serious challenge, too. Globalization, if dealt wrongly, can make China jobless, voiceless, rootless, ruthless and futureless. If handled right, it can strengthen independence, sovereignty and self reliance.[1] A correct understanding of the challenges of globalization is the important prerequisite for setting forth a focused strategy of development to make use of the advantages and avoid the disadvantages.

6.2.1 Challenges of globalization to the economic development in China

6.2.1.1 The economic security faces severe challenges.

National security is a permanent topic. In the trend of economic globalization, the content of national security is notably expanded; economic security issues increase and become the focus of national security.

---

[1] Wolfgang Deckers, "China, Globalization and the World Trade Organization", *Journal of Contemporary Asia*, 2004, Vol. 34, Issue 1.

First of all, China's foreign trade dependency increases, and Chinese economy faces growing external risks. Foreign trade dependency is a key index reflecting the degree of openness of a nation's economy, which usually is the ratio of the annual total volume of import and export and GDP. As seen from Table 6-1 and Chart 6-1, since the 1990s, foreign trade dependency of China has kept increasing; in particular it soared to 60.8% in 2003, while it rose to a new high of 70.1% recently. Such a trend drew the attention of many scholars and business professionals. Many scholars had asserted that this index could not measure the true degree of dependency of China's economy, as there were some elements influencing and exaggerating foreign trade dependency. Main elements includes exchange rate, the high proportion of processing trade, the impact of foreign-invested ventures, and the low

Table 6-1 Foreign Trade Dependency of China Since the 1990s (%)

Year	1990	1991	1992	1993	1994	1995	1996	1997
Foreign Trade Dependency	30.1	35.7	34.0	32.5	43.6	40.2	35.6	36.2
Year	1998	1999	2000	201	2002	2003	2004	
Foreign Trade Dependency	34.3	36.4	43.9	43.3	49.0	60.8	70.1	

Source: Data of 1990-2003 are calculated on the basis of statistics released in *China Statistics Yearbook 2004*, China National Statistics Bureau; data of 2004 is calculated on the basis of statistics in the *Notice of Statistics of National Economy and Social Development, 2004*.

Note: Foreign trade dependency = trade volume / GNP × 100%

Chart 6-1 Foreign Trade Dependency of China Since the 1990s Has Kept Rising

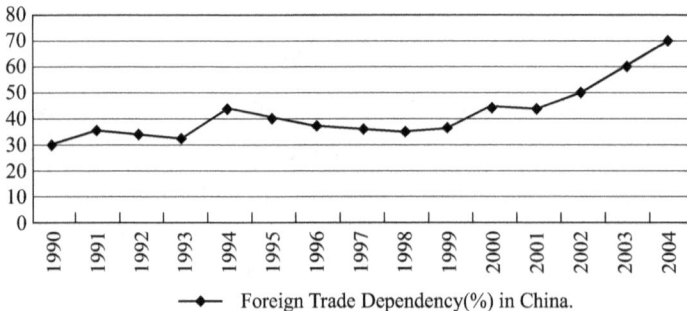

—◆— Foreign Trade Dependency(%) in China.

proportion of the tertiary industry in GDP.[1] Despite of these facts, the rising foreign trade dependency remains indisputable. It showed that China has taken the opportunity offered by economic globalization and expanded opening up, and at the same time Chinese economy has a deeper dependency which poses risks and challenges.

What needs greater attention is that there is serious imbalance and asymmetry in China's foreign trade, which results in structural risks in foreign trade. The imbalance of trade in China is not a question of the total volume, but a question of imbalance with some countries, in particular, the United States. There is also trade surplus with some countries, which easily brings trade frictions with the importing nations. Restrictions from importing nations on Chinese exports will affect the development of the related industries as well as unemployment in China. As a result, the space for China's opening up is limited, and protectionism aimed at China is prone to occur in major trade partners. More seriously, the imbalance and asymmetry of trade with some individual countries means the interdependence between China and major trade partners is uneven and asymmetric. China thus becomes more sensitive to the external environment and becomes more vulnerable, and the space for maneuvering in the arena of international politics is narrowed. For example, the United States and Japan account for nearly half of China's export market, and these two countries frequently have frictions with China. As a result, China has also to have economic considerations in political struggles in the international arena.[2] When relations with these countries become tense, there will be certainly some negative impact on Chinese economy.

The asymmetry in foreign trade is not a problem of total volume, but a problem of elasticity of demand and supply of products, mainly labor-intensive products for export, and imported energy and resource products

---

[1] Yin Xiaoshuo, "Trade Structure Is More Important: Foreign Trade Dependency and The Imbalance and Asymmetry of Import and Export", *Journal of International Trade*, 2004 (3).

[2] Zhang Youwen, "The Impact and Countermeasures of the Increase of China's Trade Dependency", *Journal of Issues of International Trade*, 2004 (8).

and machinery. The potential risks and problems of the rising foreign trade dependency have affected the healthy development of processing trade. Some export products have extremely high dependency, and some textiles products have reached the upper limit of market share. Textiles and household electronics have a high dependency. In 2003, China produced 2.51 million pieces of garment products and exported 1.77 million pieces, and the export dependency was 70.5%; in 2002, China produced 6 billion pairs of shoes and exported 4.3 billion pairs, and the export dependency was nearly 71%; China produced 87 million sets of DVD and domestically consumed only 14 million sets, and the export dependency was 84%; China produced 14.3 million motor bikes and domestically consumed only 5 million, and the export dependency was 63%; the export dependency of leather shoes, cameras, refrigerators, color TVs and air-conditioners was respectively 63%, 56%, 47%, 46% and 42%. In addition, some important products of processing trade also have a risk of high dependency for some target markets. For example, in 2001, stuffed and plush toys from China accounted for 88% of the total volume of this category of products imported by the United States, and shoe products accounted for 64% of the total import of the US, fiber luggage bags and handbags 51%, and window air-conditioners 34%. If export of these types of products encounters difficulties, related businesses in China will be greatly affected.[1] When the elasticity of demand is low, the increase of import will intensify the dependency on foreign products. High dependency on imports of energy, minerals, some key equipment and accessories will have the economic lifeline of a country subject to external control. Currently, dependency on imports of energy and important resources tends to get increasingly serious. In 2003, the import dependency of crude oil, iron ore, aluminum hydroxide in China ranged between 36% and 48%, with high monopoly risk, international shipment risk and international political risk. It becomes an important topic for importing nations as to how to prevent monopolizing exporters of minerals to raise prices of these products. Some

---

[1] Gong Zhen, "Why There Are Frequent Foreign Trade Frictions", from http://www.stock2000. com.cn/refresh/arch/2004/09/28/771453.html, 2004-09-28.

unstable factors in neighboring areas of China and in the international environment may threat the safety of international shipping routes, or even interrupt some of the routes. For example, half of China's imported oil comes from unstable Middle East, and about 4/5 marine transportation of oil need to go through the Malacca Strait. Oil safety of China is exposed to potential risks. The political risk of importing key equipment and accessories, energy and minerals lies in that the government of the exporting nations sets up barriers to check China's import of these products or terminate the cooperation with China for these products, out of strategic consideration.[1] Once such things occur, Chinese economy will be impacted.

Foreign trade dependency of China may not be as serious as shown in the index figures, and the actual situation may need further study. But the rising trend of foreign trade dependency needs due attention. If the imbalance and asymmetry mentioned afore grow with the rising dependency of foreign trade, there will be a severe negative impact.[2]

Secondly, financial security of China faces many problems. Since reform and opening up, China has been merging into the world financial system at a growing speed. After its entry into WTO, China has quickened the steps for opening its financial markets, and international finance has an increasing influence on Chinese finance. Opening up of Chinese finance and merger into the world system bring many economic benefits to China, and for a long time, the interaction between China's financial system and the world financial system is a positive one, and China has seized opportunities and benefits in the process of internationalization of her financial system. However, as financial globalization proceeds, financial safety of China faces many problems.

In the context of economic globalization, financial turmoil of one economy will rapidly spread to other economies and cause regional or global

---

[1] Fu Junwen, "International Comparison of Trade Dependency and Analysis on Structural Risk of China's Foreign Trade", *Journal of World Economic Research*, 2004 (4).

[2] Yin Xiangshuo, "Trade Structure Is More Important: Foreign Trade Dependency and The Imbalance and Asymmetry of Import and Export", *Journal of International Trade*, 2004 (3).

financial crisis, and the possibility of China being impacted by external financial crisis is increasing. After entering WTO, China gradually opens its financial and service markets, and the inflow and outflow of international financial capital become more frequent, which increases fluctuations in the international market and the domestic financial environment is more prone to impacts from international economy, financial risks and crises, as well as speculative capital in the international market. International liquid capital may flood into China and stir up troubles in the financial market of China. The large volume of flow of international capital in and out of a country likely causes sharp fluctuation in the stock market, increase volatility of prices, inflation or deflation, which in turn causes financial crisis. In particular, when domestic financial market of China is not well developed and administration is not well regulated, the opening up of the financial sector will increase the possibility of being impacted by international financial risks and crises. China had similar conditions with Southeast Asian countries before the Asian financial crisis broke out. Great cautions and effective measures must be taken to dissolve financial risks and prevent financial crisis.

The competition in China's financial market will grow after foreign-owned financial institutes enter the market and the development of financial industry in China will be impacted. On the one hand, the entry of foreign-owned banks will to some extent increase the unstable factors of the Chinese financial market and make it more difficult to adjust macro-monetary policies. On the other hand, state-owned Chinese banks will face greater competition from their foreign counterparts and be greatly impacted. Mc Kinsey report shows that among the sectors China will open in line with WTO agreements, banking is one that has the highest level of protection and will be mostly impacted after opening up. Banking industry is the sector of high risk that concerns the Chinese government after China became a member of WTO. In the process of opening up of the financial sector, local banks and foreign banks will have fierce competition in areas such as quality customers, financial professionals, intermediate business, personal financial services, consumption loans, credit card business, as well as online banking.[1]

Financial policies of China will encounter much external pressure. Financial globalization is the area of the highest degree of economic globalization and with the most rapid development in economic globalization. With the access of international liquid capital to the financial markets of China, speculative activities such as foreign exchange hedging and interest hedging increase, the effectiveness of macro-monetary policies in China will inevitably be weakened, the financial market may be under impact and financial risks grow. Financial policies of China will at the same time be restricted by many external factors, which will have negative influence on the domestic economy if they are not properly handled. Over the recent years, there is growing pressure from abroad on the exchange rate of renminbi. In early 2005, following the International Monetary Fund, the World Bank hinted that the time for reforming the mechanism of renminbi exchange rate had matured. Citigroup in USA made a bold forecast in its latest report that China might re-evaluate renminbi in three months and would allow renminbi to appreciate by 3%. These external factors might have influence on the policies of renminbi exchange rate.

Finally, merger into the world economic system will weaken the control of economy by the Chinese government and impact some industries in China. Many scholars believe that China's development increasingly relies on the international economic environment, and the international environment in the coming 15 years will bring more benefits than harms to China. But the negative impact of some unfavorable elements on the development of China cannot be underestimated. China has entered a period with many trade frictions. Protectionist measures for trade aimed at China of some countries increase. The economic development of China will be increasingly influenced by the cyclic fluctuation of the world economy. With the higher degree of opening up of Chinese economy, the deepening dependency on the world market and resources, the price volatility in energy resources,

---

[1] Zheng Guozhong, "Seven Focuses of Competition of Banks in China and in the World", *Outlook Weekly*, 2002 (20).

grain and minerals in the international market will exert greater influence on domestic market prices. As a result, the domestic economy will undergo sharp fluctuations. Participation in globalization brings about a series of new economic risks to China. Since the macro-adjustment measures and risk prevention mechanisms that can be adapted to open economy are not sound, risks that China faces will increase.

Economic globalization means that the economy of a country merges into the world economic system and integrates its own economy with the world economy. The rule of game after the integration will abide by international practices and rules. Practices indicate that, abiding by international practices and rules is the basis of participating in international economy at a deeper level and on a greater scope. The quicker China adapts to international practices and rules, the more favorably it will be positioned in economic globalization. However, connecting to international market and operating according to international practices and rules will enable a series of essential changes in all aspects, at multiple levels and in a wide spectrum of areas. The current economic operations and the system of economic laws and regulations in China will be greatly impacted, institutional contradictions and conflicts will be unavoidable, and the ability of control and protection of the economy will be weakened.

Economic globalization will have great impact on some industries in China. For a long time in the early period of reform and opening up, Chinese government had implemented extreme subsidies and advantages to foreign-invested enterprises and domestic enterprises were disadvantaged, which had limited the development of domestic companies in the same industries, and positioned the state-owned enterprises unfavorably in the competition for a long time. After China's accession to WTO, national industries not only face strong competition from foreign-invested enterprises in the domestic market, but also face keener competition in the world market. In addition, foreign-invested enterprises partly control and monopolize some industries in China and make it very difficult for domestic enterprises to develop. Economic globalization promotes the development of multinational corporations and global expansion of capital. The acquisitions and mergers of enterprises in the world reach a peak in economic history. The surge of acquisitions and mergers indicates capital accumulation and concentration is accelerated, and the power of international monopoly capital is strengthened. At present, in many areas such as aviation, telecommunication, computer, automobile, pharmaceuticals and food, many global consortiums appear with astonishingly high degree of monopoly. They are likely to monopolize industries in China when entering the Chinese market. For example, soon after its entry into China, through its joint venture Chinese partner, AT&T has become a key enterprise in the telecommunication industry in China, and its products occupy 1/4 of the market share in China. Motorola wireless communication equipment occupies a large share of the Chinese market; Schindler of Switzerland and Otis of Germany has almost monopolized the elevator market in China; Coca-cola and Pepsi-cola became well-known names in China. Multinational corporations have an intention to monopolize other sectors such as bio-medicine, optical industry, aviation and new materials. The situation brings unfavorable influence on the optimization of industrial structure and threats the industrial security of China.[1]

6.2.1.2 The industry of new and high technology in China faces severe challenges.

In the keen competition of the world economy, the competitive advantage of the new and high-tech industry represents a nation's international competitiveness. The development of new and high-tech industry has great significance in improving national strength and international competitiveness and in maintaining the nation's economic security. Since reform and opening up, a series of initiatives for the high-tech industry such as Project 863, Torch, Climbing, Sparkling Fire, have assisted China to score remarkable achievements in the information industry, biology, new materials and new energy sectors. New and high-tech industry

---

[1] Zhao Guizhi, "The Impact of Economic Globalization on Economic Safety of China and Study of Countermeasures", *Journal of Research of Financial Issues*, 2002 (5).

has gained rapid development and achievements. However, the new and high tech industry remains at the primary stage of all-round development.

At present, the new and high-tech industry is at the stage of start-up, and is not yet the dominant and driving force of the development of national economy. Chart 6-2 shows that, over recent years the proportion of added value of new and high-tech industry and the added value of manufacturing industries and in GDP has risen, but it is still low. In 2002, the added value of new and high-tech industry accounted for 9.9% of the added value of manufacturing industries, and only 3.6% of GDP. Over the recent years, the contribution of new and high-tech industry in GDP remained at a low level between 1.5% and 2%. In 1993, the contribution of new and high-tech industry in GDP was 1.56%, and rose only to 1.94% in 1999. The total number of new and high-tech industrial zones grows rapidly, but the overall level of profit of these zones is not impressive. In 2000, the net profit of new and high-tech zones accounted for 6.5% of the income of technological industries business, which decreased to 5.4% in 2001.[1] Zhongguancun zone is known as the best cluster of new and high-tech industry in Beijing. But

**Chart 6-2   The Proportions of Added Value of New and High-Tech
Industry in the Added Value of Manufacturing Industry
and in the GDP between 1998 and 2002**

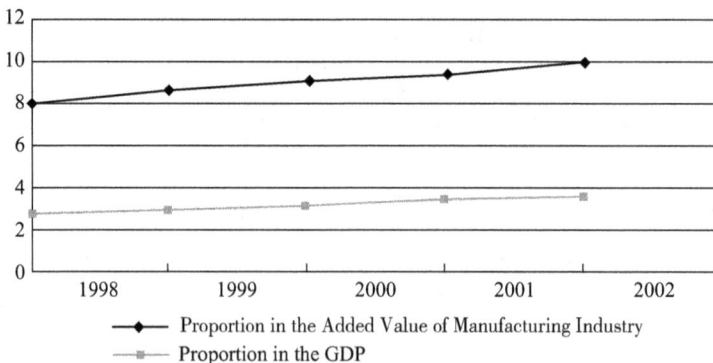

—◆— Proportion in the Added Value of Manufacturing Industry
—■— Proportion in the GDP

[1] Zhao Yumei, "To Improve the Competitiveness of China's High-Tech Industry and Meet with the Challenges of Accession to WTO", *Journal of China's Science and Technology Industry*, 2002 (6).

statistics in 2003 showed that its leading industry was modern manufacturing including automobile, which contributes nearly 50% to its GDP, but the new and high-tech industry were not well-developed and its contribution to GDP was rather limited. A few large companies started up in Zhongguancun are actually trading companies, under the name of "technology". In terms of the level of new and high-tech industry, China not only lags far behind developed nations, but also lags behind newly industrialized countries and regions.

In the international division of labor, most of the high-tech enterprises in China stay at the lower level. Most industries in China are labor-intensive. Though the product of new and high-tech industry has gained rapid growth, the key technologies, parts and accessories of new and high-tech industries are imported, and those possessing intellectual property rights are only few in numbers. A large number of enterprises mainly rely on the advantage of low-cost labor and the development of assembly processing industry. Their products mainly aim at low and middle segment of the market with low content of technology. In the exports, computers and telecommunication equipment have a large share, but the core parts, including CPU, memory and IC chips, largely rely on import or foreign-invested enterprises. What has been earned by so-called new and high-tech enterprises in China is a fee for processing. Their profitability is weak and the added value of their products is low. The average added value of new and high-tech industry in developed countries is usually 30%, but the average figure in China in 1998 was only 23.9%, even lower than the level of all manufacturing industries of 25.6%.[1] Therefore, it becomes increasingly important for high-tech enterprises in China to strengthen their core competition, and transform to a structure that focuses more on technological development and innovation.

The R&D capability of new and high technology in China lags far behind that of developed nations, though technological competitiveness of China has improved and ranks in the middle-level of developing nations.

---

[1] Sui Yinghui, "Economic Globalization: The Strategic Orientation of Technological Industres", *Journal of International Technological and Economic Research*, 2001(3)

Take R&D spending as an example. R&D spending in China is far from enough, but since the Second World War, developed nations have kept a high level of spending in R&D. The United States is the country with the strongest overall power of science and technology. The flexible administrative system of science and technology, the reasonable structure for scientific research, the huge amount of R&D spending, the effective motivation and talent recruiting and retaining system, have created a favorable environment for the development of science and technology in the United States.[1] In the past three decades, R&D spending in the United States has accounted for a high percentage in GDP and maintained above 2.5%, with only one exception of lowering to 2.2% in the 1970s. R&D spending and GDP grow at the same pace, and the huge amount of R&D spending provides strong support for all levels of scientific research in the United States. R&D spending in the United States each year makes up about 43% of the total R&D spending of the industrialized countries, higher than the total amount of countries ranking after it. Countries ranking from the second to the seventh are Japan, Canada, France, Germany, Italy, and the United Kingdom.[2] In addition, R&D investment in the United States has diversified channels. As seen from Table 6-2, the bulk of R&D spending in the United States comes from the federal government and enterprises, and a small part comes from universities and other non-profit organizations. American enterprises have long attached much importance to R&D investment, which makes up a high proportion of the total R&D investment in the United States. The period from 1994 to 2000 witnessed the most rapid growth of R&D spending, which hiked from 169.2 billion USD to 264.6 billion USD. Calculated with the constant price of US dollars in 1996 minus inflation, the actual R&D spending increased from

---

[1] Xiong Guangqing, "Why Does Science and Technology of the U. S. Lead the Globe", *Journal of Science and Technology Management in Yunnan*, 2003(6).

[2] Wang Dengqi, "Current Status of Development of Contemporary Science and Technology in the U.S.", *Journal of Science and Management*, 2000 (6).

175.9 billion US dollars in 1994 to 249.1 billion US dollars in 2000, with an annual increase rate of 6% which was much higher than the growth rate of GDP over the same period of time. The proportion of R&D spending in GDP of Germany and France has remained above 2.3% since the 1990s; but Japan had a higher level, 2.92% in 1991, 2.74% in 1994, and 2.80% in 1997.

Table 6-2 The U.S. Spending on R&D in 1993-2002 (million US dollar)

Year	Federal Government	Industrial Enterprises	Universities	Nonprofit Organizations	State Governments	Total
1993	60,516	96,549	3,708	3,387	1,557	165,717
1994	60,792	99,203	3,937	3,664	1,622	169,218
1995	62,963	110,870	4,108	3,924	1,750	183,615
1996	63,397	123,416	4,433	4,238	1,860	197,344
1997	64,583	136,227	4,836	4,589	1,921	212,156
1998	66,383	147,847	5,170	4,994	1,973	226,367
1999	67,014	163,245	5,628	5,573	2,101	243,561
2000	66,208	183,724	6,210	6,217	2,257	264,616
2001	72,920	192,873	6,830	6,757	2,387	281,767
2002	81,004	193,420	7,459	7,308	2,473	291,664

Source: Website of National Science Foundation

On the contrary, China's governmental departments and the majority of enterprises do not have a strong consciousness of research and development, and R&D spending remains at a fairly low level. Since 1996, R&D spending has started to grow, and so has its proportion in GDP, which was 0.60% in 1996, 0.83% in 1999, 1.00% in 2000, and 1.31% in 2003. The growth continued for eight consecutive years. The proportion in 2003 was higher at 0.31 percentage point than that in 2000, a remarkable increase. But R&D spending in GDP in China was lower than the world average of 1.6%, and the average of developed countries of 2.2%. The gap was quite notable.[1] As

[1] "The Percentage in GDP of the Input of R&D Expenses Grows for Eight Consecutive Years in GDP", from http://www.sts.org.cn/nwdt/gndt/document/039.html, 2005-01-24.

Table 6-3 shows, R&D intensity of manufacturing and high-tech industries in China also lags behind developed countries. R&D spending in China can not give strong support to economic development, which may result in further widening gap between China and developed countries. In the process of merging into world economic system, some high-tech enterprises with weak capability of innovation and core competitiveness may not be able to survive, and lowered tariffs will make the new and high-tech industries in China face greater challenges. Besides, the internationalization of the domestic market will narrow the space of development for China's new and high-tech industries.[1] It becomes essential to set forth practical and effective strategies of development for the new and high-tech industries in China to face up the challenge of economic globalization.

Table 6-3 R&D Intensity of Manufacturing and High-Tech Industries of Some Countries

Country / Industry	China 2002	The U.S. 2000	Japan 2001	Germany 2001	France 2001	The U.K. 2000	Canada 2000	Italy 2001	Korea 2001
Manufacturing	3.4	8.2	9.4	7.6	7.0	6.0	4.1	2.2	6.0
High-Tech	5.0	22.5	26.3	23.8	25.8	21.2	29.3	11.2	21.8
Pharmaceutical	2.6	20.2	22.9	22.3	24.8	54.1	23.9	6.5	4.8
Aerospace Vehicles	15.0	20.8	22.3	23.8	29.2	20.8	14.0	20.4	-
Electronics and Communication	5.8	18.6	18.5	44.1	40.4	13.5	36.4	16.5	29.0
Computer and Office Equipment	4.1	30.7	59.4	19.8	12.5	3.9	38.1	7.8	21.5
Medical Devices and Instruments and Meters	2.5	30.2	28.8	14.8	15.9	9.1	-	7.5	4.9

Source: Website of the Ministry of Science and Technology, China

Note: R&D intensity is calculated as the percentage of R&D budget in industrial value-added.

---

[1] Xiong Guangqing, "On the Challenges of Economic Globalization for China Developing New and High-Tech Industries", *Journal of Science and Management*, 2003 (2).

6.2.2 The challenges of globalization to the political development in China[1]

Globalization is not a sheer economic phenomenon; it will have remarkable influence on political, cultural and social life. Cultural penetration, value changes and transplantation of systems always accompany the process of globalization. Obviously, globalization of economic activities will have political requirements in line with its progress. For China, the political appeal brought along by globalization will influence the goal, value orientation and strategic choices of political development in China. It is fair to say that globalization will both promote and challenge the process of political development in China.

First of all, globalization facilitates the promotion of the strategy of "peaceful evolution" of Western countries aiming socialist countries. In the context of economic globalization, socialism and capitalism are interdependent economically, but the confrontation of the two systems exists and the struggle between them is not reconcilable. The intention of capitalist countries of overthrowing socialism does not change. Taking the favorable conditions provided by globalization, they are able to promote the strategy of "peaceful evolution". After the dramatic changes in the Soviet Union and Eastern Europe, the focus of "peaceful evolution" has shifted to socialist China, which now involves areas of economy, ideology and cultural exchanges. Western countries take economic and trade relations with China as a key link in promoting changes in China, using the advantages of economy and technology to intensify ideological penetration. After China adopted policies of reform and opening up, the United States took it as an opportunity to promote "peaceful evolution" and deems that opening up policies serve as a most reliable path for developing Western democratic values in Chinese society. Taking advantage of China's economic need for capital and technology, Western countries promote "Western civilization" with economy and technology as carriers, pressing and

---

[1] Part of this section is from the final study of "Deng Xiaoping's Thought and the Political Development of China in the 21st Century", a project of the National Fund of Philosophy and Social Sciences, steered by Prof. Li Jingzhi.

luring China. In terms of communications, publicity and cultural exchanges, Western countries use many propaganda tools to enhance penetration into ideas and culture of China and to disseminate "seeds of freedom", with an intention to shake, split apart and "evolve" socialist countries. Making full use of modernized media network and international cultural exchanges, they try to shake Chinese people's faith in Marxism and socialism through media and ideological penetration. In the territory of foreign affairs, Western countries constantly intervene in Chinese domestic affairs by making use of human rights issues. Since the 1980s, the United States has paid much attention to human rights diplomacy and taken human rights issues as a breaking point to promote "peaceful evolution" in China. In the 1990s, the United States upgraded its pressure on China in human rights issues. In its Country Reports on Human Rights of each year, State Department of the United States always attacks China. The United States also summons up some countries in the Human Rights Committee of the UN to propose motions against China. The essence of the strategy of "peaceful evolution" of Western countries is to change the political system of socialist countries and to have them evolve to capitalism. This strategy brings great international pressure for the political development of China.

Secondly, globalization has huge impact on political culture of China. Globalization in a direct way changes the political ideas of people, which in turn generate important influence on the changes of political culture. If not properly handled, it will have negative impact on political stability in China. With its influence on the political ideas of people, globalization changes the judgment of citizens on their country's political system and on their government. Western democratic ideas, values and institutional practices will exert pressure on developing countries. "Globalization is transcending national boundaries to promote the communication of thinking and ideas, which enables more regions in the world to have more active citizens."[1] At the same time, "cultural communication is changing the political stance of national

---

[1] Anthony Giddens, *Sociology*, 4th Edition, p 542.

identification, and the political stance of more general identifications."[1] Globalization will also bring along conflicts of political ideologies between China and the West. Against the backdrop of globalization, various political ideas, such as liberalism, corporatism, conservatism, and nationalism, emerge. The complicated social situation and the variety of thinking and ideas widen the vision and add to people's political experiences, but to some extent confuse people in their political life. While economic exchanges are growing between countries with different systems, the contact between political ideologies grows, too. On the one hand, the exchanges benefit China for taking in excellent cultural achievements of mankind to the end of better development. On the other hand, the exchanges inevitably result in clashes and conflicts between political consciousness between China and the West. In particular, the intentional penetration and influence of Western political consciousness poses conflicts and confrontation with socialist political ideology. The diversity of values and the standard of values will bring about brand new understanding of values and ethnical requirement, which in turn will change the values, thinking and value orientation of members in the society. To some extent, a new type of political culture will be formed and the political changes in China will be influenced.

Thirdly, globalization causes notable impact on the mainstream ideology in China. To a certain degree, the challenge to the government is greater than its challenge to the society; its challenge to politics is greater than to economy; its challenge to the ruling party is greater than to the government; and its challenge to ideology is greater than to general ideas in life. Participation in economic globalization and international cooperation and exchange is not only a major economic issue, but also a major political issue, which involves the introduction and influence of lifestyles, thinking as well as ideology that in turn relates to the guiding idea, values and the

[1] David Held, Anthony McGrew, *Globalization/Anti-Globalization*, p 32, Beijing: Social Sciences Press, 2004.

direction of development of the society. A correct understanding of the conditions and problems that face the ideas and ideology in the context of globalization and responding in a proper way are essential. The difficulty and complexity of infiltration and anti-infiltration in ideological territory which will last for a long time must be sufficiently understood. Undeniably, Marxism is deeply rooted in Chinese society in the process of guiding the great practices of the Communist Party of China and the Chinese people, and became the common theoretical base for the Party and the people of China. It has a dominating role in China's political culture. However, the development of market economy has profoundly changed the pattern of social interests. Other political cultures are being extensively communicated in Chinese society in the context of globalization. Though the political awareness of people is essentially unified under the banner of socialism and patriotism, political orientation and political emotions are diversified. At the current stage, ideological field in China shows a pattern of dominance by one idea accompanied by some diversified ideas, and sometimes the guiding position of Marxism is possibly challenged. Some schools of Western political thought that advocate cultural diversity and negate Marxism as a guiding idea already have some influence in China. In this context, China has to speed up the process of political development to face up challenges brought along to the ideological field by globalization.

6.2.3　Challenges of globalization to cultural development in China

Globalization may have unfavorable influence on the development of national culture. Globalization is a natural historical process in modern times in which human societies transcend special barriers, and communicate, contact, exchange and interact on the global scope. One of its outcomes is the clashes between different cultures. Where would world culture go amid the clashes? Would it be the assimilation of cultures, or further divisions among cultures? It is fair to say that homogeneity and heterogeneity are phenomena of the development of culture in the process of globalization, as well as the basic direction of cultural development.[1] In the exchanges and dialogues of world culture in the age of globalization, it is proper to respect the traditions and particularity of each national culture, to oppose cultural hegemony, and to promote the common development of each national culture in the world. Though cultural development shows a tendency of co-existence of homogeneity and heterogeneity, developed countries usually adopt a more positive attitude toward globalization because of their leading position in cultural exchanges. Their cultures will be spread globally along with the global spread of commodities and services, while cultures of underdeveloped countries may be distorted or turn heterogenic in the process of globalization. In this sense, globalization may have negative influence on the development of national culture in China.

With the rapid development of information technology and extensive exchanges across national borders of labor immigration, international travel, modern media, and educational cooperation, Western cultures increasingly influence the mindset and lifestyles of people, especial lifestyles and values of young people who are more easily affected by the charm of Western cultures. Western countries such as the United States take full advantage of their information communication system covering the globe, in particular the Internet, to have cultural expansion and infiltration. With the advantage in science and economy, they build a film and video recreation system led by Hollywood and Disney. Backed by strong knowledge, academy and education system, an ideological front in the production and communication of Western culture has been opened up. The Internet, known as the "fourth media" following newspapers, broadcasting and television, has an increasing influence on culture. The global application of information technology, as an essential part of as well as an enormous driving force for globalization, has become an important trend in the development of the contemporary world, which is most remarkably shown in the development of web culture. In the context of globalization, cultural development in China faces great

---

[1] Zhang Jing, "Cultural Homogeneity and Heterogeneity in the Process of Globalization", *Journal of Teaching and Research*, 2002 (5).

challenges. China Internet Network Information Center released its 15th report on the conditions of the Internet development in China on January 19, 2005. The Internet users in China exceeded 94 million, and the number of netizens soared by 1.2 million each month on average. In terms of age, about 69% were under 30, with those aged 18-24 accounted for the highest proportion of 21%, those above 60 only 0.2%. In terms of occupation, students were the main part of netizens. In terms of education, undergraduates (and above) made up 20%, and polytechnic school students made up the highest proportion of 36%.[1] In terms of information on the Internet, above 80% of online information and above 95% of service information are provided by the United States, and those provided by China only accounted for about 1%. The United States government is using the absolute advantage of the Internet to ideologically and culturally infiltrate many countries. It is explicitly raised that a new front is to be opened up, to rule the world with Western values, and to conquer socialist countries ideologically and culturally. Promoting American ideology and values of individualism as well as the neo-liberal economic policies, and attacking social reformist ideas that threaten the interests of monopoly capital, and imperceptibly influencing young people in China with the power of Rock 'n' Roll, music discs, and Hollywood movies, all these cultural infiltrations and influences inevitably generate negative impacts on cultural development in China.

6.3 China's Strategic Choice in the Context of Two Systems

Globalization means deepening interdependence and mutual restriction. To the end of co-existence and win-win in the context of globalization, history, culture, social system and mode of development of each

---

[1] Source: China Internet Network Information Center (CNNIC), "The 15th Statistical Report on the Internet Development in China", from http://it.people.com.cn/GB/8219/43564/43565/313142 4.html, 2005-01-19.

country should be respected, the reality of a diversified world should be acknowledged, and countries should supplement each other in competitions and seek common development by setting aside differences and pursuing what is reasonable. For China, globalization is both an opportunity and a challenge. Appropriate strategies, firm beliefs, correct direction and relentless endeavors will enable China to take advantage of opportunity, avoid risks, and protect national interests for greater development.

6.3.1 To enhance the global vision and face up to the challenges of globalization

In face of uncertain factors and the relative passiveness of developing countries in the process of globalization, the wise choice of any country is not to close itself, but to open up and merge into the process of globalization, solving problems encountered in the process. The future of China's economic development is destined to be closely linked with the global economy.[1]

Undeniably, with the progress of globalization and further integration into the process of globalization, China faces increasing challenges and risks. It is fair to say that against the backdrop of globalization, the existence of risks is normal. That is to say, it is normal for risks to exist since risks always exist. Sometimes risks and crises may have remarkable impacts on China. But the correct attitude is to take the right steps to handle challenges encountered in opening up, and to prevent and control the impact of various risks and crises, instead of returning to a state of closing the country from the outside world, or refraining from integrating into globalization for fear of risks. It must be sufficiently understood that, firstly, China's opening up policies are not to be wavered. Opening up is a basic policy of China in the long term, with the goal of promoting China's development. International economic and technological exchanges are the objective requests of socialized production. Without external conditions, it is difficult for China to construct and realize socialist modernization. Secondly, opening up,

---

[1] Maurice Daly, Mal Logan, *Reconstructing Asia*, Melbourne: RMIT Publishing, 1998, p167.

safeguarding the country, independency and improving ability of risk-resistance are supplementary. Opening up and safeguarding national security are attainable at the same time, and they are unity of opposites and co-exist. China should actively participate in globalization, and take full advantage of favorable conditions and opportunities to develop itself and enhance its international competitiveness. At the same time, China should understand and prevent in a timely manner any possible negative impact and risks brought by globalization.[1]

In the context of globalization, the strategy of economic development of developing countries should be directed to the gradual integration into the process of globalization. The core of traditional development strategy for developing countries was to gain external income through export, which shows the will of seeking market interests abroad. But today the accelerated process of globalization has changed the environment for implementing the development strategies of developing countries, there appears a tendency of the integration of the economy as a whole of developing countries into the world economy. The strategy of integration follows the general trend of the development of world economy with deepening interdependence. The strategy of integration is the road of development for conducting production, operation and trading activities that developing countries take in the context of globalization, in order to promote industrialization, to position themselves in integrated international production, unified world market and global capital flow, to follow the basic rules of market economy and international economic activities, to take advantage of international production factors and the international market, and to depend on the adjustment of international industrial structure.[2] Being guided by and implementing the strategy, more active policies need to be adopted to enable national economy to participate

---

[1] Zhu Niangui, "On Opening Up and Safeguarding China's Economic Security", *Journal of Theory and Reform*, 2003(4).

[2] Huang Yejing, "Economic Globalization and Transformation of Development Strategy of Developing Countries", *Journal of Academics*, 2003 (8).

in international competition more deeply and broadly, to become part of the world economic system, and to take part in international division of labor not only between industries, but also within industries and at the level of single products. National economy of developing countries needs to form close relations of interaction and interdependence, and at the same time, to connect economic system and operational system with the international system. The core of the strategy of merging into globalization lies in merging into international value-added chain, which is one of the important paths of developing countries in merging into the process of globalization.[1] Since reform and opening up, China has been constantly merging into the globalization process. As noted by a British scholar, Joshua Cooper Ramo in The Beijing Consensus, "As we have seen, China is ever-deeply woven into the international order as an essential part of many nations' hopes and livelihoods. In the late 1990s, when China was seeking WTO accession, it was probably still possible to manipulate China with broad moves like denying trade access. But those days have passed. China is both self-propelled and increasingly part of the international community."[2]

Judged by economic and technological achievements since the adoption of reform and opening up, opening up and taking part in globalization have provided the development of China with a very favorable external environment. China in fact is one of the important beneficiaries of globalization. Over the decades since reform and opening up, GDP in China grew from 362.41 billion yuan in 1978 to 13,687.6 billion yuan in 2004.[3] The annual GDP growth rate remained over 9.0%, with the highest growth rate 14.2% in 1992, and lowest 3.8% in 1990.[4] GDP per capita in

---

[1] Huang Yejing, "Economic Globalization and Transformation of Development Strategy of Developing Countries", *Journal of Academics*, 2003 (8).

[2] Joshua Cooper Ramo, *The Beijing Consensus*, The Foreign Policy Centre, 2004, from http://fpc.org.uk/fsblob/244.pdf.

[3] National Statistics Bureau of China, *China Statistics Yearbook 2005*, p 51, Beijing: China Statistics Press, 2005.

[4] National Statistics Bureau of China, *China Statistics Yearbook 2004*, p 59, Beijing: China Statistics Press, 2004.

1978 was 379 yuan, 2,287 in 1992, and 10,561 in 2004[1], showing a strong momentum of increase, too. However, the annual growth rate of price index mostly was below 10%, with only a few exceptions above 15%. On the whole, over the decades since reform and opening up, China has achieved sustained economic growth at a high speed without vicious inflation. This is rarely seen in other countries transforming from planned economy to market economy. It is a miracle that China achieves economic growth at such high rate which had lasted for so long. More importantly, the economic growth is not merely a quantitative increase, but also adjustment and upgrading of industrial structure. In 1978, the proportion of primary, secondary and tertiary industry in China was respectively 28.1%, 48.2% and 23.7%. In 2004, the proportions changed to 15.2%, 52.9% and 31.9%.[2] Though the three industries had rapid growth, the growth rate of the primary industry was slightly lower, that of secondary and tertiary industry were relatively higher. As a result, the proportion of primary industry shows a tendency of decrease, the proportion of the secondary industry remains stable and the proportion of tertiary industry increases, which is a sign of improvement of China's industrial structure. In this process, the position of agriculture as a foundation continues to be strengthened. Traditional industries are improved, and new and high-tech industries and modern service industries have speeded up the development. Many infrastructure projects of irrigation, transportation, telecommunication, energy and environmental protection have been executed. At the same time, culture, education and healthcare in China have made remarkable progress. Social security, community service and public safety situation has greatly been improved. The successful practices of China's opening up indicate that globalization can serve as a strong engine for rapid economic growth of developing countries.[3] The achievements China has scored since reform and opening up has given China a greater ability of

---

[1] National Statistics Bureau of China, *China Statistics Yearbook 2005*, p 51, Beijing: China Statistics Press, 2005.

[2] *Ibid*, p 52.

[3] Paul M. Augimeri, "The Effects of Globalization on China, a Developing, Newly Industrialized Economy", *Ecodate*, March 2001, Vol. 15, Issue 1.

resisting risks in the process of globalization, opened the international vision of the Chinese people, and consolidated the confidence in opening up.

6.3.2 To build a new security concept

Against the backdrop of rapid progress of globalization, origins and types of security issues, as well as means of dealing with security issues have undergone tremendous changes. Globalization brings human society into a risk society. While traditional security issues have not been solved, various non-conventional threats emerge. For example, Asian financial crisis, 9.11 terrorist attack, SARS epidemic in 2003, threats of bird flu, all have threatened and impacted the safety of many countries and peoples, even peace and stability of the world. Under new historical conditions, the concept of security has become one encompassing many domains such as military, politics, economy, science and technology, environment and culture.[1]

Globalization has raised non-conventional security threats. Traditional security involves threats in political and military domains, the most outstanding one being the threat to sovereignty and territory. Ever since states came into being, traditional security threat becomes the core of threats to national security. To hedge traditional security threat, usually military means are adopted, such as armament and defense, military conflicts and wars. In this sense, traditional security threats are known as military threats of security. In comparison to traditional threats, non-conventional threats to security involve mainly threats in social-economic and biological environment, including economic security, financial security, resources security, water safety, grain safety, biological environment safety, information safety, the spread of epidemics, organized cross-border criminal activities, drug smuggling, illegal immigration, piracy, money laundry, etc.[2] With the rapid progress of globalization, non-conventional threats of security seriously impact social stability and sustainable development of national economies,

---

[1] "China's Position Paper on the New Security Concept", *People's Daily*, 2002-08-02.

[2] Liu Xuecheng, "Basic Features of and Response to Non-Conventional Security Issues", *Journal of Research of Intentional Issues*, 2004 (1).

and threatens living environment and health of human beings.

Non-conventional security threats have obvious cross-border features. Not only a country faces this kind of threat, many other countries and even the whole world face this kind of threat. It not only threats the security of a country, but also the security of other countries. Non-conventional security threats do not usually come from one sovereign country, but from non-state behaviors of individuals, organizations or consortiums. Non-conventional security threats are possibly turned to traditional ones in the domain of security, and non-conventional and traditional threats intertwine. For example, terrorism and the dissemination of mass destruction weapons may turn problems into traditional ones. Non-conventional security threats constantly change with expanding contents. The progress and application of information technology raises the issue of information safety. The spread of AIDS and SARS has put the safety of public health on the agenda of governments.[1] Features of non-conventional security threats make it impossible for one single country to protect itself effectively from these threats, instead, coordination and cooperation must be strengthened. Issues in the domain of economy, information, resources, environment, international terrorist activities, and cross-border crimes are not just for one single country. All countries in the world face the threats in these aspects and share common interests, which reflects the non-confrontational and interdependent features of national security in the context of globalization, and show the necessity and importance of international cooperation in terms of security. Social stability is the cornerstone of the stability of a country, and the stability of a country is the basis for international and regional cooperation, while the safety of people is the core for both traditional and non-traditional security. In responding to issues in the domain of non-traditional security, national security, social stability and safety of the people must all be taken care of, collaboration and coordination of all departments be promoted domestically.

---

[1] Liu Xuecheng, "Basic Features of and Response to Non-Conventional Security Issues", *Journal of Research of Intentional Issues*, 2004 (1).

In turn, regional and international cooperation should be conducted on equal footing basis and respecting mutual benefits.[1] In dealing with many issues of international security, non-traditional security issues in particular, a special attention needs to be paid to the principle of "treating problems by looking into both their root causes and symptoms". Most of non-traditional security issues, such as international terrorism, cross-border crimes, ecological issues, and highly dangerous epidemics, have sophisticated origins and cannot be solved by any single measure (e.g., military means). Instead, measures can be effective only when used in a coordinated way.[2] However, it must be acknowledged that in international cooperation, due to the status of nation state in the international community, the security of a country reasonably is the last symbol of the country's sovereignty. Even in European Union, with the highest degree of integration, the issue of sovereignty transfer remains to be the issue that makes it fairly difficult for countries to have physical and effective coordination in terms of common security and defense policies. International cooperation in security sphere will not sustain if sovereignty is requested to be forfeited.[3]

At present, China needs to strengthen exchanges and communication with other countries—international cooperation—in the following aspects, in order to enhance common understanding, to shoulder its own responsibility in international security and cooperation, and to solve the security issues she faces in the process of globalization.

First of all, common security, collective security, and security awareness in the international community are to be enhanced, and a new order of international security in line with common interests of all countries should be promoted. In July 2002, at the ASEAN Regional Forum of Foreign Ministers' Meeting, Chinese delegation submitted China's position paper on the new

[1] Liu Xuecheng, "Basic Features of and Response to Non-Conventional Security Issues", *Journal of Research of Intentional Issues*, 2004 (1).

[2] Xu Jian, "Non-Traditional Security Issues and International Security Cooperation", *Journal of Modern Asia-Pacific*, 2003 (3).

[3] Li Xuebao, "Security in the Context of Globalization: Status and Role of a Country", *Journal of Modern International Relations*, 2004 (5).

security concept, which elaborated in a systematic way the view of China on new security and its policies in the new scenario. In China's view, the core of such a new security concept should include mutual trust, mutual benefit, equality and coordination. Mutual trust means that all countries should transcend differences in ideology and social system, discard the mentality of cold war and power politics and refrain from mutual suspicion and hostility. They should maintain frequent dialogues and mutual briefings on each other's security and defense policies and major operations. Mutual benefit means that all countries should meet the objective needs of social development in the era of globalization, respect each other's security interests and create conditions for others' security while ensuring their own security interests with a view of achieving common security. Equality means that all countries, big or small, are equal members of the international community and should respect each other, treat each other as equals, refrain from interfering in other countries' internal affairs and promote the democratization of the international relations. Coordination means that all countries should seek peaceful settlement of their disputes through negotiation and carry out wide ranging and deep-going cooperation on security issues of mutual concern so as to remove all potential dangers and prevent the outbreak of wars and conflicts.[1]

Secondly, China maintains that cooperation under the new security concept should be flexible and diversified in forms and models. It could be a multi-lateral security mechanism of relatively strong binding force or a forum-like multi-lateral security dialogue. It could also be a confidence-building bilateral security dialogue or a non-governmental dialogue of an academic nature. The promotion of greater interaction of economic interests is another effective mean of safeguarding security.[2]

Thirdly, relations between different types of international security cooperative institutes should be dealt with in an appropriate way, and the authority of the UN and other global security cooperative institutes should be respected and maintained. For security mechanisms led by the United States,

---

[1] "China's Position Paper on the New Security Concept", *People's Daily*, 2002-08-02.
[2] *Ibid.*

such as North Atlantic Treaty, and the U.S.-Japan Alliance, China should develop dialogue and cooperation with their members in a selective manner, in order to jointly probe into that how to handle both traditional and non-traditional security issues.[1]

Fourthly, cooperation should be strengthened in domains that are closely linked with a country's security. Security threats China faces come not only from traditional security domains, but also from non-traditional ones. Urgent issues of a country's security must be identified and more active manner is needed in foreign affairs.

On the whole, because risks and crises brought by globalization are globally interconnected, China should have extensive international cooperation to respond and prevent these risks and crises.

6.3.3 To properly handle ideological elements in external exchanges

Ideology is the superstructure of a society and the theoretical system formed by intuitively reflecting existing social relations of a society or certain social classes or groups based on their own interests. The theoretical system is composed of political, legal, philosophical, ethical, artistic or religious views and is the theoretical base for political creed, behavioral guideline, value orientation and social thinking.[2] Ideology is a very important issue in social political life and the tool for the ruling class to guide, motivate, adjust and restrict social activities of all social members. Generally speaking, the mainstream ideology of a country is the social consciousness that is elevated to superstructure. Ideology has important influence on countries' foreign policies. The ultimate goal of any country's foreign policy set is to protect national interests and ideology which are the key elements of a country's interest. It is impossible to ignore the element of ideology in international

---

[1] Xu Jian, "Non-Traditional Security Issues and International Security Cooperation", *Journal of Modern Asia-Pacific*, 2003 (3).

[2] Huang Xinhua, "Studies of Contemporary Ideology: A Summary of Literatures", *Journal of Studies of Politics*, 2003 (3).

relations. However, important as it is, ideology rarely presents the core interests of a nation's foreign affairs.

Since the 1980s, in its foreign relations, China has been trying to reduce ideological elements and in particular stressing that relations between countries should transcend barriers of "different social system". Since the 12th National Congress of the Communist Party of China in 1982, China has drawn lessons from setting forth foreign policies by lopsidedly differentiating ideology and social system. Thus China has reformed the most important contents of her foreign policies by highlighting national interests and transcending ideological differences. Deng Xiaoping made it clear: "In observing relations between countries, China does not judge by social systems."[1] "Consideration of relations between countries should mainly take the perspective of national strategic interests. The long-term strategic self-interests should be considered, and the interests of other countries should be respected. What had happened in history and the differences of social systems and ideologies should not be paid attention to. Countries should be all equal and respect each other, big or small."[2] In this way, Deng had proposed the principle of prioritizing national interests in handling foreign relations, that is, national interests is the supreme principle in discussing and handling problems.

Foreign strategies transcending ideology benefits China in making more friends and having fewer enemies in international exchanges, and also benefits China in playing greater role in international affairs. Since the 1980s, the enemy-or-friend view of Chinese diplomacy has gradually surpassed the restriction of ideology and China has made more exchanges with other countries. There are no longer fixed opponents or enemies, but more friends to make. China has shifted its focus on developing relations with countries of the Third World and achieved friendly relations with countries with various levels of development and different ideologies. China

---

[1] *Works of Deng Xiaoping*, 1ˢᵗ Edition, Vol. 3, p 168.
[2] *Ibid*, p 330.

no longer uses slogans with strong ideological coloring, such as "Down with Imperialism, Revisionism and Counter-Revolutionary", and no longer takes "establishing a unified front against imperialism" as an important part of her diplomatic work. China sincerely hopes to develop friendly relationship with all countries on the basis of the Five Principles of Peaceful Co-existence, to jointly safeguard world peace and promote development. Foreign policies of China are positively appraised in the world. With growing prestige, China has made more and more friends. The feature of China's diplomacy at this stage is concluded as "diplomacy with zero hostility" in the international community.

Since the mid-1990s, China has developed diplomatic ties in greater scope and depth, stressing the importance of establishing strategic partnership with major powers in the world. Strategic partnership focuses on strategic cooperation with major powers in the West in the new historical period, aiming at promoting and deepening trust, cooperation and friendship between China and major Western powers. Equality and mutual benefits, mutual respect, non-alignment, non-confrontation, not targeting a third country are emphasized in the strategic partnership relation. Partners should have the overall situation in mind and focus on the future. Disputes and conflicts should not affect the healthy development of bilateral relations. Effective communication and coordination mechanisms are to be established. China takes striving for and safeguarding peace as the primary task of her foreign policy, energetically develops friendly and cooperative relations with all countries on the basis of the Five Principles of Peaceful Coexistence, and advocates that countries should transcend discrepancies of social system and ideology, respect each other and co-exist peacefully. When China handles relations with other countries, it not only safeguards its interests, but also respects the interests of other countries. China endeavors to seek approaching points of common interests, and aims to expand mutually beneficial cooperation. Dialogues should be conducted to the end of peacefully solutions. Confrontation should be avoided, and disputes should escalate to military clashes and military threat should be avoided. China never markets its social system and ideology to other countries, and at the same time does not allow other countries to enforce their social systems and ideologies to China. Differences and disputes between countries should be solved through dialogue, not confrontation. Peaceful means, not military means, should be used.

However, in the existing international political environment, these high ideals which do not categorize ideology and advocate the development of relations between countries with emphasis on national interests meet challenges. Consequently, the ideological elements in China's diplomacy to a large degree become inevitable due to ideological elements deployed in the diplomacy of some big powers in the world.

It should be acknowledged that in the external relations of Western countries, national interests are also a priority, and besides there is also strong ideological coloring. This is particularly true when they are dealing with countries with different values or ideology. Through their imputation on a hostile ideology, a different civilization or a "traditional view of sovereignty", they defame that socialist countries and some other developing countries are illegal, backward, failing or even evil. They advocate Western values and ideologies, e.g., democracy, freedom, human rights as self-justified, legal and universal. They strive for the dominance of Western civilization considering both pros and cons. At the same time they argue for the legitimacy of "humanistic intervention", and military intervention in domestic affairs of other countries, on the basis that interdependence of countries deepens and domestic issues become internationalized in the age of globalization. The purpose is to publicize and argue for the inevitability and legitimacy of a global order led by the United States and dominated by the Western world. I am indeed pleased to observe that some ideas with extreme ideological coloring such as "the end of history" that had emerged after the Cold War has proven to be incredible and is no longer paid attention to. But theories such as "Democratic Peace Theory", theory of new imperialism, theory that "human rights have higher value than sovereignty", have been instigating conflicts and deceiving.

Western countries, the United States in particular, are prone to attack and defame others in the domain of international politics with tools of ideology. After the disintegration of the Soviet Union and the end of the Cold War, China had become the only major socialist power in the world, and was regarded as "the last bastion of communism", and the main target of "peaceful evolution". The strategic need shared by China and Western countries, with the United States as the leader, to resist the Soviet Union in 70ies, no longer exists today. Though common interests between China and Western countries increase, in terms of economy and trade, regional stability and prosperity, and handling global issues, they do not present similar urgency as in the Cold War period. In addition, frictions and conflictions along with these common interests stand out. China actively develops multilateral diplomacy and fully participates in international system, with increasing role in regional and global affairs, and remarkably increases its national strength as well as international influence.[1] On the other hand, after the dramatic changes in the Soviet Union and Eastern Europe, China was pushed to the frontline in international political struggles. Whether China "hides its capacities and bids for the time", or "aims not to stand out among others", any actions in both its domestic or foreign affairs may cause chain reactions in the international community. Just as the saying goes, detraction pursues the great. The international role of China differs from that in the Cold War period and also from that in the early period after the Cold War. Once a secondary actor on the game board of international strategy, China is now regarded as a major rival or potential threat, a country that is to be guarded against or to be contained. On the contrary, big powers target to play on India and ASEAN countries, who profit from conflicts between China and the United States, and between China and Japan. It is impossible for China to pull herself out of the contradictions among big powers, and this fact has

---

[1] Meng Xiangqing, "On the Changing International Role of China and the Basic Positioning of Foreign Strategy of Security", *Journal of World Economy and Politics*, 2002 (7).

become one of the issues taken advantage of by some other countries.[1] In a more complex international environment, many countries regard ideology as a tool to exert pressure on China or vilify the image of China. For example, in October 1997, right before Jiang Zemin, former President of China, paid a visit to the United States, Bill Clinton had given an address about China and U.S national interests through radio (Voice of America). After pointing out that many common interests exist between China and the United States, and developing Sino-US relations is in the national interest of the United States, he had remarked, "We strongly believe that over some time, growing interdependence would have a liberalization effect on China; but it does not mean that we in the meantime should or can ignore to oppose human rights abuses or religious freedom abuses in China. Nor does it mean that there is nothing we can do to speed the process of liberalization." He had further claimed, "The United States, therefore, must and will continue to stand up for human rights, to speak out against abuses in China or anywhere else in the world. To do otherwise would run counter to everything we stand for as Americans."[2] As a matter of fact, anti-communism remains a vein running through America's policy toward China.[3]

Though China proposes to transcend ideology in handling international relations, China cannot ignore the role of ideology in external relations under the ideological pressure of Western countries. The following aspects need to be noticed for a clear understanding of international positioning of China: Firstly, China is a socialist country, which is the most determining position of the system that regulates and push other kinds of positioning of China. The history of the past century has proven that, socialist system is the only choice for China to grow strong. "Building socialism in China is not to be

[1] Meng Xiangqing, "On the Changing International Role of China and the Basic Positioning of Foreign Strategy of Security", *Journal of World Economy and Politics*, 2002 (7).

[2] Xing Hua as compiler *Background Documents of the United States Policies Toward China*, p 11, Beijing: Xinhua Press, 1998.

[3] Liu Jianfei, *The United States and Anti-Communism—On the United States' Ideological Diplomacy Toward Socialist Countries*, pp 133-143, Beijing: China Social Sciences Press, 2001.

wavered."[1] For China with complex conditions, large population and weak economic foundation, "only socialism can unite the country, solve difficulties of the people, avoid polarization between the rich and the poor, and gradually lead all the people to common prosperity."[2] Secondly, the short-term goal of economic development of China is to reach a moderate level of development. China has made brilliant achievement in its reform and opening up, but there is a large gap when compared with developed countries. Deng Xiaoping had pointed out for many times that by the mid-21st century, "it will be a marvelous achievement for a country with a population of 1.5 billion to reach the moderate level of development."[3] China should not overestimate its strength, and there is no need to underestimate, too. Thirdly, the positioning of China in international relations is that it will stand with countries in the Third World forever. Even its economy reaches to the level of moderately developed countries, its per capita production and income level are in the rank of developing countries. China will never become a super power, will go against hegemonies, and will always promote peace and development and take the establishment of a new international order as her sacred mission. Fourthly, in face of the strategy of peaceful evolution of Western countries, China needs to adopt an active stance and effective tactics. It is to be acknowledged that the strategy of peaceful evolution of Western countries will be thawed only by actively responding to it with a clear-cut attitude. Meanwhile, China should not be afraid and only mention the risks of "peaceful evolution", and thus reject many excellent achievements of Western countries. In the course of her development, China should draw upon and absorb outstanding achievements of human civilization on the one hand, and should be highly vigilant against "war without the smoke of gunpowder" and "peaceful evolution" on the other hand.

There needs to be a correct and comprehensive understanding of the view of transcending ideology when handling international relations. First

---

[1] *Works of Deng Xiaoping*, 1st Edition, Vol. 3, p 328.

[2] *Ibid*, p 357.

[3] *Ibid*, p 305.

of all, "transcending" does not mean ignorance. Ideological difference remains, and admitting the difference is the precondition of transcending ideology. Aim is to prevent the difference escalating to a major gap, and the independent choice of ideology of each nation should be respected. Secondly, "to lessen the dose in degrees" does not equal to assimilation. The ideological erosion and infiltration risks always exist, which should be recognized. But there should be no ideological confrontation, no expansion of controversies, no forcing of one's own view on others. China should not demand from others to change their stance or hesitate on her own stance. Thirdly, "transcending" is only a precondition, and its aim is to put aside discrepancies, seek common points while reserving differences, and promote common development. Fourthly, China should not fully "lessen the dose in degrees" of ideological content in its external relations, or expect other countries do the same. Wisdom is to fit ideology in the historical, cultural and political traditions, assure that it pleases and accepted by the majority of the people. At the same time, China should keep up with the trends of times, adapt to the world trend of development and let ideology play positive role in China's external relations.[1]

6.3.4 Correct understanding and proper handling of the relation between two systems

In the course of merging into globalization, the relation between two systems needs to be correctly understood and properly handled, which is a basic request for socialist countries to take part in globalization when capitalism and socialism co-exist. Globalization has helped many countries with different economic and political systems integrate into the international community, and resulted in new characteristics and reforms in the relation between two systems. Yong Dong and Thomas G. Moore assert that, "Globalization has not diminished competition completely, but in an increasingly globalized world, rules and regulations ease rivaling

---

[1] Xing Yue, "The Role of Ideology in Foreign Policies", *Pacific Journal*, 2004 (9).

politics."[1] Under this circumstance, the confrontation of two systems has weakened, which provides conditions for cooperation between countries with different systems. Following the dramatic changes in Eastern Europe and the disintegration of the Soviet Union and the establishment of socialist market economy in China, market economy had expanded in the world, and a unified single world market was basically formed. Since China was forced into the world system since the Opium War, China had remained at the periphery of the world economic system. To achieve the best economic benefits, China on the one hand needs to join in the world economic system and make full use of the internationalization of capital flow. On the other hand, China should contribute to reforms in the world economic system favoring developing countries.[2] To take part in the common economic system, countries with different systems should abide by common international practices, international rules and international laws. They are having increasing dialogues, cooperation and exchanges, and facing common international problems.[3] As a result, in order to strengthen communication and cooperation, the relation between countries with different systems is no longer confrontational, but both co-existing and competitive. In the context of globalization, clashes between two systems often occur, but features of clashes and means of solving them have changed, and the intensity of clashes can be controlled to certain extent. Confrontation of the two systems may evolve to more cooperation, which could be deepened over a long time. Peaceful co-existence and learning from each seem highly possible. It should be recognized that as globalization proceeds, countries with different systems tend to seek consensus and what's in common, and the influence of ideology on international relations will be gradually weakened. In its external exchanges, China needs to handle relations with different countries

[1] Yong Dong, Thomas G. Moore, "China Views Globalization: Toward a New Great Power Politics?" *Washington Quarterly*, Summer 2004, Vol. 27, Issue 3.

[2] Wang Zhengyi, *Theory of World System and China*, p 349, Beijing: Commercial Press, 2000.

[3] Chen Shaokang, "Challenges of Economic Globalization for Socialism and Countermeasures", *Journal of Theories*, 2003 (4).

positively, and thus create a favorable external environment for the peaceful development of China.

On the basis of the proper handling of relations of countries with different systems, outstanding achievements accumulated in the process of social development should be drawn upon and absorbed with the aim of speeding up development of China in all aspects and in all the spheres. At present, capitalist countries have some advantages, such as the mature managerial system and sound economic basis, but socialist countries have relatively low level of productive forces and some structural defects in the economic system due to many reasons. On the basis of adhering to socialist road, China should further emancipate her thinking mode, seek truth from facts, and actively learn from Western countries' advanced practices. China needs to develop friendly and cooperative relations with capitalist countries, in particular developed countries, to learn from others' strong points to offset its weaknesses, and to absorb civilization fruits accumulated in the process of economic and political development. At the same time, China needs to set forth policies and strategies in line with its national conditions, and to protect its sovereignty and national interests. China needs to absorb not only scientific and technological achievements, advanced business management expertise, but also political achievements that could benefit the course of political development in China. Economically, China has gained great interests in absorbing and drawing upon advanced technologies and management expertise of foreign countries, and it has become a consensus for the Chinese society to absorb advanced technologies and management expertise. But when it comes to political domain, there remain some doubts as to whether China can absorb the political achievements of mankind, and also some people think it will be hard to realize this idea.

In order to promote political development of China, it must be insisted to proceed from the actual historical conditions of China, and at the same time, make full use of the achievements of the political civilization of mankind, including the advanced experiences and best practices of capitalist countries. In the long course of the historical development of capitalism, its political civilization has scored many achievements. Is there a need, or is it possible to learn from the political civilization of capitalism in the process of socialist political development? The answer to this question is to further emancipate the mode of thinking and to hold indeed an objective stance toward capitalist political civilization. Political civilization of mankind has a historical continuation, inner logic and contents which may fit different systems. As an important component of political civilization of mankind, capitalist political civilization covers, inherits and develops these contents of political civilization of mankind, which are common assets of mankind, instead of being solely owned by the capitalist society. Good systems, rules and practices of political civilization of mankind can be used both by capitalism and socialism. It is not that socialism can no longer make use of them if capitalism has used them, as they do not uniquely belong to capitalism.[1] Socialism is the most advanced social political system in human history, a social order superior to capitalism. The construction of socialist democratic politics needs to draw upon and absorbs all beneficial achievements of political civilization of mankind, in order to create a better and more advanced political civilization. In fact, China has absorbed many political achievements of mankind in its course of political progress, such as representative democracy, democratic elections, democratic decision-making, republican system, modern political party system, etc. A combination of these systems with Chinese socialism create a political system with Chinese characteristics, including the system of people's congress, multi-party cooperation and political consultation under the leadership of the Communist Party of China, the system of self-government of ethnic autonomous areas and the system of one country, two systems. A favorable primary foundation for constructing socialist political civilization of China has been laid and the political development of China has been pushed forward.[2]

At the same time, the experiences and lessons of world democratic waves need to be carefully summarized. World democratic wave is the result

---

[1] Li Jingzhi, "To Vigorously Draw Upon the Achievements of Political Civilization of Mankind", *Journal of Academia*, 2003 (5).

[2] Li Jingzhi, "To Vigorously Draw Upon the Achievements of Political Civilization of Mankind", *Journal of Academia*, 2003 (5).

of the internal causes of political changes in developing countries, besides the external promotion of Western countries as well as the role of globalization, and have profound influences on the whole world. Problems emerged and lessons accumulated in world democratic waves need to be summarized in order to avoid future mistakes. Faced by democratic waves, some countries with no tradition of Western democracy, or social conditions necessary for the Western democracy, often display dramatic in-capabilities in absorbing Western democracy. This is the reason why, the democratic process of some countries is ephemeral. Some countries possess the shell of Western democracy but indeed lack the essence and contents of democracy, with real power remaining in the hands of a few political elites or authoritative people. Democracy, as such is an "elite democracy", and not a democracy for the people. Besides, the democratic waves bring disaster to some developing countries. Some countries, in particular some African countries, have constant political turmoil. Some countries witness growing political conflicts after democratization, resulting in economic stagnation or even retrogression. In some countries defects of Western democracy appear after democratization, as corrupt "money democracy" or "money" politics. It is proven that, as the important component of political civilization of mankind, democracy is a developing process growing from lower to a higher level, and political systems keep improving. The development of democracy must be combined with the national historical conditions. In terms of the transformation of traditional politics to modern politics, undoubtedly there are internal laws for political development which are of universal significance, and also the experiences of some developing countries should not be completely excluded.[1] China needs to actively absorb lessons and experiences of world democratization in its own political development and explore a road of political development in line with China's actual conditions. For China, there is still much to examine and reflect on, in the sphere of transforming political culture. China should set proper goals for political development, choose appropriate strategies for political development, and promote political reforms while checking her political stability.

---

[1] Chen Zhenming, *Politics: Concepts, Theories, Methods*, p 383, Beijing: China Social Sciences Press, 2004.

Bibliography

Gao Fang, *Probe into the World Affairs*, Beijing: China Books Press, 2002.

Gao Fang, Li Jingzhi and Pu Guoliang as compilers, *Theories and Practices of Scientific Socialism*, 4th Edition, Beijing: China Renmin University Press, 2005.

Huang Zongliang, Kong Hanbing, *The Relationship Between Socialism and Capitalism: Theories, History and Evaluation*, Beijing: Peking University Press, 2002.

Huang Zongliang, Kong Hanbing, *The History of World Socialism*, Beijing: Peking University Press, 2004.

National Statistics Bureau of China, *China Statistics Yearbook 2004*, Beijing: China Statistics Press, 2004.

National Statistics Bureau of China, *China Statistics Yearbook 2005*, Beijing: China Statistics Press, 2005.

Hu Yuanzi, Xue Xiaoyuan, *Globalization and China*, Beijing: Central Compilation and Translation Press.

Li Jingzhi, *Evolution and Conflicts of the Contemporary Capitalism*, Beijing: China Renmin University Press, 2001.

Li Jingzhi, Lin Su, *Contemporary World Economy and Politics*, Beijing: China Renmin University Press, 2003.

Li Jingzhi, et al, *Political Development and System Innovation in Contemporary China*, Beijing: Peking University Press, 2006.

Li Huibin, *Globalization and Citizen Society*, Guilin: Guangxi Normal

University Press, 2003.

Li Cong as chief compiler, *A New Anthology of World Economics*, Beijing: Economic Science Press, 2000.

Li Cong, *The New Evolution of Modern Capitalism*, Beijing: Economic Science Press, 1998.

Liu Jianfei, *The United States and Anti-Communism—On the United States' Ideological Diplomacy Toward Socialist Countries*, Beijing: China Social Sciences Press, 2001.

Liu Dexi, *WTO and Sovereignty*, Beijing: People's Press, 2003.

Liu Shucheng, Zhang Ping, *Probing into the "New Economy"*, Beijing: Social Sciences Literature Press, 2001.

Pu Guoliang, *Introduction to Contemporary Socialism in Other Countries*, Beijing: China Renmin University Press, 2006.

Shi Yinhong, *New Trend, New Pattern and New Norms,* Beijing: Law Press House, 2000.

Wang Yizhou, *Analysis on Modern International Politics*, Shanghai: Shanghai People's Press, 1995.

Wang Zhengyi, *Theory of World System and China*, Beijing: Commercial Press, 2000.

Wu Jiang, *On the Communication of Socialism and Capitalism*, Beijing: China Social Sciences Press, 2003.

Xu Chongwen, *New Changes of the Contemporary Capitalism*, Chongqing: Chongqing Press, 2004.

Xu Juezai, *The History of the Schools of Socialism*, Shanghai: Shanghai People's Press, 1999.

Xiao Feng, *Socialim: Transition and Innovation*, Beijing: Contemporary World Press, 2003.

Yu Keping, *"Socialism" in the Age of Globalization*, Beijing: Central Compilation and Translation Press, 1998.

Yu Keping, *"Marxism" in the Age of Globalization*, Beijing: Central Compilation and Translation Press, 1998.

Yu Keping and Huang Weiping as chief compilers, *The Paradox of*

Globalization, Beijing: Central Compilation and Translation Press, 1998.

Yu Keping, *Globalization and Political Development*, Beijing: Social Sciences Literature Press, 2005.

Zhang Zesen, Tian Xiwen, *Capitalism and Socialism in the 20th Century*, Beijing: China Yanshi Press, 2005.

Zhao Mingyi as chief compiler, *Contemporary Socialism*, Jinan: Shandong Univeristy Press, 2001.

Edward W. Said, *Culture and Imperialism*, Beijing: SDX Joint Publishing Company, 2003.

Iov H. Daalder, James M. Lindsay, *America Unbound: The Bush Revolution in Foreign Policy*, Beijing: Xinhua Press, 2004.

Francis Fukuyama, *The End of History and the Last Man*, Beijing: China Academy of Social Sciences Press, 2003.

Robert Keohane, *Liberalism, Power and Governance in a Partially Globalized World*, Beijing: Peking University Press, 2004.

David Held, Anthony McGrew, *Globalization/Anti-Globalization*, Beijing: Social Sciences Literature Press, 2004.

Joseph E. Stiglitz, *Globalization and Its Discontents*, Beijing: China Machine Press, 2004.

Gerald Boxberger and Harald Klimenta, *Die 10 Globalisierungslügen*, Beijing: Xinhua Press, 2000.

Akiyoshi Hoshino, *World Politics in the Age of Globalization: The Actors and Structures of World Politics*, Beijing: Social Sciences Academic Press, 2004.

Robert Gilpin, *War and Change in World Politics*, Beijing: China Renmin University Press, 1994.

Paul Kennedy, *Grand Strategies in War and Peace*, Beijing: World Affairs Press, 2005.

Ernest Mandel, *Money and Power: A Marxist Theory of Bureaucracy*, Beijing: Central Compilation and Translation Press, 2002.

Ernest Mandel, *Marxism and the Fourth International*, Hong Kong: October Books, 1996.

Ernest Mandel, *From Capitalism to Socialism*, Hong Kong: October Books, 1997.

Gorbachev, Brant, *The Future Socialism*, Beijing: Central Compilation and Translation Press, 1994.

John Eatwell, Peter Newman, Murray Milgate, *The New Palgrave Dictionary of Economics*, Vol. 3, Beijing: Economic Science Press, 1992.

John E. Roemer, *A Future for Socialism*, Chongqing: Chongqing Press, 1997.

David Schweickart, *Against Capitalism*, Beijing: China Renmin University Press, 2002.

István Mészáros, *Beyond Capital: Toward a Theory of Transition*, Beijing: Renmin University Press, 2003.

David McLellan, *Marxism after Marx*, 3rd Edition, Beijing: China Renmin University Press, 2004.

Alan Woods, *Neo-Socialism*, Nanjing: Jiangsu People's Press, 2005.

Leste C. Thurow, *The Future of Capitalism: How Today's Economic Forces Shape Tomorrow's World*, Beijing: China Social Sciences Press, 1998.

Anthony Giddens, *Sociology*, Beijing: Peking University Press, 2003.

Samuel P. Huntington, Peter Burger, *Many Globalizations: Cultural Diversity in the Contemporary World*, Beijing: Xinhua Press, 2004.

Samuel P. Huntington, *The Third Wave: Democratization in the Late Twentieth Century*, Shanghai: SDX Joint Publishing Company, 1998.

Robert Keohane, Helen Milner, *Internationalization and Domestic Politics*, Beijing: Peking University Press, 2003.

Jr. Joseph Nye, *Understanding International Conflicts: An Introduction to Theory and History*, Shanghai: Shanghai People's Press, 2002.

Cai Wu, "Current Situation and Characteristics of Socialist Movement in the World", *Journal of Teaching and Research*, 2004 (1).

Chai Shangjin, "The Current Status and Prospects of the Communist Parties in Other Countries", *Journal of the Contemporary World*, 2005 (2).

Chen Shaokang, "Challenges of Economic Globalization for Socialism and Countermeasures", *Journal of Theories*, 2003 (4).

Cui Guitian, "On American-Cuban Relation and the Characteristics of Cuban Socialism", *Contemporary World and Socialism*, 2003 (1).

Dai Lu, "A Few Thoughts on Cultural Globalization", *China Youth Daily*, 2001-12-06.

Han Zhaozhu, "Analysis on Ecological Socialism", *Academic Research*, 2004 (8).

Hu An'gang, Zhou Shaojie, "New Gap Between the Rich and the Poor in the World: Increasingly Expanding 'Digital Gap'", *China Social Sciences*, 2002 (3).

Hu Guoliang, "Globalization and Protection of Economic Security", *Journal of China Statistics*, 2002 (11).

Fu Junwen, "International Comparison of Trade Dependency and Analysis on Structural Risk of China's Foreign Trade", *Journal of World Economic Research*, 2004 (4).

Guo Liancheng, "Positive and Negative Effects of Economic Globalization", *World Economy and Politics*, 2000 (8).

Huang Yejing, "Economic Globalization and Transformation of Development Strategy of Developing Countries", *Journal of Academics*, 2003 (8).

Jiang Yong, "On the Uncertainties of World Economy", *Qiushi Monthly*, 2003 (15).

Jiang Xiaojuan, "Take the Opportunities Provided by Economic Globalization and Develop China's Economy", *Journal of Shanxi University of Finance and Economics*, 2004 (1).

Jin Canrong, "On the United States' International Position from a Perspective of Internal Balancing Mechanism", *Modern International Relations*, 2004 (3).

Li Chunyu, "On Economic Globalization and Cultural Diversity", *Journal of Business Economics*, 2004 (11).

Li Jingzhi, "To Vigorously Draw Upon the Achievements of Political Civilization of Mankind", *Journal of Academia*, 2003 (5).

Li Jinqi, "Globalization and Cultural Security in China", *Journal of*

Philosophy Research, 2005 (1).

Li Shenzhi, "Globalization and Chinese Culture", *Journal of Pacific Studies*, 1994 (2).

Li Xuebao, "Security in the Context of Globalization: Status and Role of a Country", *Journal of Modern International Relations*, 2004 (5).

Li Cong, "On Economic Integration", *Journal of China Social Sciences*, 1993 (1).

Liu Dachun, "On the Essence of Modern Technological Revolution", *Journal of Adult Higher Education*, 2005(5).

Liu Jianfei, "The Influence of Democracy on the International Relations in the 21st Century", *Strategy and Management*, 2002 (3).

Liu Xuelian, "Globalization and the New Development of International Relationship", *Social Sciences Journal of Jilin University*, 2001 (6).

Liu Yumei and Zhang Peng, "Quantitative Research of the Degree of Economic Globalization", *Statistics Research*, 2003 (12).

Liu Xuecheng, "Basic Features of and Response to Non-Conventional Security Issues", *Journal of Research of Intentional Issues*, 2004 (1).

Luo Wendong, "On the 'New Social Elements' Inside the Contemporary Capitalism", *Journal of Theoretical Frontier*, 2004 (14).

Lu Renzhu, "Economic Globalization and Chinese Culture", *World Economy and Politics*, 1997 (11).

Niu Jianguo, "Transnational Corporations and Economic Globalization", *Journal of China's Economy and Trade*, 2003 (9).

Long Yongtu, "Actively Participate in Economic Globalization and Seize Opportunities for Development", *Journal of Zhejiang Wanli College*, 2004 (4).

Meng Xiangqing, "On the Changing International Role of China and the Basic Positioning of Foreign Strategy of Security", *Journal of World Economy and Politics*, 2002 (7).

Peng Guohua, "National Culture in the Process of Globalization: An Interview on Professor Zhang Shiying, (Department of Philosophy, Peking University)", *People's Daily*, 2001-11-24.

Pu Guoliang, "The Origin and Nature of the Nuclear Crisis on the Korean Peninsula", *Research of Socialism of Chinese Characteristics*, 2003 (5).

Ren Junying, "The Strategic Direction of Socialist Development in the Context of Globalization", *Journal of Henan Normal University* (Philosophy and Social Sciences Edition), 2001 (6).

Shi Yinhong, "On the Limitation of Interdependence and the Restrain of National Policies on the Impact of Globalization", *Research of International Issues*, 2002 (2).

Sui Yinghui, "Economic Globalization: The Strategic Orientation of Technological Industries", *Journal of International Technological and Economic Research*, 2001 (3).

Tao Wenzhao, "Internal and External Resistance: The Interpretation of the New Changes of Capitalism by Socialist Movement", *Journal of Teaching and Research*, 1999 (4).

Tao Chengde, Ye Guanglin, "New Changes of the Contemporary Capitalism and the Growth of Socialist Elements", *Journal of Theoretical Horizon*, 2002 (3).

Wang Yizhou, "Ideology and International Relationship—A Brief Review of the Concepts and the Representations", *Europe*, 1994 (5).

Wang Dengqi, "Current Status of Development of Contemporary Science and Technology in the U.S.", *Journal of Science and Management*, 2000 (6).

Wang Zhenya, "A Multi-Dimensional Analysis on the Values of Ecological Socialism", *Journal of Marxism Research*, 2003 (1).

Xiao Feng, "Current Status of World Socialist Movement", *Journal of Party Life*, 2000 (10).

Xie Hao, "Uneven Distribution of Benefit in Economic Globalization and the Theoretical Origin", *Economic Issue Studies*, 2004 (7).

Xiong Guangqing, "On the Opportunities of Maintaining State Sovereignty by Developing Nations in the Era of Globalization", *Capital Normal University Journal* (Social Sciences Edition), 2002 (4).

Xiong Guangqing, "Economic Globalization: Major Driving Force of America's New Economy", *Chongqing Business School Journal*, 2002 (4).

Xiong Guangqing, "Challenges of Economic Globalization to Developing New and High-Tech Industries in China", *Journal of Science, Technology and Management*, 2003 (2).

Xiong Guangqing, "The Current Situation of Socialist Development in the World", *Qiushi Monthly*, 2004 (10).

Xiong Guangqing, "Iraq War Weakens the Soft Power of the United States", *Journal of Academic Exploration*, 2005 (2).

Xing Yue, "The Role of Ideology in Foreign Policies", *Pacific Journal*, 2004 (9).

Xu Jian, "Non-Traditional Security Issues and International Security Cooperation", *Journal of Modern Asia-Pacific*, 2003 (3).

Yang Mengying, "Chen Demian, Digital Gap Between Developing Countries and Developed Countries", *Modern Scientific Management*, 2003 (11).

Yang Xuedong, "Risk Society in the Context of Economic Globalization", *Study Times*, 2005-01-17.

Yang Shuang, "The Basic Features of Ruling Social Democratic Parties", *Research of Marxism*, 2005 (3).

Yin Dengxiang, "Basic Features of the Development of the Contemporary Revolution of Science and Technology", *Research of Party Building*, 2003 (5).

Yuan Zushe, "The Formation of Global Civil Society and Its Cultural Significance, the Implication of 'Personality' of World Citizen and the Awareness of Global 'Public Value'", *Peking University Journal* (Philosophy and Social Sciences Edition), 2004 (4).

Yu Pei, "Anti-Cultural Globalization—Thoughts on Cultural Diversity in the Context of Economic Globalization", *Research of History Theories*, 2004 (4).

Zhao Bin, "New Changes of the Contemporary Capitalism and Their Influence on World Socialism", *Journal of Contemporary World and*

Socialism, 2004 (1).

Zhang Senlin, Liu Taiping, "The Features of the Relations of Socialism and Capitalism in Economic Globalization", *Journal of the Party School of Changchun City Committee*, 2003 (2).

Zhao Ziwen, "Globalization Process in the 21st Century and the Historical Opportunity for China", *Journal of International Business Research*, 2005 (1).

Zhao Guizhi, "The Impact of Economic Globalization on Economic Safety of China and Study of Countermeasures", *Journal of Research of Financial Issues*, 2002 (5).

Zhao Yuhai, "To Improve the Competitiveness of High-Tech Industries in China to Face the Challenge of Entry of WTO", *China Science and Technology Industry*, 2002(6).

Zhang Jing, "Cultural Homogeneity and Heterogeneity in the Process of Globalization", *Journal of Teaching and Research*, 2002 (5).

Zhang Youwen, "The Impact and Countermeasures of the Increase of China's Trade Dependency", *Journal of Issues of International Trade*, 2004 (8).

Zheng Guozhong, "Seven Focuses of Competition of Banks in China and in the World", *Outlook Weekly*, 2002(20).

Zhu Qinjun, "Ten Influences of Economic Globalization on International Politics", *World Economic Research*, 2001(5).

Zhu Niangui, "On Opening Up and Safeguarding China's Economic Security", *Journal of Theory and Reform*, 2003(4).

Ernest Mandel, "Socialism or Neo-Liberalism", *Research of Theories From Overseas*, 2002(12).

Alberto Rodriguez Arufe, "Current Situation in Cuba", *Journal of Latin America Research*, 2005(2).

Adam Schaff, "Creative Marxist—A New Type of Socialism (Part One)", *Contemporary World Socialist Issues*, 2000 (4).

Adam Schaff, "Creative Marxist—A New Type of Socialism (Part Two)", *Contemporary World Socialist Issues*, 2001 (1).

Adam Schaff, "A Call for New Left", *Contemporary World Socialist Issues*, 1996 (4).

Adam Schaff, "New Left is Needed", *Contemporary World Socialist Issues*, 1997 (4).

Adam Schaff, "Thoughts on Future Socialism", *Contemporary World Socialist Issues*, 1997 (1).

Cal Jillson, *American Government: Political Change and Institutional Development*. Belmont, CA: Thomson/Wadsworth, 2005.

Doroth Riddle, *Service-Led Growth*. New York: Praeger, 1986.

Ernst B. Haas, *Beyond the Nation-State*. Stanford: Stanford University Press, 1964.

James A. Yunker, *On the Political Economy of Market Socialism: Essays and Analyses*. Aldershot, Hampshire, England; Burlington, VT, USA: Ashgate Publishing Ltd, 2001.

James A. Yunker, *Economic Justice: The Market Socialist Vision*. Lanham, Maryland: Rowman & Littlefield Publishers, 1997.

Johan K. De Vree, *Political Integration: The Formation of Theory and Its Problems*. The Hague Paris, Mouton, 1972.

Karl W. Deutsch, *The Analysis of International Relations*, 2nd ed. Englewood Cliffs, New Jersey: Prentice Hall, Inc. 1988.

Maurice Daly, Mal Logan, *Reconstructing Asia*. Melbourne: RMIT Publishing, 1998.

Mahathir Mohamad, *A New Deal for Asia*. Malaysia: Pelanduk Publications, 1999.

R. Keohane and J. Nye, eds, *Power and Interdependence: Transnational Relations and World Politics*. Cambridge, Massachusetts: Harvard University Press, 1977.

Oxford Dictionary of New Words. London: Oxford University Press, 1991.

Webster's Ninth Collegiate Dictionary. Massachusetts: Webster Co. Ltd., 1991.

William J. Baumol etc., *Productivity and American Leadership*.

Cambridge, Massachusetts: MIT Press, 1989.

Adam Roberts, "Humanitarian War: Military Intervention and Human Rights". In *International Affairs*. Vol. 69, No. 3, July 1993.

Albert Wohsstetter, "The Delicate Balance of Terror". In *Foreign Affairs*. XXXVIII, January 1959.

Andreas Osiander, "Sovereignty, International Relations, and the Westphalian Myth". In *International Organization*. Vol. 55, No. 2, Spring 2001.

Elena Safronova, "Globalization from the Perspective of the PRC and Developing Countries". In *Far Eastern Affairs*. Vol. 31, Issue 4, 2003.

Foreign Policy & A. T. Kearney, "Measuring Globalization: 2005 A. T. Kearney/FOREIGN POLICY Globalization Index". http://www.foreignpolicy.com/story/cms.php?story_id=2823, May/June 2005.

Gao Fang, "The Origin of the Term Globalization". In *Latin American Studies (Beijing)*. June, 1999.

Jean-Pierre Lehmann, "Developing Economies and the Demographic and Democratic Imperatives of Globalization". In *International Affairs*. Jan 2001, Vol. 77.

Jin Zhouying, "Globalization, Technological Competitiveness and the 'Catch-Up' Challenge for Developing Countries: Some Lessons of Experience". In *International Journal of Technology Management & Sustainable Development*. Vol. 4, Issue 1, 2005.

Joseph S. Nye, "The New Rome Meets the New Barbarians". In *The Economist*, 3/23/2002, Vol.362, Issue 8265.

Joseph S. Nye, "The American National Interest and Global Public Goods". In *International Affairs*. Apr 2002, Vol. 78, Issue 2.

Joshua Cooper Ramo, "The Beijing Consensus". The Foreign Policy Centre, 2004. http://fpc.org.uk/fsblob/244.pdf.

Jürgen Habermas, "What Does Socialism Mean Today? The Rectifying Revolution and the Need for New Thinking on the Left". In *New Left Review*. No. 183, Sept/Oct 1990.

Kofi Annan, "International: Two Concepts of Sovereignty". In *The*

Economist, Sept 18, 1999.

Paul M. Augimeri, "The Effects of Globalisation on China, A Developing, Newly Industrialised Economy". In *Ecodate,* Mar 2001, Vol.15, Issue 1.

Mark Beeson, Alex J. Bellamy, "Globalisation, Security and International Order After 11 September". In *Australian Journal of Politics & History,* Sept 2003, Vol.49, Issue 3.

Mikhail Titarenko, "China and Globalization". In *Far Eastern Affairs.* 2003, Vol. 31, Issue 4.

Michael Glennon, "The New Interventionism". In *Foreign Affairs.* May/June 1999.

Wolfgang Deckers, "China, Globalisation and the World Trade Organisation". In *Journal of Contemporary Asia.* Vol. 34, Issue 1, 2004.

William W. Kaufmann, "The Requirements of Deterrence". In W.W. Kaufmann, ed: *Military Policy and National Security.* Princeton: Princeton University Press, 1956.

Rhoda E. Howard Hassman, "Culture, Human Rights, and the Politics of Resentment in the Era of Globalization". In *Human Rights Review.* Oct/Dec 2004, Vol.6, Issue 1.

Robert Hunter Wade, "Inequality of World Incomes: What Should Be Done?" http://www.opendemocracy.net/globalization/article_257.jsp.

Robert Hunter Wade, "The Rising Inequality of World Income Distribution". In *Finance and Development.* Dec 2001, Vol.38, Issue 4.

Russell B. Scholl, "The International Investment Position of the United States at Yearend 1999". In *Survey of Current Business.* Vol. 80, No. 7, July 2000.

Rhoda E. Howard Hassman, "Culture, Human Rights, and the Politics of Resentment in the Era of Globalization". In *Human Rights Review.* Oct/Dec 2004, Vol. 6, Issue 1.

Ryokichi Hirono, "Globalization in the 21st Century: Blessing or Threat to Developing Countries". In *Asia-Pacific Review.* Nov 2001, Vol. 8, Issue 2.

Samuel P. Huntington, "The Lonely Superpower". In *Foreign Affairs.*

Mar/Apr 1999, Vol. 78, Issue 2.

Yong Dong, Thomas G. Moore, "China Views Globalization: Toward a New Great-Power Politics?" In *Washington Quarterly*. Summer 2004, Vol. 27, Issue 3.

Yuri Shishkov, "Economic Globalization: The Result of the Industrialization and Informatization of Society". In *Social Sciences*. Vol. 33 Issue 3, 2002.

Printed in P. R. C. by order of Canut-Berlin.